ECONOMIC FREEDOM AND INTERVENTIONISM

Titles in the Liberty Fund Library of the Works of
    Ludwig von Mises

LUDWIG VON MISES

Economic Freedom and Interventionism

An Anthology of Articles and Essays

ᘚ **LUDWIG VON MISES**

Selected and Edited by Bettina Bien Greaves

LIBERTY FUND   *Indianapolis*

This book is published by Liberty Fund, Inc., a foundation established to encourage study of the ideal of a society of free and responsible individuals.

𒂼𒉿

The cuneiform inscription that serves as our logo and as the design motif for our endpapers is the earliest-known written appearance of the word "freedom" (*amagi*), or "liberty." It is taken from a clay document written about 2300 B.C. in the Sumerian city-state of Lagash.

First published in 1990 by The Foundation for Economic Education, Inc., Irvington-on-Hudson, New York

Front cover photograph of Ludwig von Mises used by permission of the Ludwig von Mises Institute, Auburn, Alabama

Frontispiece courtesy of Bettina Bien Greaves

Printed in the United States of America

11 10 09 08 07 C 5 4 3 2 1
11 10 09 08 07 P 5 4 3 2 1

Library of Congress Cataloging-in-Publication Data

Von Mises, Ludwig, 1881–1973.
  Economic freedom and interventionism: an anthology of articles and essays / by Ludwig von Mises; selected and edited by Bettina Bien Greaves.
        p.   cm.
  Originally published: Irvington-on-Hudson: Foundation for Economic Education, 1990.
  Includes bibliographical references and index.
  ISBN-13: 978-0-86597-672-6 (hardcover: alk. paper)
  ISBN-10: 0-86597-672-4 (hardcover: alk. paper)
  ISBN-13: 978-0-86597-673-3 (pbk.: alk. paper)
  ISBN-10: 0-86597-673-2 (pbk.: alk. paper)
  1. Free enterprise.   2. Central planning.   3. Economic policy.
I. Greaves, Bettina Bien. II. Title.
HB95 .V66   2007
338.9 — dc22   2006019383

Liberty Fund, Inc.
8335 Allison Pointe Trail, Suite 300
Indianapolis, Indiana 46250-1684

To Percy L. Greaves, Jr.,
my husband and mentor,
who introduced me to the teachings
of Professor Mises

CONTENTS

PART III   Mises as Critic

PART IV   Economics and Ideas

FOREWORD

When Professor Ludwig von Mises died in 1973, he was mourned by friends, associates, and students. His admirers at that time, though not numerous, had recognized him for decades as an intellectual giant and the leading spokesman of the subjective value, marginal utility, "Austrian" school of economics. Yet most of the world paid little attention to his passing.

Throughout his long life, Mises had gone quietly about his business—studying, writing, and lecturing. He persisted, even though his ideas appeared to be having little impact. In time, the quantity and quality of his contributions were prodigious. To give the reader some indication of the importance of his work, his major books, and the dates of their first editions, include *The Theory of Money and Credit* (1912), *Nation, State and Economy* (1919), *Socialism* (1922), *Liberalism* (1927), *Monetary Stabilization and Cyclical Policy* (1928), *Epistemological Problems of Economics* (1933), *Bureaucracy* (1944), *Omnipotent Government* (1944), *Human Action* (1949), *The Anti-capitalistic Mentality* (1956), *Theory and History* (1957), and *The Ultimate Foundation of Economic Science* (1962).

Since Mises's death in 1973, his contributions have been gaining wider recognition. Many articles about him have appeared. His ideas and those of his students are being more widely studied and discussed. New organizations have sprung up to treat his teachings seriously. Interest in studying his works is on the rise, not only in this hemisphere but also apparently in eastern Europe and in the U.S.S.R.

Significant changes are taking place in the climate of opinion. The main doctrines of Mises's principal antagonists—Karl Marx and John Maynard Keynes—have been discredited. Their names are not so widely cited as authorities. Their collectivist theories are no longer taken as "gospel" by the man in the street. The attitude of people toward government has shifted somewhat. Many find government corrupt and expensive and have come to doubt its effectiveness. To ask for government help is no longer as popular as it once was. At the same time, people still do not completely trust free markets and open competition. Thus, the most important ideas of both Marx and Keynes linger on in "mainstream" thinking and have been incorporated in legislation.

With respect to the ideas of Marx, most people still assume that a certain amount of government regulation and control is necessary to preserve the capitalistic system and to prevent the "exploitation" by big businessmen of employees and consumers. There is less talk of confiscatory taxation than there was during the heyday of the "welfare state." Yet Marxian egalitarianism continues to find expression in programs such as progressive taxation, public housing, relief, welfare, and subsidies for students, the unemployed, and the elderly.

When it comes to the ideas of Keynes, most people still believe that the government, through the Federal Reserve, should use monetary policy to assure economic prosperity and employment. Deficit financing and pump priming may not be as openly advocated as in the days of the New Deal, the Fair Deal, and the Great Society. Yet when tax funds fail to cover government expenses, governments resort to deficit financing, inflation, and credit expansion. Our own Federal Reserve, consistent with Keynes, continues to follow an expansionist policy. High interest rates are considered bad for business. Bankers and businessmen are eager for "easy money," fostered by artificially low interest rates to spur business activity. People do not realize that nonmanipulated *market* interest rates have an important role to play. Thus, even though the infatuation with Keynes per se has declined, his doctrine of deficit financing and monetary manipulation survives and the value of the U.S. dollar has declined, although fortunately, thanks to the relative caution of the "Fed," not as much as has the value of the national currencies of other more expansionist central banks.

Dramatic changes have taken place in the international field since Mises's death. The U.S.S.R* no longer appears to pose the threat to

---

* The U.S.S.R. was officially disbanded on December 26, 1991. Mikhail Gorbachev, General Secretary of the Communist Party, had introduced *perestroika* and *glasnost*. The U.S.S.R. had undergone unrest, economic turmoil, and on August 19, 1991, a general strike called by Boris Yeltsin, president of the Russian Republic. On August 24, 1991, Mikhail Gorbachev resigned as leader of the Communist Party. Several republics declared independence. The Soviet Parliament suspended all activities of the Communist Party on August 29, 1991, and the U.S.S.R. broke up officially on December 26, 1991. The former Soviet Republics then became independent states.

international peace that it did in the years just after World War II when these articles were written. The popularity and power of communism has declined. There is also somewhat less tendency to blame the poverty of the "Third World" on the success of the industrialized nations. People here and abroad now give lip service to free enterprise, entrepreneurship, and the market forces of supply and demand.

Yet most people are still fearful of completely free laissez faire. They do not realize the importance of protecting the unadulterated right to own, use, and dispose of private property. They are not prepared to leave the determination of wages, prices, and interest rates to the market. They reject out of hand any thought of the gold standard. On the one hand, they ask government to regulate businesses lest they exploit workers and produce shoddy and dangerous products that would harm consumers. On the other hand, they want to give some businesses special protection, lest they fail and force workers into unemployment. Moreover, many people want government to undertake programs they are not willing to pay for in taxes, programs that, therefore, can only be financed by inflation or credit expansion. They remain ideological, if not intellectual, Marxians and Keynesians.

The articles in this collection were written at a time when the spread of Communism, Progressivism, and the power of labor unions were major national concerns. Although these no longer appear to be such immediate threats, they continue to influence government policies with respect to spending, special privileges, inflation, credit expansion, unemployment, and wage rates.

One recurring theme throughout Mises's writings is that men act on the basis of ideas. Today is the product of past ideas. And the ideas of today will produce tomorrow. The idea that government has the power to cure almost any social ill permitted big government to triumph throughout the world. To reverse this trend, to create a world of free markets, to change governments, to repeal government programs, the ideas men hold must be changed. Government should stick to its fundamental role of protecting the people against those who would violate their rights to life and property. Market checks and balances and free and open competition would then protect the interests of consumers, minimize the injury private industry could cause, and keep unemployment at a minimum.

People must come to respect and protect private property. They must realize that entrepreneurs should be free to make their own decisions and then to benefit, or suffer the consequences. They must insist that governments not interfere with voluntary transactions among private individuals. They must not allow the dividing line between capitalism and interventionism to blur. As Mises points out, big government is a far greater threat to people than are the mistakes and the misdeeds of big business.

"Nothing is more important today," Mises wrote in 1957, "than to enlighten public opinion about the basic differences between genuine liberalism, which advocates the free market economy, and the various interventionist parties which are advocating government interference with prices, wages, the rate of interest, profits and investment, confiscatory taxation, tariffs and other protectionist measures, huge government spending, and finally inflation." This is the goal to which Mises devoted his life. And this is the purpose for which Mises wrote the articles in this book.

ʖ

If an author's contributions are worth preserving, his works must be published and available in libraries. English-language editions of Mises's major works are still in print. Although quite a few of his articles have been collected in anthologies, many of his short pieces that appeared in ephemeral sources, newspapers, and little-known journals have been practically inaccessible. The purpose of this collection is to rescue some of those articles from obscurity and make them available to future generations of students. Quite a few others still remain to be resurrected, including several that appeared in European publications not available in many U.S. libraries. These should be translated one day, published in book format, and preserved in libraries where students can read them and future generations of scholars will be able to find them.

Bettina Bien Greaves
March 1990

ACKNOWLEDGMENTS

Most of the articles in this collection were published during the years when I was attending Professor Ludwig von Mises's graduate seminar at New York University. At that time I was trying to assemble all his writings for a bibliography of his works and Mises would always give me copies of any of his articles that appeared in journals I might not otherwise see. Thus Professor Mises deserves special thanks for making this collection possible.

Thanks are due, also, to Mrs. Mises, who approves of my resurrecting many of her late husband's articles that might otherwise be forgotten.

Many of the articles in this collection were published first in *The Freeman*, the monthly journal of The Foundation for Economic Education. Others appeared in newspapers and magazines now defunct. However, special thanks must go to the several firms that are still publishing, who gave us permission to reprint Mises articles that appeared within their pages: *The Commercial and Financial Chronicle*, the Institute for Humane Studies, Liberty Fund (publisher of the reprinted *New Individualist Review*), *National Review*, *New American* (successor to *American Opinion*), *New Guard* (publication of the Young Americans for Freedom), and Regnery Gateway, Inc. Thanks go to The Foundation for Economic Education, of course, for their support of this project. Mary Ann Murphy did an excellent job of entering all these articles on the computer. I am grateful also for the helpful editorial advice of Beth Hoffman and the careful proofreading of Debra Anderson and Deane Brasfield.

Side-heads have been added to make for ease of reading. Also for the sake of clarity, a few sentences have been edited slightly. The Foundation's style of punctuation and capitalization has been followed throughout.

In addition to being a profound and thoughtful economist, Mises had a remarkable understanding of history and a wealth of historical knowledge, as evidenced by his frequent references to historical personages and events. With the hope of helping future generations of students appreciate Mises's contributions to economic understanding, the editor has added symboled footnotes to identify the more obscure individuals and historical events mentioned in this anthology.

ECONOMIC FREEDOM AND INTERVENTIONISM

Economic Freedom

At one of his seminars, a student asked Professor Mises, "Why aren't all businessmen in favor of capitalism?"

"That very question," Mises answered, "is Marxist."

Mises's response shocked me at the time. It took me some time to realize what he meant. The questioner assumed, as had Karl Marx, that businessmen had a special group or "class" interest in capitalism that other people didn't.

"Capitalism," Mises went on, "benefits everyone — consumers, the masses. It doesn't benefit only businessmen. As a matter of fact, under capitalism some businessmen suffer losses. A businessman's position on the market is never secure; the door is always open to competitors who may challenge his position and deprive him of profits. Yet it is this very competition under capitalism that assures consumers that businessmen will do their best to furnish them, the consumers, with the goods and services they want."

In the articles and papers in this first section, Mises reveals again and again that he is no apologist for business or businessmen. He is interested in determining the economic system which best improves the welfare of individuals and the living conditions of the masses. And that economic system is economic freedom under capitalism. Only with economic freedom, Mises says, are more goods and services produced. Only under capitalism do wages rise and the living standards of the masses improve. The reason? Consumers are sovereign in capitalist free markets. They are in a position to let entrepreneurs know what they want most urgently, by rewarding with profits those who satisfy their wants and by imposing losses and thus withdrawing wealth from those who fail. This system of rewards and penalties guides production and makes sure that more of the goods and services consumers want will be produced, thus raising the wages of workers and the living standards of everyone.

The market is the outcome of peaceful social cooperation and economic freedom. And it is the market that makes individual freedom, justice, morality, innovation, and social harmony possible. As Mises writes in this section:

"A man has freedom as far as he shapes his life according to his own plans," and

"[M]orality makes sense only when addressing individuals who are free agents."

1

The Economic Foundations of Freedom

Animals are driven by instinctive urges. They yield to the impulse which prevails at the moment and peremptorily asks for satisfaction. They are the puppets of their appetites.

Man's eminence is to be seen in the fact that he chooses between alternatives. He regulates his behavior deliberatively. He can master his impulses and desires; he has the power to suppress wishes the satisfaction of which would force him to renounce the attainment of more important goals. In short: man acts; he purposively aims at ends chosen. This is what we have in mind in stating that man is a moral person, responsible for his conduct.

Freedom as a Postulate of Morality

All the teachings and precepts of ethics, whether based upon a religious creed or whether based upon a secular doctrine like that of the Stoic philosophers, presuppose this moral autonomy of the individual and therefore appeal to the individual's conscience. They presuppose that the individual is free to choose among various modes of conduct and require him to behave in compliance with definite rules, the rules of morality. Do the right things, shun the bad things.

It is obvious that the exhortations and admonishments of morality make sense only when addressing individuals who are free agents. They are vain when directed to slaves. It is useless to tell a bondsman what is morally good and what is morally bad. He is not free to determine his comportment; he is forced to obey the orders of his master. It is difficult to blame him if he prefers yielding to the commands of his master to

Reprinted from *The Freeman*, April 1960.

the most cruel punishment threatening not only him but also the members of his family.

This is why freedom is not only a political postulate, but no less a postulate of every religious or secular morality.

The Struggle for Freedom

Yet for thousands of years a considerable part of mankind was either entirely or at least in many regards deprived of the faculty to choose between what is right and what is wrong. In the status society of days gone by the freedom to act according to their own choice was, for the lower strata of society, the great majority of the population, seriously restricted by a rigid system of controls. An outspoken formulation of this principle was the statute of the Holy Roman Empire that conferred upon the princes and counts of the Reich (Empire) the power and the right to determine the religious allegiance of their subjects.

The Orientals meekly acquiesced in this state of affairs. But the Christian peoples of Europe and their scions that settled in overseas territories never tired in their struggle for liberty. Step by step they abolished all status and caste privileges and disabilities until they finally succeeded in establishing the system that the harbingers of totalitarianism try to smear by calling it the bourgeois system.

The Supremacy of the Consumers

The economic foundation of this bourgeois system is the market economy in which the consumer is sovereign. The consumer, i.e., everybody, determines by his buying or abstention from buying what should be produced, in what quantity and of what quality. The businessmen are forced by the instrumentality of profit and loss to obey the orders of the consumers. Only those enterprises can flourish that supply in the best possible and cheapest way those commodities and services which the buyers are most anxious to acquire. Those who fail to satisfy the public suffer losses and are finally forced to go out of business.

In the precapitalistic ages the rich were the owners of large landed estates. They or their ancestors had acquired their property as gifts — feuds or fiefs — from the sovereign who — with their aid — had conquered the country and subjugated its inhabitants. These aristocratic landowners were real lords as they did not depend on the patronage of buyers. But the rich of a capitalistic industrial society are subject to the supremacy of the market. They acquire their wealth by serving the consumers better than other people do and they forfeit their wealth when other people satisfy the wishes of the consumers better or cheaper than they do. In the free market economy the owners of capital are forced to invest it in those lines in which it best serves the public. Thus ownership of capital goods is continually shifted into the hands of those who have best succeeded in serving the consumers. In the market economy private property is in this sense a public service imposing upon the owners the responsibility of employing it in the best interests of the sovereign consumers. This is what economists mean when they call the market economy a democracy in which every penny gives a right to vote.

The Political Aspects of Freedom

Representative government is the political corollary of the market economy. The same spiritual movement that created modern capitalism substituted elected officeholders for the authoritarian rule of absolute kings and hereditary aristocracies. It was this much-decried bourgeois liberalism that brought freedom of conscience, of thought, of speech, and of the press and put an end to the intolerant persecution of dissenters.

A free country is one in which every citizen is free to fashion his life according to his own plans. He is free to compete on the market for the most desirable jobs and on the political scene for the highest offices. He does not depend more on other people's favor than these others depend on his favor. If he wants to succeed on the market, he has to satisfy the consumers; if he wants to succeed in public affairs he has to satisfy the voters. This system has brought to the capitalistic countries of Western Europe, America, and Australia an unprecedented increase in population figures and the highest standard of living ever known in history. The much talked-about common man has at his disposal amenities of which the richest men in precapitalistic ages did not even dream. He is in a position to enjoy the spiritual and intellectual achievements of science, poetry, and art that in earlier days were accessible only to a small elite of well-to-do people. And he is free to worship as his conscience tells him.

The Socialist Misrepresentation of the Market Economy

All the facts about the operation of the capitalistic system are misrepresented and distorted by the politicians and writers who arrogated to themselves the label of liberalism, the school of thought that in the nineteenth century crushed the arbitrary rule of monarchs and aristocrats and paved the way for free trade and enterprise. As these advocates of a return to despotism see it, all the evils that plague mankind are due to sinister machinations on the part of big business. What is needed to bring about wealth and happiness for all decent people is to put the corporations under strict government control. They admit, although only obliquely, that this means the adoption of socialism, the system of the Union of Soviet Socialist Republics. But they protest that socialism will be something entirely different in the countries of Western civilization from what it is in Russia. And anyway, they say, there is no other method to deprive the mammoth corporations of the enormous power they have acquired and to prevent them from further damaging the interests of the people.

Against all this fanatical propaganda there is need to emphasize again and again the truth that it is big business that brought about the unprecedented improvement of the masses' standard of living. Luxury goods for a comparatively small number of well-to-do can be produced by small-size enterprises. But the fundamental principle of capitalism is to produce for the satisfaction of the wants of the many. The same people who are employed by the big corporations are the main consumers of the goods turned out. If you look around in the household of an average American wage-earner, you will see for whom the wheels of the machines are turning. It is big business that makes all the achievements of modern technology accessible to the common man. Everybody is benefited by the high productivity of big scale production.

It is silly to speak of the "power" of big business. The very mark of capitalism is that supreme power in all economic matters is vested in the consumers. All big enterprises grew from modest beginnings into bigness because the patronage of the consumers made them grow. It would be impossible for small- or medium-size firms to turn out those products which no present-day American would like to do without. The bigger a corporation is, the more does it depend on the consumers' readiness to buy its wares. It was the wishes — or, as some say, the folly — of the consumers that drove the automobile industry into the production of ever bigger cars and forces it today to manufacture smaller cars. Chain stores and department stores are under the necessity to adjust their operations daily anew to the satisfaction of the changing wants of their customers. The fundamental law of the market is: the customer is always right.

A man who criticizes the conduct of business affairs and pretends to know better methods for the provision of the consumers is just an idle babbler. If he thinks that his own designs are better, why does he not try them himself? There are in this country always capitalists in search of a profitable investment of their funds who are ready to provide the capital required for any reasonable innovations. The public is always eager to buy what is better or cheaper or better and cheaper. What counts in the market is not fantastic reveries, but doing. It was not talking that made the "tycoons" rich, but service to the customers.

Capital Accumulation Benefits All of the People

It is fashionable nowadays to pass over in silence the fact that all economic betterment depends on saving and the accumulation of capital. None of the marvelous achievements of science and technology could have been practically utilized if the capital required had not previously been made available. What prevents the economically backward nations from taking full advantage of all the Western methods of production and thereby keeps their masses poor is not unfamiliarity with the teachings of technology but the insufficiency of their capital. One badly misjudges the problems facing the underdeveloped countries if one asserts that what they lack is technical knowledge, the "know-how." Their businessmen and their engineers, most of them graduates of the best schools of Europe and America, are well acquainted with the state of contemporary applied science. What ties their hands is a shortage of capital.

A hundred years ago America was even poorer than these backward nations. What made the United States become the most affluent country of the world was the fact that the "rugged individualism" of the years before the New Deal did not place too serious obstacles in the way of enterprising men. Businessmen became rich because they consumed only a small part of their profits and plowed the much greater part back into their businesses. Thus they enriched themselves and all of the people. For it was this accumulation of capital that raised the marginal productivity of labor and thereby wage rates.

Under capitalism the acquisitiveness of the individual businessman benefits not only himself but also all other people. There is a reciprocal relation between his acquiring wealth by serving the consumers and accumulating capital and the improvement of the standard of living of the wage-earners who form the majority of the consumers. The masses are in their capacity both as wage-earners and as consumers interested in the flowering of business. This is what the old liberals had in mind when they declared that in the market economy there prevails a harmony of the true interests of all groups of the population.

Economic Well-Being Threatened by Statism

It is in the moral and mental atmosphere of this capitalistic system that the American citizen lives and works. There are still in some parts of the United States conditions left which appear highly unsatisfactory to the prosperous inhabitants of the advanced districts which form the greater part of the country. But the rapid progress of industrialization would have long since wiped out these pockets of backwardness if the unfortunate policies of the New Deal had not slowed down the accumulation of capital, the irreplaceable tool of economic betterment. Used to the conditions of a capitalistic environment, the average American takes it for granted that every year business makes something new and better accessible to him. Looking backward upon the years of his own life, he realizes that many implements that were totally unknown in the days of his youth and many others which at that time could be enjoyed only by a small minority are now standard equipment of almost every household. He is fully confident that this trend will prevail also in the future. He simply calls it the "American way of life" and does not give serious thought to the question of what made this continuous improvement in the supply of material goods possible. He is not earnestly disturbed by the operation of factors that are bound not only to stop further accumulation of capital but may very soon bring about capital decumulation. He does not oppose the forces that—by frivolously increasing public expenditure, by cutting down capital accumulation, and even making for consumption of parts of the capital invested in business, and, finally, by inflation—are sapping the very foundations of his material well-being. He is not concerned about the growth of statism that wherever it has been tried resulted in producing and preserving conditions which in his eyes are shockingly wretched.

No Personal Freedom Without Economic Freedom

Unfortunately many of our contemporaries fail to realize what a radical change in the moral conditions of man, the rise of statism, the substitution of government omnipotence for the market economy, is bound to bring about. They are deluded by the idea that there prevails a clear-cut dualism in the affairs of man, that there is on the one side a sphere of economic activities and on the other side a field of activities that are considered as noneconomic. Between these two fields there is, they think, no close connection. The freedom that socialism abolishes is "only" the economic freedom, while freedom in all other matters remains unimpaired.

However, these two spheres are not independent of each other as this doctrine assumes. Human beings do not float in ethereal regions. Everything that a man does must necessarily in some way or other affect the economic or material sphere and requires his power to interfere with this sphere. In order to subsist, he must toil and have the opportunity to deal with some material tangible goods.

The confusion manifests itself in the popular idea that what is going on in the market refers merely to the economic side of human life and action. But in fact the prices of the market reflect not only "material concerns" — like getting food, shelter, and other amenities — but no less those concerns which are commonly called spiritual or higher or nobler. The observance or nonobservance of religious commandments — to abstain from certain activities altogether or on specific days, to assist those in need, to build and to maintain houses of worship, and many others — is one of the factors that determines the supply of, and the demand for, various consumers' goods and thereby prices and the conduct of business. The freedom that the market economy grants to the individual is not merely "economic" as distinguished from some other kind of freedom. It implies the freedom to determine also all those issues which are considered as moral, spiritual, and intellectual.

In exclusively controlling all the factors of production the socialist regime controls also every individual's whole life. The government assigns to everybody a definite job. It determines what books and papers ought to be printed and read, who should enjoy the opportunity to embark on writing, who should be entitled to use public assembly halls, to broadcast and to use all other communication facilities. This means that those in charge of the supreme conduct of government affairs ultimately determine which ideas, teachings, and doctrines can be propagated and which not. Whatever a written and promulgated constitution may say about the freedom of conscience, thought, speech, and the press and about neutrality in religious matters must in a socialist country remain a dead letter if the government does not provide the material means for the exercise of these rights. He who monopolizes all media of communication has full power to keep a tight hand on the individuals' minds and souls.

What makes many people blind to the essential features of any socialist or totalitarian system is the illusion that this system will be operated precisely in the way which they themselves consider as desirable. In supporting socialism, they take it for granted that the "state" will always do what they themselves want it to do. They call only that brand of totalitarianism "true," "real," or "good" socialism the rulers of which comply with their own ideas. All other brands they decry as counterfeit. What they first of all expect from the dictator is that he will suppress all those ideas of which they themselves disapprove. In fact, all these supporters of socialism are, unbeknown to themselves, obsessed by the dictatorial or authoritarian complex. They want all opinions and plans with which they disagree to be crushed by violent action on the part of the government.

The Meaning of the Effective Right to Dissent

The various groups that are advocating socialism, no matter whether they call themselves communists, socialists, or merely social reformers, agree in their essential economic program. They all want to substitute state control — or, as some of them prefer to call it, social control — of production activities for the market economy with its supremacy of the individual consumers. What separates them from one another are not issues of economic management, but religious and ideological convictions. There are Christian socialists — Catholic and Protestant of different denominations — and there are atheist socialists. Each of these varieties of socialism takes it for granted that the socialist commonwealth will be guided by the precepts of their own faith or of their rejection of any religious creed. They never give a thought to the possibility that the socialist regime may be directed by men hostile to their own faith and moral principles who may consider it as their duty to use all the tremendous power of the socialist apparatus for the suppression of what in their eyes is error, superstition, and idolatry.

The simple truth is that individuals can be free to choose between what they consider as right or wrong only where they are economically independent of the government. A socialist government has the power to make dissent impossible by discriminating against unwelcome religious and ideological groups and denying them all the material implements that are required for the propagation and the practice of their convictions. The one-party system, the political principle of socialist rule, implies also the one-religion and one-morality system. A socialist government has at its disposal means that can be used for the attainment of rigorous conformity in every regard, *Gleichschaltung* (political conformity) as the Nazis called it. Historians have pointed out what an important role in the Reformation was played by the printing press. But what chances would the reformers have had if all the printing presses had been operated by the governments headed by Charles V of Germany and the Valois kings of France?* And, for that matter, what chances would Marx have had under a system in which all the means of communication had been in the hands of the governments?

Whoever wants freedom of conscience must abhor socialism. Of course, freedom enables a man not only to do the good things but also to do the wrong things. But no moral value can be ascribed to an action, however good, that has been performed under the pressure of an omnipotent government.

---

* Charles V of Germany (1500–1558), a devoted Catholic, persecuted religious heresy in the Netherlands and struggled to suppress Lutheranism in the German principalities. During the reign of the Valois kings of France (1328–1589) religious wars were fought as French Protestants, including the Huguenots, struggled for freedom of worship.

2

The Individual in Society

The words freedom and liberty signified for the most eminent representatives of mankind one of the most precious and desirable goods. Today it is fashionable to sneer at them. They are, trumpets the modern sage, "slippery" notions and "bourgeois" prejudices.

Freedom and liberty are not to be found in nature. In nature there is no phenomenon to which these terms could be meaningfully applied. Whatever man does, he can never free himself from the restraints which nature imposes upon him. If he wants to succeed in acting, he must submit unconditionally to the laws of nature.

Freedom and liberty always refer to interhuman relations. A man is free as far as he can live and get on without being at the mercy of arbitrary decisions on the part of other people. In the frame of society everybody depends upon his fellow citizens. Social man cannot become independent without forsaking all the advantages of social cooperation.

The fundamental social phenomenon is the division of labor and its counterpart—human cooperation.

Experience teaches man that cooperative action is more efficient and productive than isolated action of self-sufficient individuals. The natural conditions determining man's life and effort are such that the division of labor increases output per unit of labor expended. These natural facts are: (1) the innate inequality of men with regard to their ability to perform various kinds of labor, and (2) the unequal distribution of the nature-given, nonhuman opportunities of production on the surface of the earth. One may as well consider these two facts as one and the same fact, namely, the manifoldness of nature which makes the universe a complex of infinite varieties.

Excerpts from *Human Action* (1949). Reprinted from the pamphlet published by the Foundation for Economic Education in 1952, with the permission of the publisher.

Innate Inequality

The division of labor is the outcome of man's conscious reaction to the multiplicity of natural conditions. On the other hand, it is itself a factor bringing about differentiation. It assigns to the various geographic areas specific functions in the complex of the processes of production. It makes some areas urban, others rural; it locates the various branches of manufacturing, mining, and agriculture in different places. Still more important, however, is the fact that it intensifies the innate inequality of men. Exercise and practice of specific tasks adjust individuals better to the requirements of their performance; men develop some of their inborn faculties and stunt the development of others. Vocational types emerge, people become specialists.

The division of labor splits the various processes of production into minute tasks, many of which can be performed by mechanical devices. It is this fact that made the use of machinery possible and brought about the amazing improvements in technical methods of production. Mechanization is the fruit of the division of labor, its most beneficial achievement, not its motive and fountain spring. Power-driven specialized machinery could be employed only in a social environment under the division of labor. Every step forward on the road toward the use of more specialized, more refined, and more productive machines requires a further specialization of tasks.

Within Society

Seen from the point of view of the individual, society is the great means for the attainment of all his ends. The preservation of society is an essential condition of any plans an individual may want to realize by any action whatever. Even the refractory delinquent who fails to adjust his conduct to the requirements of life within the societal system of cooperation does not want to miss any of the advantages derived from the division of labor. He does not consciously aim at the destruction of society. He wants to lay his hands on a greater portion of the jointly produced wealth than the social order assigns to him. He would feel miserable if antisocial behavior were to become universal and its inevitable outcome, the return to primitive indigence, resulted.

Liberty and freedom are the conditions of man within a contractual society. Social cooperation under a system of private ownership of the means of production means that within the range of the market the individual is not bound to obey and to serve an overlord. As far as he gives and serves other people, he does so of his own accord in order to be rewarded and served by the receivers. He exchanges goods and services, he does not do compulsory labor and does not pay tribute. He is certainly not independent. He depends on the other members of society. But this dependence is mutual. The buyer depends on the seller and the seller on the buyer.

Self-Interest

The main concern of many writers of the nineteenth and twentieth centuries was to misrepresent and to distort this obvious state of affairs. The workers, they said, are at the mercy of their employers. Now, it is true that the employer has the right to fire the employee. But if he makes use of this right in order to indulge in his whims, he hurts his own interests. It is to his own disadvantage if he discharges a better man in order to hire a less efficient one. The market does not directly prevent anybody from arbitrarily inflicting harm on his fellow citizens; it only puts a penalty upon such conduct. The shopkeeper is free to be rude to his customers provided he is ready to bear the consequences. The consumers are free to boycott a purveyor provided they are ready to pay the costs. What impels every man to the utmost exertion in the service of his fellow men and curbs innate tendencies toward arbitrariness and malice is, in the market, not compulsion and coercion on the part of gendarmes, hangmen, and penal courts; it is self-interest. The member of a contractual society is free because he serves others only in serving himself. What restrains him is only the inevitable natural phenomenon of scarcity. For the rest he is free in the range of the market.

In the market economy the individual is free to act within the orbit of private property and the market. His choices are final. For his fellow men his actions are data which they must take into account in their own acting. The coordination of the autonomous actions of all individuals is accomplished by the operation of the market. Society does not tell a man what to do and what not to do. There is no need to enforce cooperation by special orders or prohibitions. Noncooperation penalizes itself. Adjustment to the requirements of society's productive effort and the pursuit of the individual's own concerns are not in conflict. Consequently no agency is required to settle such conflicts. The system can work and accomplish its tasks without the interference of an authority issuing special orders and prohibitions and punishing those who do not comply.

Compulsion and Coercion

Beyond the sphere of private property and the market lies the sphere of compulsion and coercion; here are the dams which organized society has built for the protection of private property and the market against violence, malice, and fraud. This is the realm of constraint as distinguished from the realm of freedom. Here are rules discriminating between what is legal and what is illegal, what is permitted and what is prohibited. And here is a grim machine of arms, prisons, and gallows and the men operating it, ready to crush those who dare to disobey.

It is important to remember that government interference always means either violent action or the threat of such action. Government is in the last resort the employment of armed men, of policemen, gendarmes, soldiers, prison guards, and hangmen. The essential feature of government is the enforcement of its decrees by beating, killing, and imprisoning. Those who are asking for more government interference are asking ultimately for more compulsion and less freedom.

Liberty and freedom are terms employed for the description of the social conditions of the individual members of a market society in which the power of the indispensable hegemonic bond, the state, is curbed lest the operation of the market be endangered. In a totalitarian system there is nothing to which the attribute "free" could be attached but the unlimited arbitrariness of the dictator.

There would be no need to dwell upon this obvious fact if the champions of the abolition of liberty had not purposely brought about a semantic confusion. They realized that it was hopeless for them to fight openly and sincerely for restraint and servitude. The notions liberty and freedom had such prestige that no propaganda could shake their popularity. Since time immemorial in the realm of Western civilization, liberty has been considered as the most precious good. What gave to the West its eminence was precisely its concern about liberty, a social ideal foreign to the oriental peoples. The social philosophy of the Occident is essentially a philosophy of freedom. The main content of

the history of Europe and the communities founded by European em-
igrants and their descendants in other parts of the world was the
struggle for liberty. "Rugged" individualism is the signature of our civilization. No open attack upon the freedom of the individual had any
prospect of success.

New Definitions

Thus the advocates of totalitarianism chose other tactics. They reversed the meaning of words. They call true or genuine liberty the condition of the individuals under a system in which they have no right
other than to obey orders. They call themselves true *liberals* because
they strive after such a social order. They call democracy the Russian
methods of dictatorial government. They call the labor union methods
of violence and coercion "industrial democracy." They call freedom of
the press a state of affairs in which only the government is free to pub-
lish books and newspapers. They define liberty as the opportunity to do
the "right" things, and, of course, they arrogate to themselves the determination of what is right and what is not. In their eyes government
omnipotence means full liberty. To free the police power from all restraints is the true meaning of their struggle for freedom.

The market economy, say these self-styled liberals, grants liberty only
to a parasitic class of exploiters, the bourgeoisie; that these scoundrels
enjoy the freedom to enslave the masses; that the wage earner is not
free; that he must toil for the sole benefit of his masters, the employers;
that the capitalists appropriate to themselves what according to the inalienable rights of man should belong to the worker; that under socialism the worker will enjoy freedom and human dignity because he will
no longer have to slave for a capitalist; that socialism means the emancipation of the common man, means freedom for all; that it means,
moreover, riches for all.

These doctrines have been able to triumph because they did not encounter effective rational criticism. It is useless to stand upon an alleged "natural" right of individuals to own property if other people assert that the foremost "natural" right is that of income equality. Such
disputes can never be settled. It is beside the point to criticize nonessen-
tial, attendant features of the socialist program. One does not refute socialism by attacking the socialist stand on religion, marriage, birth control, and art.

A New Subterfuge

In spite of these serious shortcomings of the defenders of economic freedom it was impossible to fool all the people all the time about the essential features of socialism. The most fanatical planners were forced to admit that their projects involve the abolition of many freedoms people enjoy under capitalism and "plutodemocracy." Pressed hard, they resorted to a new subterfuge. The freedom to be abolished, they emphasize, is merely the spurious "economic" freedom of the capitalists that harms the common man; that outside the "economic sphere" freedom will not only be fully preserved, but considerably expanded. "Planning for Freedom" has lately become the most popular slogan of the champions of totalitarian government and the Russification of all nations.

The fallacy of this argument stems from the spurious distinction between two realms of human life and action, the "economic" sphere and the "noneconomic" sphere. Strictly speaking, people do not long for tangible goods as such, but for the services which these goods are fitted to render them. They want to attain the increment in well-being which these services are able to convey. It is a fact that people, in dealing on the market, are motivated not only by the desire to get food, shelter, and sexual enjoyment, but also by manifold "ideal" urges. Acting man is always concerned both with "material" and "ideal" things. He chooses between various alternatives, no matter whether they are to be classified as material or ideal. In the actual scales of value, material and ideal things are jumbled together.

Freedom, as people enjoyed it in the democratic countries of Western civilization in the years of the old liberalism's triumph, was not a product of constitutions, bills of rights, laws, and statutes. Those documents aimed only at safeguarding liberty and freedom, firmly established by the operation of the market economy, against encroachments on the part of officeholders. No government and no civil law can guarantee and bring about freedom otherwise than by supporting and defending the fundamental institutions of the market economy. Government means always coercion and compulsion and is by necessity the opposite of liberty. Government is a guarantor of liberty and is compatible with liberty only if its range is adequately restricted to the preservation of economic freedom. Where there is no market economy, the best-intentioned provisions of constitutions and laws remain a dead letter.

Competition

The freedom of man under capitalism is an effect of competition. The worker does not depend on the good graces of an employer. If his employer discharges him, he finds another employer. The consumer is not at the mercy of the shopkeeper. He is free to patronize another shop if he likes. Nobody must kiss other people's hands or fear their disfavor. Interpersonal relations are businesslike. The exchange of goods and services is mutual; it is not a favor to sell or to buy, it is a transaction dictated by selfishness on either side.

It is true that in his capacity as a producer every man depends either directly, as does the entrepreneur, or indirectly, as does the hired worker, on the demands of the consumers. However, this dependence upon the supremacy of the consumers is not unlimited. If a man has a weighty reason for defying the sovereignty of the consumers, he can try it. There is in the range of the market a very substantial and effective right to resist oppression. Nobody is forced to go into the liquor industry or into a gun factory if his conscience objects. He may have to pay a price for his conviction; there are in this world no ends the attainment of which is gratuitous. But it is left to a man's own decision to choose between a material advantage and the call of what he believes to be his duty. In the market economy the individual alone is the supreme arbiter in matters of his satisfaction.

Consumers Choose

Capitalist society has no means of compelling a man to change his occupation or his place of work other than to reward those complying with the wants of the consumers by higher pay. It is precisely this kind of pressure that many people consider as unbearable and hope to see abolished under socialism. They are too dull to realize that the only alternative is to convey to the authorities full power to determine in what branch and at what place a man should work.

In his capacity as a consumer man is no less free. He alone decides what is more and what is less important for him. He chooses how to spend his money according to his own will.

The substitution of economic planning for the market economy removes all freedom and leaves to the individual merely the right to obey. The authority directing all economic matters controls all aspects of a man's life and activities. It is the only employer. All labor becomes compulsory labor because the employee must accept what the chief deigns to offer him. The economic tsar determines what and how much the consumer may consume. There is no sector of human life in which a decision is left to the individual's value judgments. The authority assigns a definite task to him, trains him for this job, and employs him at the place and in the manner it deems expedient.

The "Planned" Life Is Not Free

As soon as the economic freedom which the market economy grants to its members is removed, all political liberties and bills of rights become humbug. Habeas corpus and trial by jury are a sham if, under the pretext of economic expediency, the authority has full power to relegate every citizen it dislikes to the arctic or to a desert and to assign him "hard labor" for life. Freedom of the press is a mere blind if the authority controls all printing offices and paper plants. And so are all the other rights of men.

A man has freedom as far as he shapes his life according to his own plans. A man whose fate is determined by the plans of a superior authority, in which the exclusive power to plan is vested, is not free in the sense in which the term "free" was used and understood by all people until the semantic revolution of our day brought about a confusion of tongues.

3

The Elite under Capitalism

A long line of eminent authors, beginning with Adam Ferguson,* tried to grasp the characteristic feature that distinguishes the modern capitalistic society, the market economy, from the older systems of the arrangement of social cooperation. They distinguished between warlike nations and commercial nations, between societies of a militant structure and those of individual freedom, between the society based on status and that based on contract. The appreciation of each of the two "ideal types" was, of course, different with the various authors. But they all agreed in establishing the contrast between the two types of social cooperation as well as in the cognition that no third principle of the arrangement of social affairs is thinkable and feasible.[1] One may disagree with some of the characteristics that they ascribed to each of the two types, but one must admit that the classification as such makes us comprehend essential facts of history as well as of contemporary social conflicts.

There are several reasons that prevent a full understanding of the significance of the distinction between these two types of society. There is in the first place the popular repugnance to assign to the inborn inequality of various individuals its due importance. There is furthermore the failure to realize the fundamental difference that exists between the meaning and the effects of private ownership of the means of production in the precapitalistic and in the capitalistic society. Finally, there is serious confusion brought about by the ambiguous employment of the term "economic power."

Reprinted from *The Freeman,* January 1962.
1. See Ludwig von Mises, *Human Action* (New Haven: Yale, 1949), pp. 196–99; (Chicago: Regnery, 1966), pp. 195–98.
* Adam Ferguson (1723–1816), Scottish philosopher and historian, a contemporary and friend of Adam Smith (1723–90).

Inborn Inequality

The doctrine that ascribed all differences among individuals to post-natal influences is untenable. The fact that human beings are born unequal in regard to physical and mental capacities is not denied by any reasonable man, certainly also not by pediatrists. Some individuals surpass their fellow men in health and vigor, in brain power and aptitude for various performances, in energy and resolution. Some people are better fit for the pursuit of earthly affairs, some less. From this point of view we may—without indulging in any judgment of value—distinguish between superior and inferior men. Karl Marx referred to "the inequality of individual endowment and therefore productive capacity (*Leistungsfähigkeit*) as natural privileges" and was fully aware of the fact that men "would not be different individuals if they were not unequal."[2]

In the precapitalistic ages the better endowed, the "superior" people, took advantage of their superiority by seizing power and enthralling the masses of weaker, i.e., "inferior" men. Victorious warriors appropriated to themselves all the land available for hunting and fishing, cattle raising and tilling. Nothing was left to the rest of the people than to serve the princes and their retinue. They were serfs and slaves, landless and penniless underlings.

Such was by and large the state of affairs in most parts of the world in the ages in which the "heroes"[3] were supreme and "commercialism" was absent. But then, in a process that, although again and again frustrated by a renascence of the spirit of violence, went on for centuries and is still going on, the spirit of business, i.e., of peaceful cooperation under the principle of the division of labor, undermined the mentality of the "good old days." Capitalism—the market economy—radically transformed the economic and political organization of mankind.

In the precapitalistic society the superior men knew no other method of utilizing their own superiority than to subdue the masses of inferior people. But under capitalism the more able and more gifted men can profit from their superiority only by serving to the best of their abilities the wishes and wants of the majority of less gifted men.

In the market economy the consumers are supreme. Consumers determine, by their buying or abstention from buying, what should be

2. Karl Marx, *Critique of the Social-Democratic Program of Gotha* (Letter to Bracke, May 5, 1875).
3. Werner Sombart, *Händler und Helden* (Hucksters and Heroes) (Munich, 1915).

produced, by whom and how, of what quality and in what quantity. The entrepreneurs, capitalists, and landowners who fail to satisfy in the best possible and cheapest way the most urgent of the not yet satisfied wishes of the consumers are forced to go out of business and forfeit their preferred position. In business offices and in laboratories the keenest minds are busy fructifying the most complex achievements of scientific research for the production of ever better implements and gadgets for people who have no inkling of the scientific theories that make the fabrication of such things possible. The bigger an enterprise is, the more it is forced to adjust its production activities to the changing whims and fancies of the masses, its masters. The fundamental principle of capitalism is mass production to supply the masses. It is the patronage of the masses that makes enterprises grow into bigness. The common man is supreme in the market economy. He is the customer "who is always right."

In the political sphere representative government is the corollary of the supremacy of the consumers in the market. The officeholders depend on the voters in a way similar to that in which the entrepreneurs and investors depend on the consumers. The same historical process that substituted the capitalistic mode of production for precapitalistic methods substituted popular government — democracy — for royal absolutism and other forms of government by the few. And wherever the market economy is superseded by socialism, autocracy makes a comeback. It does not matter whether the socialist or communist despotism is camouflaged by the use of aliases such as "dictatorship of the proletariat" or "people's democracy" or "*Führer* (leader) principle." It always amounts to a subjection of the many to the few.

It is hardly possible to misconstrue more improperly the state of affairs prevailing in the capitalistic society than by dubbing the capitalists and entrepreneurs a "ruling" class intent upon "exploiting" the masses of decent men. We do not have to raise the question as to how the men who under capitalism are businessmen would have tried to take advantage of their superior talents in any other thinkable organization of production activities. Under capitalism they are vying with one another in serving the masses of less gifted men. All their thoughts aim at perfecting the methods of supplying the consumers. Every year, every month, every week, something unheard of before appears on the market and is very soon made accessible to the many. Precisely because they are producing for profit, the businessmen are producing for the use of the consumers.

Confusion Concerning Property

The second deficiency of the customary treatment of the problems of society's economic organization is the confusion produced by the indiscriminate employment of juridical concepts, first of all the concept of private property.

In the precapitalistic ages there prevailed by and large economic self-sufficiency, first of every household, later — with the gradual progress toward commercialism — of small regional units. The much greater part of all products did not reach the market. They were consumed without having been sold and bought. Under such conditions there was no essential difference between private ownership of producers' goods and that of consumers' goods. In each case property served the owner exclusively. To own something, whether a producers' good or a consumers' good, meant to have it for oneself alone and to deal with it for one's own satisfaction.

But it is different in the frame of a market economy. The owner of producers' goods, the capitalist, can derive advantage from his ownership only by employing them for the best possible satisfaction of the wants of the consumers. In the market economy property in the means of production is acquired and preserved by serving the public and is lost if the public becomes dissatisfied with the way in which it is served. Private property of the material factors of production is a public mandate, as it were, which is withdrawn as soon as the consumers think that other people would employ the capital goods more efficiently for their, viz., the consumers', benefit. By the instrumentality of the profit and loss system the capitalists are forced to deal with "their" property as if it were other people's property entrusted to them under the obligation to utilize it for the best possible provision of the virtual beneficiaries, the consumers. This real meaning of private ownership of the material factors of production under capitalism could be ignored and misinterpreted because all people — economists, lawyers, and laymen — had been led astray by the fact that the legal concept of property as developed by the juridical practices and doctrines of precapitalistic ages has been retained unchanged or only slightly altered while its effective meaning has been radically transformed.[4]

4. It was the great Roman poet Quintus Horatius Flaccus who first alluded to this characteristic feature of property of producers' goods in a market economy. See Mises, *Socialism* (Yale, 1951), p. 42 n; (Liberty Fund, 1981), p. 31 n.

In the feudal society the economic situation of every individual was determined by the share allotted to him by the powers that be. The poor man was poor because little land or no land at all had been given to him. He could with good reason think (to say it openly would have been too dangerous): "I am poor because other people have more than a fair share." But in the frame of a capitalistic society the accumulation of additional capital by those who succeeded in utilizing their funds for the best possible provision of the consumers enriches not only the owners but all of the people, on the one hand by raising the marginal productivity of labor and thereby wages, and on the other hand by increasing the quantity of goods produced and brought to the market. The peoples of the economically backward countries are poorer than the Americans because their countries lack a sufficient number of successful capitalists and entrepreneurs.

A tendency toward an improvement of the standard of living of the masses can prevail only when and where the accumulation of new capital outruns the increase in population figures.

The formation of capital is a process performed with the cooperation of the consumers: only those entrepreneurs can earn surpluses whose activities best satisfy the public. And the utilization of the once accumulated capital is directed by the anticipation of the most urgent of the not yet fully satisfied wishes of the consumers. Thus capital comes into existence and is employed according to the wishes of the consumers.

Two Kinds of Power

When in dealing with market phenomena we apply the term "power," we must be fully aware of the fact that we are employing it with a connotation that is entirely different from the traditional connotation attached to it in dealing with issues of government and affairs of state.

Governmental power is the faculty to beat into submission all those who would dare to disobey the orders issued by the authorities. Nobody would call government an entity that lacks this faculty. Every governmental action is backed by constables, prison guards, and executioners. However beneficial a governmental action may appear, it is ultimately made possible only by the government's power to compel its subjects to do what many of them would not do if they were not threatened by the police and the penal courts. A government-supported hospital serves charitable purposes. But the taxes collected that enable the authorities to spend money for the upkeep of the hospital are not paid voluntarily. The citizens pay taxes because not to pay them would bring them to prison and physical resistance to the revenue agents could bring them to the gallows.

It is true that the majority of the people willy-nilly acquiesce in this state of affairs and, as David Hume* put it, "resign their own sentiments and passions to those of their rulers." They proceed in this way because they think that in the long run they serve better their own interests by being loyal to their government than by overturning it. But this does not alter the fact that governmental power means the exclusive faculty to frustrate any disobedience by the recourse to violence. As human nature is, the institution of government is an indispensable means to make civilized life possible. The alternative is anarchy and the law of the stronger. But the fact remains that government is the power to imprison and to kill.

The concept of *economic* power as applied by the socialist authors means something entirely different. The fact to which it refers is the capacity to influence other people's behavior by offering them something the acquisition of which they consider as more desirable than the avoidance of the sacrifice they have to make for it. In plain words: it means the invitation to enter into a bargain, an act of exchange. I will give you *a* if you give me *b*. There is no question of any compulsion nor of any threats. The buyer does not "rule" the seller and the seller does not "rule" the buyer.

Of course, in the market economy everybody's style of life is adjusted to the division of labor, and a return to self-sufficiency is out of the question. Everybody's bare survival would be jeopardized if he were forced suddenly to experience the autarky of ages gone by. But in the regular course of market transactions there is no danger of such a relapse into the conditions of the primeval household economy. A faint image of the effects of any disturbance in the usual course of market exchanges is provided when labor union violence, benevolently tolerated or even openly encouraged and aided by the government, stops the activities of vital branches of business.

In the market economy every specialist — and there are no other people than specialists — depends on all other specialists. This mutuality is

---

* David Hume (1711–76), prominent Scottish philosopher and historian. His skeptical philosophy had a profound influence on later thinkers.

the characteristic feature of interpersonal relations under capitalism. The socialists ignore the fact of mutuality and speak of economic power. For example, as they see it, "the capacity to determine product" is one of the powers of the entrepreneur.[5] One can hardly misconstrue more radically the essential features of the market economy. It is not business, but the consumers who ultimately determine what should be produced. It is a silly fable that nations go to war because there is a munitions industry and that people are getting drunk because the distillers have "economic power." If one calls economic power the capacity to choose — or, as the socialists prefer to say, to "determine" — the product, one must establish the fact that this power is fully vested in the buyers and consumers.

"Modern civilization, nearly all civilization," said the great British economist Edwin Cannan, "is based on the principle of making things pleasant for those who please the market and unpleasant for those who fail to do so."[6] The market, that means the buyers; the consumers, that means all of the people. To the contrary, under planning or socialism the goals of production are determined by the supreme planning authority; the individual gets what the authority thinks he ought to get. All this empty talk about the economic power of business aims at obliterating this fundamental distinction between freedom and bondage.

The "Power" of the Employer

People refer to economic power also in describing the internal conditions prevailing within the various enterprises. The owner of a private firm or the president of a corporation, it is said, enjoys within his outfit absolute power. He is free to indulge in his whims and fancies. All employees depend on his arbitrariness. They must stoop and obey or else face dismissal and starvation.

Such observations, too, ascribe to the employer powers that are vested in the consumers. The requirement to outstrip its competitors by serving the public in the cheapest and best possible way enjoins upon every enterprise the necessity to employ the personnel best fitted for the performance of the various functions entrusted to them. The

5. Cf., for instance, A. A. Berle, Jr., *Power without Property* (New York: Harcourt, Brace, Inc., 1959), p. 82.
6. Edwin Cannan, *An Economist's Protest* (London: P. S. King & Son, Ltd., 1928), pp. vi–vii.

individual enterprise must try to outdo its competitors not only by the employment of the most suitable methods of production and the purchase of the best fitted materials, but also by hiring the right type of workers. It is true that the head of an enterprise has the faculty to give vent to his sympathies or antipathies. He is free to prefer an inferior man to a better man; he may fire a valuable assistant and in his place employ an incompetent and inefficient substitute. But all the faults he commits in this regard affect the profitability of his enterprise. He has to pay for them in full. It is the very supremacy of the market that penalizes such capricious behavior. The market forces the entrepreneurs to deal with every employee exclusively from the point of view of the services he renders to the satisfaction of the consumers.

What curbs in all market transactions the temptation of indulging in malice and venom is precisely the costs involved in such behavior. The consumer is free to boycott for some reasons, popularly called noneconomic or irrational, the purveyor who would in the best and cheapest way satisfy his wants. But then he has to bear the consequences; he will either be less perfectly served or he will have to pay a higher price. Civil government enforces its commandments by recourse to violence or the threat of violence. The market does not need any recourse to violence because neglect of its rationality penalizes itself.

The critics of capitalism fully acknowledge this fact in pointing out that for private enterprise nothing counts but the striving after profit. Profit can be made only by satisfying the consumers better or cheaper or better *and* cheaper, than others do. The consumer has in his capacity as customer the right to be full of whim and fancies. The businessman *qua* producer has only one aim: to provide for the consumer. If one deplores the businessman's unfeeling preoccupation with profit-seeking, one has to realize two things. First, that this attitude is prescribed to the entrepreneur by the consumers who are not prepared to accept any excuse for poor service. Secondly, that it is precisely this neglect of "the human angle" that prevents arbitrariness and partiality from affecting the employer-employee nexus.

To establish these facts does not amount either to a commendation or to a condemnation of the market economy or its political corollary, government by the people (representative government, democracy). Science is neutral with regard to any judgments of value. It neither approves nor condemns; it just describes and analyzes what is.

A Duty of the Elite

Stressing the fact that under unhampered capitalism the consumers are supreme in determining the goals of production does not imply any opinion about the moral and intellectual capacities of these individuals. The individuals *qua* consumers as well as *qua* voters are mortal men liable to error and may very often choose what in the long run will harm them. Philosophers may be right in severely criticizing the conduct of their fellow citizens. But there is, in a free society, no other means to avoid the evils resulting from one's fellows' bad judgment than to induce them to alter their ways of life voluntarily. Where there is freedom, this is the task incumbent upon the elite.

Men are unequal and the inherent inferiority of the many manifests itself also in the manner in which they enjoy the affluence capitalism bestows upon them. It would be a boon for mankind, say many authors, if the common man would spend less time and money for the satisfaction of vulgar appetites and more for higher and nobler gratifications. But should not distinguished critics rather blame themselves than the masses? Why did they, whom fate and nature have blessed with moral and intellectual eminence, not better succeed in persuading the masses of inferior people to drop their vulgar tastes and habits? If something is wrong with the behavior of the many, the fault rests no more with the inferiority of the masses than with the inability or unwillingness of the elite to induce all other people to accept their own higher standards of value. The serious crisis of our civilization is caused not only by the shortcomings of the masses. It is no less the effect of a failure of the elite.

4

The Economic Role of Saving
and Capital Goods

As the popular philosophy of the common man sees it, human wealth and welfare are the products of the cooperation of two primordial factors: nature and human labor. All the things that enable man to live and to enjoy life are supplied either by nature or by work or by a combination of nature-given opportunities with human labor. As nature dispenses its gifts gratuitously, it follows that all the final fruits of production, the consumers' goods, ought to be allotted exclusively to the workers whose toil has created them. But unfortunately in this sinful world conditions are different. There the "predatory" classes of the "exploiters" want to reap although they have not sown. The landowners, the capitalists, and the entrepreneurs appropriate to themselves what by rights belongs to the workers who have produced it. All the evils of the world are the necessary effect of this originary wrong.

Such are the ideas that dominate the thinking of most of our contemporaries. The socialists and the syndicalists conclude that in order to render human affairs more satisfactory it is necessary to eliminate those whom their jargon calls the "robber barons," i.e., the entrepreneurs, the capitalists, and the landowners, entirely; the conduct of all production affairs ought to be entrusted either to the social apparatus of compulsion and coercion, the state (in the Marxian terminology called Society), or to the men employed in the individual plants or branches of production.

Other people are more considerate in their reformist zeal. They do not intend to expropriate those whom they call the "leisure class" entirely. They want only to take away from them as much as is needed

Reprinted from *The Freeman*, August 1963.

to bring about "more equality" in the "distribution" of wealth and income.

But both groups, the party of the thoroughgoing socialists and that of the more cautious reformers, agree on the basic doctrine according to which profit and interest are "unearned" income and therefore, morally objectionable. Both groups agree that profit and interest are the cause of the misery of the great majority of all honest workingmen and their families, and, in a decent and satisfactory organization of society, ought to be sharply curbed, if not entirely abolished.

Yet this whole interpretation of human conditions is fallacious. The policies engendered by it are pernicious from whatever point of view we may judge them. Western civilization is doomed if we do not succeed very soon in substituting reasonable methods of dealing with economic problems for the present disastrous methods.

Three Factors of Production

Mere work—that is, effort not guided by a rational plan and not aided by the employment of tools and intermediary products—brings about very little for the improvement of the worker's condition. Such work is not a specifically human device. It is what man has in common with all other animals. It is bestirring oneself instinctively and using one's bare hands to gather whatever is eatable and drinkable that can be found and appropriated.

Physical exertion turns into a factor of human production when it is directed by reason toward a definite end and employs tools and previously produced intermediary products. Mind—reason—is the most important equipment of man. In the human sphere, labor counts only as *one* item in a combination of natural resources, capital goods, and labor; all these three factors are employed, according to a definite plan devised by reason, for the attainment of an end chosen. Labor, in the sense in which this term is used in dealing with human affairs, is only one of several factors of production.

The establishment of this fact demolishes entirely all the theses and claims of the popular doctrine of exploitation. Those saving and thereby accumulating capital goods, and those abstaining from the consumption of previously accumulated capital goods, contribute their share to the outcome of the processes of production. Equally indispensable in the conduct of affairs is the role played by the human mind. Entrepreneurial judgment directs the toil of the workers and the employment of the capital goods toward the ultimate end of production, the best possible removal of what causes people to feel discontented and unhappy.

What distinguishes contemporary life in the countries of Western civilization from conditions as they prevailed in earlier ages — and still exist for the greater number of those living today — is not the changes in the supply of labor and the skill of the workers and not the familiarity with the exploits of pure science and their utilization by the applied sciences, by technology. It is the amount of capital accumulated. The issue has been intentionally obscured by the verbiage employed by the international and national government agencies dealing with what is called foreign aid for the underdeveloped countries. What these poor countries need in order to adopt the Western methods of mass production for the satisfaction of the wants of the masses is not information about a "know how." There is no secrecy about technological methods. They are taught at the technological schools and they are accurately described in textbooks, manuals, and periodical magazines. There are many experienced specialists available for the execution of every project that one may find practicable for these backward countries. What prevents a country like India from adopting the American methods of industry is the paucity of its supply of capital goods. As the Indian government's confiscatory policies are deterring foreign capitalists from investing in India and as its prosocialist bigotry sabotages domestic accumulation of capital, their country depends on the alms that Western nations are giving to it.

Consumers Direct the Use of Capital

Capital goods come into existence by saving. A part of the goods produced is withheld from immediate consumption and employed for processes the fruits of which will only mature at a later date. All material civilization is based upon this "capitalistic" approach to the problems of production.

"Roundabout methods of production," as Böhm-Bawerk* called them, are chosen because they generate a higher output per unit of input. Early man lived from hand to mouth. Civilized man produces

---

* Eugen von Böhm-Bawerk (1851–1914), Austrian economist, professor to Ludwig von Mises, renowned for his scholarly study of interest theory, *Capital and Interest*. Böhm-Bawerk also served as Finance Minister in the Austro-Hungarian government, 1895, 1897, and 1900–1904.

tools and intermediary products in the pursuit of long-range designs that finally bring forth results which direct, less time-consuming methods could never have attained, or could have attained only with an incomparably higher expenditure of labor and material factors.

Those saving—that is consuming less than their share of the goods produced—inaugurate progress toward general prosperity. The seed they have sown enriches not only themselves but also all other strata of society. It benefits the consumers.

The capital goods are for the owner a dead fund, a liability rather than an asset, if not used in production for the best possible and cheapest provision of the people with the goods and services they are asking for most urgently. In the market economy the owners of capital goods are forced to employ their property as if it were entrusted to them by the consumers under the stipulation to invest it in those lines in which it best serves those consumers. The capitalists are virtually mandataries of the consumers, bound to comply with their wishes.

In order to attend to the orders received from the consumers, their real bosses, the capitalists must either themselves proceed to investment and the conduct of business or, if they are not prepared for such entrepreneurial activity or distrust their own abilities, hand over their funds to men whom they consider as better fitted for such a function. Whatever alternative they may choose, the supremacy of the consumers remains intact. No matter what the financial structure of the firm or company may be, the entrepreneur who operates with other people's money depends no less on the market, that is, the consumers, than the entrepreneur who fully owns his outfit.

There is no other method to make wage rates rise than by investing more capital per worker. More investment of capital means to give to the laborer more efficient tools. With the aid of better tools and machines, the quantity of the products increases and their quality improves. As the employer consequently will be in a position to obtain from the consumers more for what the employee has produced in one hour of work, he is able—and, by the competition of other employers, forced—to pay a higher price for the man's work.

Intervention and Unemployment

As the labor union doctrine sees it, the wage increases that they are obtaining by what is euphemistically called "collective bargaining" are not to burden the buyers of the products but should be absorbed by the employers. The latter should cut down what in the eyes of the communists is called "unearned income," that is, interest on the capital invested and the profits derived from success in filling wants of the consumers that until then had remained unsatisfied. Thus the unions hope to transfer step-by-step all this allegedly "unearned income" from the pockets of the capitalists and entrepreneurs into those of the employees.

What really happens on the market is, however, very different. At the market price m of the product p, all those who were prepared to spend m for a unit of p could buy as much as they wanted. The total quantity of p produced and offered for sale was s. It was not larger than s because with such a larger quantity the price, in order to clear the market, would have to drop below m to $m-$. But at this price of $m-$ the producers with the highest costs would suffer losses and would thereby be forced to stop producing p. These marginal producers likewise incur losses and are forced to discontinue producing p if the wage increase enforced by the union (or by a governmental minimum wage decree) causes an increase of production costs not compensated by a rise in the price of m to $m+$. The resulting restriction of production necessitates a reduction of the labor force. The outcome of the union's "victory" is the unemployment of a number of workers.

The result is the same if the employers are in a position to shift the increase in production costs fully to the consumers, without a drop in the quantity of p produced and sold. If the consumers are spending more for the purchase of p, they must cut down their buying of some other commodity q. Then the demand for q drops and brings about unemployment of a part of the men who were previously engaged in turning out q.

The union doctrine qualifies interest received by the owners of the capital invested in the enterprise as "unearned" and concludes that it could be abolished entirely or considerably shortened without any harm to the employees and the consumers. The rise in production costs caused by wage increases could therefore be borne by shortening the company's net earnings and a corresponding reduction of the dividends paid to the shareholders. The same idea is at the bottom of the unions' claim that every increase in what they call productivity of labor (that is, the sum of the prices received for the total output divided by the number of man hours spent in its production) should be added to wages. Both methods mean confiscating for the benefit of the employees the whole or at least a considerable part of the returns on the capital provided by the saving of the capitalists. But what induces the capitalists to abstain from consuming their capital and to increase it by new saving is the fact that their forbearance is counterbalanced by the proceeds of their investments. If one deprives them of these proceeds, the only use they can make of the capital they own is to consume it and thus to inaugurate general progressive impoverishment.

The Only Sound Policy

What elevates the wage rates paid to the American workers above the rates paid in foreign countries is the fact that the investment of capital per worker is higher in this country than abroad. Saving, the accumulation of capital, has created and preserved up to now the high standard of living of the average American employee.

All the methods by which the federal government and the governments of the states, the political parties, and the unions are trying to improve the conditions of people anxious to earn wages and salaries are not only vain but directly pernicious. There is only one kind of policy that can effectively benefit the employees, namely, a policy that refrains from putting any obstacles in the way of further saving and accumulation of capital.

5

Luxuries into Necessities

About sixty years ago Gabriel Tarde (1843–1904), the great French sociologist, dealt with the problem of the popularization of luxuries. An industrial innovation, he pointed out, enters the market as the extravagance of an elite before it finally turns, step-by-step, into a need of each and all and is considered indispensable. What was once a luxury becomes in the course of time a necessity.

The history of technology and marketing provides ample exemplification to confirm Tarde's thesis. There was in the past a considerable time lag between the emergence of something unheard of before and its becoming an article of everybody's use. It sometimes took many centuries until an innovation was generally accepted at least within the orbit of Western civilization. Think of the slow popularization of the use of forks, of soap, of handkerchiefs, and of a great variety of other things.

From its beginnings capitalism displayed the tendency to shorten this time lag and finally to eliminate it almost entirely. This is not a merely accidental feature of capitalistic production; it is inherent in its very nature. Capitalism is essentially mass production for the satisfaction of the wants of the masses. Its characteristic mark is big-scale production by big business. For big business there cannot be any question of producing limited quantities for the sole satisfaction of a small elite. The bigger big business becomes, the more and the quicker it makes accessible to the whole people the new achievements of technology.

Centuries passed before the fork turned from an implement of effeminate weaklings into a utensil of all people. The evolution of the motor car from a plaything of wealthy idlers into a universally used means of transportation required more than twenty years. But nylon

Reprinted from the New York University Graduate School of Business Administration *Newsletter* 1, no. 4 (Spring 1956).

stockings became, in this country, an article of every woman's wear within hardly more than two or three years. There was practically no period in which the enjoyment of such innovations as television or the products of the frozen food industry was restricted to a small minority.

The disciples of Marx are anxious to describe in their textbooks the "unspeakable horrors of capitalism" which, as their master had prognosticated, results "with the inexorability of a law of nature" in the progressing impoverishment of the "masses." Their prejudices prevent them from noticing the fact that capitalism tends, by the instrumentality of big-scale production, to wipe out the striking contrast between the mode of life of a fortunate elite and that of the rest of a nation.

The gulf that separated the man who travelled in a coach-and-six and the man who stayed at home because he lacked the fare has been reduced to the difference between the railroad traveller who went by Pullman car, or first class, and the traveller who went coach class.

6

The Saver as a Voter

In the phrase, "protection of savers," the word "protection" has a different meaning from that usually attributed to it in present-day political circles. Generally speaking, protection of the "little man" or of agriculture means protecting firms from competition on the market at the expense of consumers. Privileges to advance the special interests of particular groups at the expense of the entire population are recommended. Policies are proposed which must reduce total production.

Protection of savers and of savings involves something very different from this, namely, preservation of the very foundations of justice on which the capitalistic order of society is based and, consequently, of capitalism itself. The unprecedented increase in the standard of living of the masses in the capitalistic West is due to the fact that the formation of capital increased much more than the population. Real wages went up because the marginal productivity of capital goods went down in comparison with that of labor or, more popularly expressed, because the worker in a modern, well-equipped plant can produce many times more than can a worker with primitive tools.

Unrecognized Dangers

It was possible for savings and capital accumulation to increase on an ever larger scale in the West because the right of private property, in contrast to the arbitrary might of military and political rulers, had been firmly established as the result of a gradual development based on Roman law. Conditions in the constitutional state permitted sizeable accumulations of savings and capital investment. What separates West

Translated by Bettina Bien Greaves from the German, as it appeared in *Zeitschrift für das gesamte Kreditwesen* 10, no. 1 (January 1, 1957): pp. 24–25.

from East is precisely the idea which social reformers ridicule as the "sanctity" of property, and which has not penetrated the Orient at all.* Capitalistic saving and investment cannot develop in lands where it is generally believed that the wealth of the businessman causes the poverty of the many, and where the successful trader is sacrificed to the predatory desires of the rulers and their representatives. The short interlude of "colonialism" and "imperialism" now belongs to history. One day, also, the United States will discontinue its gifts of billions to the enemies of capitalism. Many hundreds of millions in Asia and Africa will suffer increasing want because the policies of their governments obstruct domestic saving and capital formation and keep foreign capital out.

In view of the situation in the United States, there is certainly no cause to wonder that the Orientals lack understanding of the problem of capital creation and capital preservation. The fact that every year the quantity of newly accumulated capital in the United States far exceeds the amount consumed in production and otherwise used up is due neither to the policies of the government nor to the doctrines propagated by the universities, the two political parties, and the press. It is a result of the fact that American capitalism still operates satisfactorily in spite of all the obstacles placed in its way under the misleading label of "welfare economics."

The market economy under the directorship of the entrepreneur has never better demonstrated its unparalleled productivity than in its adaptation to this system so full of traps and snares. Still the official political economists, self-styled "progressives," misinterpret this great success of entrepreneurial initiative. Prejudiced by their socialistic ideas, they seek to discover in every improvement in the standard of living of the masses a new argument for the continuation of the New and Fair Deal reforms and the related policies of inflation and credit expansion through low interest rates.

For some time it has seemed that public opinion was beginning to recognize the dangers of continued inflation, and that this would lead to an end of the policy of credit expansion. Yet the Federal Reserve Banks' interest rate was allowed to increase only slightly before a strong countermovement set in. Everyone protests that he is against inflation.

* A rigid system of privilege and castes prevailed for centuries in China and Japan; wealth was a question of rank, and the common man had little opportunity to improve his situation. Savings in Japan and the other nations of the Pacific Rim are a relatively recent development.

Yet what is usually meant by "inflation" is not an increase in the supply of money and credit but an increase of prices. People do not want to hear that an increase in prices is the inevitable consequence of an increase in the money supply. To bolster purchasing power, they demand cheap credit and price ceilings.

After a period of decreased saving, the amount of new savings is once again rising in the United States. Also, the increase in the amount of life insurance taken out each year is considerable. Nevertheless it would be premature to conclude from this that the masses do not realize that the progressive decline in the dollar's purchasing power is a threat to their savings and their provision for the future. However, there is no other possible means of saving open to the employee or worker who is not familiar with business or the stock market. (Even the entirely insufficient makeshift of hoarding gold coins is in the United States illegal and practically impossible.*) The people cling to the hope that no further decline in the dollar's purchasing power will take place.

"Do You Know That You Are a Creditor?"

The coming years will determine whether the United States, whose spokesmen never tire of noting that the American standard of living is much higher and better than that of any other time or place, will succeed in managing its finances without inflation or credit expansion. The number of persons is not large who fully recognize the dangers of government's mislabelled "expansionist" monetary policy, and only a few politicians are ready to listen to their words of warning. The "practical" person has no interest in "long-run" policies. For him, nothing matters but the outcome of the next Congressional election, which is never more than two years off.

When National Socialism (Nazism) attained success in Germany with its slogan "Wipe out interest slavery!" one daily paper—I believe it was the *Frankfurter Zeitung*— carried an article under the headline "Do you know that you are a creditor?" The American "common man," as a saver and especially as an owner of life insurance policies, is a creditor to a much greater degree than was the average German of the Weimar Republic. Still he is not aware of it. He trusts the inflationists who tell

---

* For more than forty years, from June 5, 1933, until December 31, 1974, U.S. citizens were denied the right to own monetary gold.

him that "cheap money" hurts only the "international bankers." Just as he supports politicians, who spend billions in tax dollars to raise food prices, he is supporting a monetary policy that threatens his economic future.

There is only one way to improve the situation. That is to try to explain these matters to the voter.

7

The Market and the State

For every species of animals and plants the means of subsistence are limited. Hence every living being's vital interests are implacably opposed to those of all members of its own species. Only human beings know how to overcome this irreconcilable nature-given conflict by embarking upon cooperation. The higher productivity of work performed under the principle of the division of labor substitutes for the grim antagonism created by the scarcity of food the solidarity of interests of people intentionally aiming at common goals. The peaceful exchange of commodities and services, the market process, becomes the standard type of interhuman relations. Mutual agreement of the parties displaces the recourse to violence, to the law of the stronger.

Cooperation versus Violence

The inherent deficiency of this method of solving mankind's fundamental problem (and there is no other method available) is to be seen in the fact that it depends on full and unconditional cooperation of all human beings and can be frustrated by the noncooperation of any individual. There is no other means available to eliminate violent interference with human affairs than the recourse to more powerful violence. Against individuals or groups of individuals who are resorting to violence or are not complying with their obligations resulting from contracts nothing avails but the recourse to violent action. The market system of voluntary agreements cannot work if not backed up by an apparatus of compulsion and coercion ready to resort to violence against individuals who are not strictly abiding by the terms and rules of mutual agreement. The market needs the support of the state.

Reprinted from Mises's original manuscript, first published in German translation in *Schweizer Monatshefte* 48, no. 1 (April 1968): pp. 13–16.

The market in the broadest sense of the term is the process that encompasses all voluntary and spontaneous actions of men. It is the realm of human initiative and freedom and the soil upon which all human achievements thrive.

The state, the power protecting the market against destructive recourse to violence, is a grim apparatus of coercion and compulsion. It is a system of orders and prohibitions, and its armed servants are always ready to enforce these laws. Whatever the state does is done by those subject to its commands. State power forced its subjects to build pyramids and other monuments, hospitals, research institutes, and schools. People see these achievements and praise their authors to the skies. They do not see the buildings that state power destroyed. Nor do they see those structures that were never constructed because the government had taxed away the means that individual citizens had destined for their erection.

There is today practically no limit to the people's and their rulers' prostatist or, as one says today, prosocialist enthusiasm. Hardly anybody is courageous enough to raise objections if some expansion of state power — popularly styled the "public sector of the economy" — is suggested. What slows down and in most fields almost stops the progress toward more socialization of business enterprises is the manifest financial failure of almost all nationalization and municipalization ventures. In this regard reference to the U.S. Post Office plays an important role in present-day social philosophies and economic policies. Its well-known inefficiency and its enormous financial deficit demolish the popular fables about the virtues of the conduct of affairs by the state, the social apparatus of violent action.

It is impossible to defend honestly the case for violence against the case for peaceful cooperation. Thus the advocates of violence are resorting to the trick of calling the methods of violence and threat of violence to which they resort "non-violence." The outstanding case is that of labor-unionism. Its essential procedure, the use of violent action of various kinds [1] or the threat of such action, is to prevent enterprises from working with the aid of people who do not obey the unions' orders. They have succeeded in giving to the military term "picketing" a

1. Cf. Roscoe Pound, *Legal Immunities of Labor Unions* (Washington, D.C.: American Enterprise Association, 1957).

"peaceful" connotation. Yet, precisely in the way they apply it, it includes the willingness to kill and destroy by brute force.

The fundamental antagonism between the realm of mutual peaceful agreement and that of compulsion and coercion cannot be eradicated by idle talk about two "sectors" of the economy, the private and the public. There is no conciliation between constraint and spontaneity. The attempts to resuscitate the totalitarianism of the Pharaohs of Egypt or of the Incas of Peru are doomed. And violence does not lose its antisocial character by being rebaptized "nonviolence." All that man has created was a product of voluntary human cooperation. All that violence has contributed to civilization consists in the — certainly indispensable — services it renders to the endeavors of peace-loving people to restrain potential peace-breakers.

Socialist Planning

Western civilization appreciates and always appreciated liberty as the greatest good. The history of the West is a record of struggles against tyranny and for freedom. In the nineteenth century the idea of the individual's freedom as developed by the ancient Greeks and resuscitated by the Europeans of the Renaissance and the Enlightenment seemed even to work upon the backward people of the East. Optimists were talking about a coming age of freedom and peace.

What really happened was just the opposite. The nineteenth century, very successful in the natural sciences and their technological utilization, begot and made popular social doctrines that depicted the total state as the ultimate design of human history. Pious Christians as well as radical atheists rejected the market economy, vilifying it as the worst of all evils. While capitalism increased the productivity of economic effort in an unprecedented degree and the standard of living of the masses in the capitalistic countries improved from year to year, the Marxian doctrine of the unavoidable progressive pauperization of the "exploited classes" was accepted as an incontestable dogma. Self-styled intellectuals, yearning and striving hard for what they style the dictatorship of the proletariat, pretend to continue the endeavors of all the great champions of freedom.

The social and political ideal of our age is planning. No longer should the individuals have the right and the opportunity of choosing the mode of their integration into the system of social cooperation. Everybody will have to comply with the orders issued by society's — i.e., the state's, the police power's — supreme office. From the cradle to the coffin everybody will be forced to behave precisely as he is ordered to behave by the makers of the "plan." These orders will determine his training and the place and the kind of his work as well as the wages he will receive. He will not be in a position to raise any objections against the orders received; according to the philosophy underlying the system, the planning authority alone is in a position to know whether or not the order is or is not in accordance with its plan for the "socially" most desirable conduct of affairs.

The total enslavement of all members of society is not a merely accidental attendant phenomenon of the socialist management. It is rather the essential feature of the socialist system, the very effect of any thinkable kind of a socialist conduct of business. It is precisely this that the socialist authors had in mind when they stigmatized capitalism as "anarchy of production" and asked for the transfer of all authority and power to "society." Either a man is free to live according to his own plan or he is forced to submit unconditionally to the plan of the great god state.

It does not matter that the socialists call themselves today "leftists" and smear the advocates of limited government and the market economy as "rightists." These terms "left" and "right" have lost any political significance. The only meaningful distinction is that between the advocates of the market economy and its corollary, limited government, and the advocates of the total state.

For the first time in human history there is perfect agreement between the majority of the so-called intellectuals and the vast majority of all other classes and groups of people. Passionately and vehemently they all want planning, i.e., their own total enslavement.

Individual Freedom and the Market Economy

The characteristic feature of the capitalistic society is the sphere of activity it assigns to the initiative and responsibility of its members. The individual is free and supreme as long as he does not restrict the freedom of his fellow citizens in pursuance of his own ends. In the market he is sovereign in his capacity as a consumer. In the governmental sphere he is a voter and in this capacity a part of the sovereign lawgiver. Political democracy and democracy of the market are congeneric.

In the terminology of Marxism one would have to say: Representative government is the superstructure of the market economy as despotism is the superstructure of socialism.

The market economy is not merely one of various thinkable and possible systems of mankind's economic cooperation. It is the only method that enables man to establish a social system of production to which the unswerving tendency is inwrought to aim at the best possible and cheapest provisioning of the consumers.

8

The Outlook for Saving and Investment

Writing in 1817, David Ricardo in his *Principles of Political Economy and Taxation* pointed to the experience that "the fancied or real insecurity of capital, when not under the immediate control of its owner," checks the emigration of capital. Thus most men of property prefer a low rate of profit in their own country to a more advantageous employment for their wealth in foreign nations.[1] This was said precisely on the eve of the age that will be remembered in history as the period in which the insulation of the various local and national markets gave way to the evolution of an effective world trade not only in consumers' goods but also in capital goods.

Foreign Investment

British capitalists inaugurated the new methods of foreign investment; they were very soon followed by the businessmen of Western and Central Europe and of the United States. An unprecedented improvement in the average standard of living resulted. Observing the benefits that this system brought both to the investors and to the people of the countries in which the investments were made, optimists hopefully looked forward to the coming of an era of perpetual peace and goodwill among all nations. They were poor prophets.

They overrated the mental power and they underrated the malicious envy not only of the uncultured masses but no less of the crowd of self-styled intellectuals. They did not foresee that in the light of doctrines, elaborated in England and France and perfected in Germany and Russia, foreign investors would appear as the worst enemies of all decent

Reprinted from 75th anniversary issue of *Farmand* (Oslo, Norway), February 12, 1966.
1. Cf. Ricardo, *Works*, ed. by McCulloch, 2d ed. (London, 1852), p. 77.

people, as exploiters and usurers. They could not divine the impetuous vehemence of the passions stirred up by unscrupulous demagogues. The Americans and the British are hated in the economically under-developed countries because they have provided the capital for invest-ments the inhabitants were not able to provide.

Every account of the history of modern culture must first of all dis-tinguish between two groups of nations, viz. those that have developed a system which made domestic saving and the large-scale accumula-tion of capital possible and those that did not. The lamentable failure of all "leftist" economic doctrines from Saint-Simonism and Marxism down to the "imperialism" theory of Luxembourg, Lenin, and Hilfer-ding and to Keynesianism is precisely to be seen in their misconstruc-tion of the meaning of saving, capital accumulation, and investment.* In the great ideological conflict of the nineteenth century the Liberals and their spokesmen, the much abused "vulgar economists," were right in proclaiming as their main thesis: there is but one means to improve the material conditions of all of the people, viz., to accelerate the ac-cumulation of capital as against the increase in population.

The great age of foreign investment came to an inglorious end when the twentieth century's doctrinaires were no longer prepared to see any difference between the devastation of a country by military action and the investment of foreign capital for the construction of factories and transportation facilities. Each of these two entirely different procedures is called conquest and imperialism. The expropriation of foreign invest-ments is styled "liberation." It is, if at all, only mildly censured by the ju-rists and economists of the "capitalistic sector" of the world. No wonder that the eagerness to invest in foreign countries disappeared. Foreign aid tries now to fill the gap. As Miss Ayn Rand defined it, this new doctrine requests that our wealth should be given away to the peoples of Asia and Africa, "with apologies for the fact that we have produced it while they haven't."[2]

The joint operation of the ideas of socialism and nationalism has not only almost entirely suppressed saving and the accumulation of capital (for non-military purposes) in the communist countries and in

2. Cf. Ayn Rand, *For the New Intellectual* (New York, 1961), p. 4.
* Claude Henri de Saint-Simon (1760–1825), founder of French socialism; Rosa Luxembourg (1870–1919), Marxist revolutionary; Nikolai Vladimir Lenin (1870–1924), leader of the 1917 Rus-sian Communist revolution; and Rudolf Hilferding (1877–1941), German Social Democrat, were all ideological socialists.

the orbit of the nations commonly called today underdeveloped. It made the industrial countries of Western and Central Europe and North America adopt conceptions the application of which must sooner or later result in the complete cessation of any voluntary saving and capital formation on the part of individual citizens.

The "Productivity of Labor"

Thus the official doctrine of the United States operates with a concept of productivity of labor that defines it as the market value (in terms of money) added to the products by the processing (of the firm in question or by all the firms of the branch of industry), divided by the number of workers employed. Or, in other words, output per man-hour of work. It pretends that every improvement in this figure means an "increase in the productivity of labor" that is caused by the workers' effort and which by rights belongs entirely to them. In wage negotiations the unions claim this "productivity gain" as their members' due. The employers as a rule neither question this concept of productivity of labor nor do they contest the resulting claims of the unions. They accept it implicitly in occasionally pointing out that wage rates have already risen to the extent of the increase in productivity, computed according to this method. The government in formulating its "guidelines" for the determination of wage rates and product prices adopts the unions' point of view.

It is obvious that the theory underlying this doctrine radically misconstrues the essential facts about industrial production. The difference between the "productivity" of a worker handling the tools of a bygone state of technology and another working in a plant equipped with the most modern machines is not due to the personal qualities and the effort of the worker but to the quality of the shop's equipment. If the worker is to get all the "increase in productivity" brought about by the investment of additional capital, nothing is left for the people whose saving created this capital and made its investment possible. (For the sake of simplicity we may omit referring to the role of the entrepreneurs and to that of the managers and the technologists.) Saving, capital accumulation and investment will no longer pay and will come to an end. There will no longer be any economic progress.[3]

3. See my *Human Action*, 4th rev. ed. (Chicago, 1996), pp. 608–10.

Anti-capitalistic Ideas

It cannot be denied that also in the noncommunist countries an out-spoken anti-capitalistic tendency prevails in fiscal policies. The taxation of personal incomes, corporations, and inheritance tends more or less openly toward a complete confiscation of such allegedly "unearned" intake. The joint effects of these anti-capitalistic measures are to some extent still veiled by inflationary monetary and banking policies. But sooner or later the main problem will become visible: how to provide for new additional investments when the individuals and corporations are prevented — either by the methods of taxation or by the methods applied to the determination of wage rates — from deriving any benefit from saving and capital investment.

9

Inequality of Wealth and Incomes

The market economy — capitalism — is based on private ownership of the material means of production and private entrepreneurship. The consumers, by their buying or abstention from buying, ultimately determine what should be produced and in what quantity and quality. They render profitable the affairs of those businessmen who best comply with their wishes and unprofitable the affairs of those who do not produce what they are asking for most urgently. Profits convey control of the factors of production into the hands of those who are employing them for the best possible satisfaction of the most urgent needs of the consumers, and losses withdraw them from the control of the inefficient businessmen. In a market economy not sabotaged by the government the owners of property are mandataries of the consumers as it were. On the market a daily repeated plebiscite determines who should own what and how much. It is the consumers who make some people rich and other people penniless.

Inequality of wealth and incomes is an essential feature of the market economy. It is the implement that makes the consumers supreme in giving them the power to force all those engaged in production to comply with their orders. It forces all those engaged in production to the utmost exertion in the service of the consumers. It makes competition work. He who best serves the consumers profits most and accumulates riches.

In a society of the type that Adam Ferguson, Saint-Simon, and Herbert Spencer (1820–1903) called militaristic and present-day Americans call feudal, private property of land was the fruit of violent usurpation or of donations on the part of the conquering warlord. Some people owned more, some less, and some nothing because the chieftain had

Reprinted from *Ideas on Liberty*, May 1955.

determined it that way. In such a society it was correct to assert that the abundance of the great landowners was the corollary of the indigence of the landless. But it is different in a market economy. Bigness in business does not impair, but improves the conditions of the rest of the people. The millionaires are acquiring their fortunes in supplying the many with articles that were previously beyond their reach. If laws had prevented them from getting rich, the average American household would have to forgo many of the gadgets and facilities that are today its normal equipment. This country enjoys the highest standard of living ever known in history because for several generations no attempts were made toward "equalization" and "redistribution." Inequality of wealth and incomes is the cause of the masses' well-being, not the cause of anybody's distress. Where there is a "lower degree of inequality," there is necessarily a lower standard of living of the masses.

Demand for "Distribution"

In the opinion of the demagogues inequality in what they call the "distribution" of wealth and incomes is in itself the worst of all evils. Justice would require an equal distribution. It is therefore both fair and expedient to confiscate the surplus of the rich or at least a considerable part of it and to give it to those who own less. This philosophy tacitly presupposes that such a policy will not impair the total quantity produced. But even if this were true, the amount added to the average man's buying power would be much smaller than extravagant popular illusions assume. In fact the luxury of the rich absorbs only a slight fraction of the nation's total consumption. The much greater part of the rich men's incomes is not spent for consumption, but saved and invested. It is precisely this that accounts for the accumulation of their great fortunes. If the funds which the successful businessmen would have ploughed back into productive employments are used by the state for current expenditure or given to people who consume them, the further accumulation of capital is slowed down or entirely stopped. Then there is no longer any question of economic improvement, technological progress, and a trend toward higher average standards of living.

When Marx and Engels in the *Communist Manifesto* recommended "a heavy progressive or graduated income tax" and "abolition of all right of inheritance" as measures "to wrest, by degrees, all capital from the bourgeoisie," they were consistent from the point of view of the ultimate end they were aiming at, viz., the substitution of socialism for the market economy. They were fully aware of the inevitable consequences of these policies. They openly declared that these measures are "economically untenable" and that they advocated them only because "they necessitate further inroads" upon the capitalist social order and are "unavoidable as a means of entirely revolutionizing the mode of production," i.e., as a means of bringing about socialism.

But it is quite a different thing when these measures which Marx and Engels characterized as "economically untenable" are recommended by people who pretend that they want to preserve the market economy and economic freedom. These self-styled middle-of-the-road politicians are either hypocrites who want to bring about socialism by deceiving the people about their real intentions, or they are ignoramuses who do not know what they are talking about. For progressive taxes upon incomes and upon estates are incompatible with the preservation of the market economy.

The middle-of-the-road man argues this way: "There is no reason why a businessman should slacken in the best conduct of his affairs only because he knows that his profits will not enrich him but will benefit all people. Even if he is not an altruist who does not care for lucre and who unselfishly toils for the common weal, he will have no motive to prefer a less efficient performance of his activities to a more efficient. It is not true, that the only incentive that impels the great captains of industry is acquisitiveness. They are no less driven by the ambition to bring their products to perfection."

Supremacy of the Consumers

This argumentation entirely misses the point. What matters is not the behavior of the entrepreneurs but the supremacy of the consumers. We may take it for granted that the businessmen will be eager to serve the consumers to the best of their abilities even if they themselves do not derive any advantage from their zeal and application. They will accomplish what according to their opinion best serves the consumers. But then it will no longer be the consumers that determine what they get. They will have to take what the businessmen believe is best for them. The entrepreneurs, not the consumers, will then be supreme. The consumers will no longer have the power to entrust control of production to those businessmen whose products they like most and to relegate those whose products they appreciate less to a more modest position in the system.

If the present American laws concerning the taxation of the profits of corporations, the incomes of individuals, and inheritances had been introduced about sixty years ago, all those new products whose consumption has raised the standard of living of the "common man" would either not be produced at all or only in small quantities for the benefit of a minority. The Ford enterprises would not exist if Henry Ford's profits had been taxed away as soon as they came into being. The business structure of 1895 would have been preserved. The accumulation of new capital would have ceased or at least slowed down considerably. The expansion of production would lag behind the increase of population. There is no need to expatiate about the effects of such a state of affairs.

Profit and loss tell the entrepreneur what the consumers are asking for most urgently. And only the profits the entrepreneur pockets enable him to adjust his activities to the demand of the consumers. If the profits are expropriated, he is prevented from complying with the directives given by the consumers. Then the market economy is deprived of its steering wheel. It becomes a senseless jumble.

People can consume only what has been produced. The great problem of our age is precisely this: Who should determine what is to be produced and consumed, the people or the State, the consumers themselves or a paternal government? If one decides in favor of the consumers, one chooses the market economy. If one decides in favor of the government, one chooses socialism. There is no third solution. The determination of the purpose for which each unit of the various factors of production is to be employed cannot be divided.

Demand for Equalization

The supremacy of the consumers consists in their power to hand over control of the material factors of production and thereby the conduct of production activities to those who serve them in the most efficient way. This implies inequality of wealth and incomes. If one wants to do away with inequality of wealth and incomes, one must abandon capitalism and adopt socialism. (The question whether any socialist system would really give income equality must be left to an analysis of socialism.)

But, say the middle-of-the-road enthusiasts, we do not want to abolish inequality altogether. We want merely to substitute a lower degree of inequality for a higher degree.

These people look upon inequality as upon an evil. They do not assert that a definite degree of inequality which can be exactly determined by a judgment free of any arbitrariness and personal evaluation is good and has to be preserved unconditionally. They, on the contrary, declare inequality in itself as bad and merely contend that a lower degree of it is a lesser evil than a higher degree in the same sense in which a smaller quantity of poison in a man's body is a lesser evil than a larger dose. But if this is so, then there is logically in their doctrine no point at which the endeavors toward equalization would have to stop. Whether one has already reached a degree of inequality which is to be considered low enough and beyond which it is not necessary to embark upon further measures toward equalization is just a matter of personal judgments of value, quite arbitrary, different with different people and changing in the passing of time. As these champions of equalization appraise confiscation and "redistribution" as a policy harming only a minority, viz., those whom they consider to be "too" rich, and benefiting the rest — the majority — of the people, they cannot oppose any tenable argument to those who are asking for more of this allegedly beneficial policy. As long as any degree of inequality is left, there will always be people whom envy impels to press for a continuation of the equalization policy. Nothing can be advanced against their inference: If inequality of wealth and incomes is an evil, there is no reason to acquiesce in any degree of it, however low; equalization must not stop before it has completely leveled all individuals' wealth and incomes.

The history of the taxation of profits, incomes, and estates in all countries clearly shows that once the principle of equalization is adopted, there is no point at which the further progress of the policy of equalization can be checked. If, at the time the Sixteenth Amendment was adopted, somebody had predicted that some years later the income tax progression would reach the height it has really attained in our day, the advocates of the Amendment would have called him a lunatic. It is certain that only a small minority in Congress will seriously oppose further sharpening of the progressive element in the tax rate scales if such a sharpening should be suggested by the Administration or by a congressman anxious to enhance his chances for reelection. For, under the sway of the doctrines taught by contemporary pseudo-economists, all but a few reasonable men believe that they are injured by the mere fact that their own income is smaller than that of other people and that it is not a bad policy to confiscate this difference.

There is no use in fooling ourselves. Our present taxation policy is headed toward a complete equalization of wealth and incomes and thereby toward socialism. This trend can be reversed only by the cognition of the role that profit and loss and the resulting inequality of wealth and incomes play in the operation of the market economy. People must learn that the accumulation of wealth by the successful conduct of business is the corollary of the improvement of their own standard of living and vice versa. They must realize that bigness in business is not an evil, but both the cause and effect of the fact that they themselves enjoy all those amenities whose enjoyment is called the "American way of life."

PART II

Interventionism

It is self-evident that human beings are not omniscient; they cannot know everything. And they are not omnicompetent; they make mistakes. However, Mises was convinced that they would have *more* knowledge and would make *fewer* mistakes if they were free and if their voluntary actions were not hampered. Mises's understanding of economic theory convinced him that men who are free to seek their respective goals by peaceful means, to compete, cooperate, bargain, and exchange with one another, to adjust and adapt to changing conditions, will learn by reason and experience. They will often be able to correct their mistakes, misjudgments, and miscalculations before the effects become serious. Everyone concerned will benefit as a result.

Realizing the advantages of peaceful social cooperation, Mises was led to advocate the protection of free markets and private property. The role of government was to act as "night watchman." It should not otherwise interfere with the peaceful and voluntary actions of individuals. It should not try to be both God and Santa Claus. Government should use its power, as Mises says, "only to protect decent law-abiding people against violent or fraudulent attacks."

The articles in this section point out the unfortunate consequences when government goes beyond this limited role. Some of the articles in this section date from the period of the post–World War II "Cold War" against communism and the Korean War (1950–53). The effects of inflation (monetary expansion) were then in the news and price controls were imposed temporarily. Among the issues discussed here are government spending, special privileges, artificially maintained wage rates, credit expansion, and inflation, all of which persist to this day.

The people, Mises said, must come to understand the consequences of these programs. It is "diabolic," Mises writes in one article, "to egg various pressure groups on to ask for more and more government spending to be financed by credit expansion. The bill for such government extravagance is always footed by the most industrious and provident people," to the disadvantage of all the people.

10

The Why of Human Action

There are no ivory towers to house economists. Whether he likes it or not, the economist is always dragged into the turmoil of the arena in which nations, parties, and pressure groups are battling. Nothing absorbs the minds of our contemporaries more intensely than the pros and cons of economic doctrines. Economic issues engross the attention of modern writers and artists more than any other problem. Philosophers and theologians today deal more often with economic themes than with those topics which were once considered as the proper field of philosophical and theological studies. What divides mankind into two hostile camps, whose violent clash may destroy civilization, is antagonistic ideas with regard to the economic interpretation of human life and action.

Politicians proclaim their utter contempt for what they label as "mere theory." They pretend that their own approach to economic problems is purely practical and free from any dogmatic prepossessions. They fail to realize that their policies are determined by definite assumptions about causal relations, i.e., that they are based on definite theories. Acting man, in choosing certain means for the attainment of ends aimed at, is necessarily always guided by "mere theory"; there is no practice without an underlying doctrine. In denying this truth, the politician tries in vain to withdraw the faulty, self-contradictory, and a hundred-times refuted misapprehensions directing his conduct of affairs from the criticism of the economists.

The social function of economic science consists precisely in developing sound economic theories and in exploding the fallacies of vicious reasoning. In the pursuit of this task the economist incurs the deadly enmity of all mountebanks and charlatans whose shortcuts to an

Reprinted from *Plain Talk*, September 1949.

earthly paradise he debunks. The less these quacks are able to advance plausible objections to an economist's argument, the more furiously do they insult them.

Sound Money versus Inflationism and Expansionism

At the beginning of our century the governments of the civilized nations were committed either to the so-called classical gold standard or to the gold exchange standard. Their conduct of monetary and credit policies was, to be sure, not free from mistakes, and they indulged in a certain amount of credit expansion. But when compared with conditions after 1914, they were moderate in their expansionist ventures and spurned the fantastic projects of the so-called "monetary cranks" who advocated boundless inflation and credit expansion as the patent medicine for all economic ills.

Yet this rejection of the plans which aimed at making people prosperous through increasing the quantity of money and fiduciary media was not founded upon a satisfactory cognition of the inevitable and undesired consequences of such a policy. The governments were disinclined to deviate from traditional standards of monetary management because the troubles engendered by earlier inflations had not yet been obliterated from the memory of the older statesmen and some vestiges of the prestige of the classical economists still prevailed. Professors and bankers loathed the writings of Ernest Solvay (1838–1922), Silvio Gesell (1862–1930), and a host of other expansionists. But hardly anybody knew why these authors were wrong or how to refute them. In fact the doctrines generally accepted by the treasuries, the central banks, the financial press, and the universities did not differ essentially from the ideas advanced by the "monetary cranks." These champions of a sweeping social reform to be accomplished by monetary measures only carried the official doctrine to its ultimate logical consequences. It was to be expected that in a coming emergency, such as a great war or revolution, those in office would turn away from their cautious reserve and that orgies of inflation and credit expansion would be rife.

Such was the state of monetary and credit theory when my *Theory of Money and Credit* was published.[1] I tried to construct a theory based

---

1. *Die Theorie des Geldes und der Umlaufsmittel,* first German-language edition, 1912; English translation, *The Theory of Money and Credit* (J. Cape, 1934; Yale, 1953; FEE, 1971; Liberty Fund, 1980).

entirely upon the modern subjectivist methods of dealing with economic issues, the marginal utility concept. What was called "inflation" at that time and is passionately praised today under the labels of deficit spending and pump-priming can never make a nation more prosperous. It may bring about a shift of income and wealth from some groups of the population to other groups, but it invariably tends to impair the prosperity of the whole nation. In my book, I pointed out that the phenomenon of interest, i.e., the higher valuation of present goods as against future goods, is an ineluctable category of human conduct which does not depend on the particular structure of society's economic organization; it cannot be abolished by any statutes or reforms. Endeavors to keep the rate of interest below the height it would attain on a market not sabotaged by credit expansion are doomed to failure in the long run. In the short run they result in an artificial boom which inevitably ends in a crash and slump. The recurrence of periods of economic depression is not a phenomenon inherent in the very course of affairs under laissez-faire capitalism. It is, on the contrary, the outcome of the reiterated attempts to "improve" the operation of capitalism by "cheap money" and credit expansion. If one wants to avert depressions, one must abstain from any tampering with the rate of interest. Thus was elaborated the theory which supporters and critics of my ideas very soon began to call the "Austrian theory of the trade cycle."

As expected, my theses were furiously vilified by the apologists of the official doctrine. Especially abusive was the response on the part of the German professors, the self-styled "intellectual bodyguard of the House of Hohenzollern." In exemplifying one point, a hypothetical assumption was made that the purchasing power of the German mark might drop to one-millionth of its previous equivalent. "What a muddle-headed man who dares to introduce — if only hypothetically — such a fantastic assumption!" shouted one of the reviewers. But a few years later the purchasing power of the mark was down not to one-millionth, but to one-billionth of its prewar amount!

It is a sad fact that people are reluctant to learn from either theory or experience. Neither the disasters manifestly brought about by deficit spending and low interest-rate policies, nor the confirmation of the theories in my *Theory of Money and Credit* by such eminent thinkers as Friedrich von Hayek, Henry Hazlitt, and the late Benjamin M. Anderson have up to now been able to put an end to the popularity

of the fiat money frenzy.* The monetary and credit policies of all nations are headed for a new catastrophe, probably more disastrous than
any of the older slumps.

The Economic Theory of Socialism

Sixty years ago Sidney Webb boasted that the economic history of the
century is an almost continuous record of the progress of socialism. A
few years later an eminent British statesman, Sir William Harcourt,
asserted: "We are all Socialists now." There cannot be any doubt that
all nations were pursuing policies which were bound to result finally in
the establishment of all-round planning exclusively by the government,
i.e., socialism or communism.

Yet nobody ventured to analyze the economic problems of a socialist
system. Karl Marx had outlawed such studies as merely "utopian" and
"unscientific." As he saw it, the mythical productive forces which inevitably determine the course of history and direct the conduct of men
"independently of their wills" would in due time arrange everything in
the best possible way; it would be a vain presumption of mortal men to
arrogate to themselves a judgment in these matters. This Marxian taboo
was strictly observed. Hosts of pseudo-economists and pseudo-experts
dealt with alleged shortcomings of capitalism and praised the blessings
of government control of all human activities; but hardly anybody
had the intellectual honesty to investigate the economic problems of
socialism.

To put an end to this intolerable state of affairs I wrote several essays
and finally a book on socialism.[2] The main result of my studies was to
prove that a socialist commonwealth would not be in a position to
apply economic calculation. When socialism is limited to one or to a
few countries only, the socialists can still resort to economic calculation on the basis of prices determined on the markets of nonsocialist
countries. But once all countries adopted socialism, there would no
longer be any market for the factors of production, the factors of pro-

---

2. *Die Gemeinwirtschaft*, first German-language edition, 1922; English language translation,
Socialism (J. Cape, 1936; Yale, 1951; J. Cape, 1969; Liberty Fund, 1981).
* F. A. Hayek (1899–1992), author of *The Road to Serfdom* (1944), was appointed Nobel Laureate
economist in 1974. Henry Hazlitt (1894–1993), economic journalist, was the author of the popular *Economics in One Lesson* (1946). B. M. Anderson (1886–1949) was well known as the economist for the Chase Bank.

duction would no longer be sold and bought, and no prices would be determined for them.

This means that it would become impossible for a socialist management to reduce the various factors of production to a common denominator and thereby resort to calculation in planning future action and in appraising the result of past action. Such a socialist management would simply not know whether what it planned and executed was the most appropriate procedure to attain the ends sought. It would operate in the dark. It would squander scarce factors of production, both material and human (labor). The paradox of planning is precisely that it abolishes the conditions required for rational action based on weighing cost (input) and result (output). What is advocated as conscious planning is in fact the elimination of conscious purposive action.

The socialist and communist authors could not help admitting that my demonstration was irrefutable. To save face they radically reversed their argument. Until 1920, the year in which my thesis on economic calculation was first published, all socialists had declared that the essence of socialism was the elimination of the market and market prices. All the blessings which they expected from the realization of socialism were described as the result of this abolition of the price system. But now they are anxious to show that markets and market prices can be preserved even under socialism. They are drafting spurious and self-contradictory schemes for a socialism in which people "play" market in the way children play war or railroad. They do not comprehend in what respect such childish play differs from the real thing it tries to imitate.

The Middle Way

Many politicians and authors believe that they could avoid the necessity of choosing between capitalism (laissez faire) and socialism (communism, planning). They recommend a third solution which — as they say — is as far from capitalism as it is from socialism. In imperial Germany this third system was called *Sozialpolitik*; in the United States it is known as the New Deal. Economists prefer the term used by the French, *interventionism*. The idea is that private ownership of the means of production should not be entirely abolished; but the government should "improve" and correct the operation of the market by interfering with the operations of the capitalists and entrepreneurs — by means of orders and prohibitions, taxes, and subsidies.

But interventionism cannot work as a permanent system of society's economic organization. The various measures recommended must necessarily bring about results which — from the point of view of their own advocates and the governments resorting to them — are more unsatisfactory than the previous state of affairs which they were designed to alter. If the government neither acquiesces in this outcome nor derives from it the conclusion that it is advisable to abstain from all such measures, it is forced to supplement its first steps by more and more interference until it has abolished private control of the means of production entirely and thus established socialism. The conduct of economic affairs, i.e., the determination of the purposes for which the factors of production should be employed, can ultimately be directed either by buying and abstention from buying on the part of consumers, or by government decrees. There is no middle way. Control is indivisible.

It is interventionism that produces all those evils for which a misguided public opinion indicts laissez-faire capitalism. As has been pointed out above, the endeavors to lower the rate of interest by means of credit expansion generate the recurrence of depression. Attempts to raise wage rates above the height they would attain in an unhampered market result in prolonged mass unemployment. "Soak-the-rich" taxation results in capital consumption. The joint outcome of all interventionist measures is general impoverishment. It is a misnomer to call the interventionist state the welfare state. What it ultimately achieves is not improving but lowering the common man's welfare, his standard of living. The unprecedented economic development of the United States and the high standard of living of its population were achievements of the free enterprise system.

The Interconnectedness of All Economic Phenomena

Economics does not allow any breaking up into special branches. It invariably deals with the interconnectedness of all phenomena of acting and economizing. All economic facts mutually condition one another. Each of the various economic problems must be dealt with in the frame of a comprehensive system assigning its due place and weight to every aspect of human wants and desires. All monographs remain fragmentary if not integrated into a systematic treatment of the whole body of social and economic relations.

To provide such a comprehensive analysis is the task of my book *Human Action, a Treatise on Economics* (New Haven: Yale University Press, 1949). It is the consummation of lifelong studies and investigations, the precipitate of half a century of experience. I saw the forces operating which could not but annihilate the high civilization and prosperity of Europe. In writing my book, I was hoping to contribute to the endeavors of our most eminent contemporaries to prevent this country from following the path which leads to the abyss.

11

Deception of Government Intervention

The intellectual and moral faculties of man can thrive only where people associate with one another peacefully. Peace is the origin of all human things, not—as the ancient Greek philosopher Heraclitus said—war. But as human nature is, peace can be established and preserved only by a power fit and ready to crush all peacebreakers.

Government or state is the social apparatus of coercion and compulsion. Its purpose is to make the world safe for peaceful human cooperation by protecting society against attacks on the part of foreign aggressors or domestic gangsters. The characteristic mark of a government is that it has, within a definite part of the earth's surface, the exclusive power and right to resort to violence.

Within the orbit of Western civilization the power and the functions of government are limited. Many hundreds, even thousands of years of bitter conflicts resulted in a state of affairs that granted to the individual citizens effective rights and freedom, not mere freedoms. In the market economy the individuals are free from government intervention as long as they do not offend against the duly promulgated laws of the land. The government interferes only to protect decent law-abiding people against violent or fraudulent attacks.

There are people who call government an evil, although a necessary evil. However, what is needed in order to attain a definite end must not be called an evil in the moral connotation of the term. It is a *means*, but not an *evil*. Government may even be called the most beneficial of all earthly institutions as without it no peaceful human cooperation, no civilization, and no moral life would be possible. In this sense the apostle declared that "the powers that be are ordained of God."

Reprinted from *Christian Economics*, February 4, 1964.

But the very existence of a government apparatus of coercion and compulsion makes a new problem arise. The men handling this apparatus yield too easily to the temptation of misusing their power. They turn their weapons against those whom they were expected to serve and to protect. The main political problem of all ages was and is: how to prevent the rulers from turning into despots and making the state totalitarian. Defense of the individual's liberty against the encroachments of tyrannical governments, against the dangers of a totalitarian regime, was and is the essential issue of the history of Western civilization.

Now in our age the cause of totalitarianism has won new vigor through the adoption of a ruse. The radical suppression of every individual's freedom to choose his own way for the benefit of the supreme political authority is praised, under the labels of socialism, communism, or planning, as the attainment of true liberty. Those aiming at a state of affairs in which every individual will be reduced to the status of a mere cog in the plans of the "social engineers" are parading as the successors of the great champions of freedom. The subjugation of a free nation by the forces of the most tyrannical regime history has ever known is called "liberation."

Middle-of-the-Road Policy

Faced with the tremendous challenge of totalitarianism, the ruling parties of the West do not venture to preserve the system of free enterprise that gave to their nations the highest standard of living ever attained in history. They ignore the fact that conditions for all citizens of the United States and those other countries which have not put too many obstacles in the way of free enterprise are much more favorable than conditions for the inhabitants of the totalitarian countries. They think that it is necessary to abandon the market economy and to adopt a middle-of-the-road policy that is supposed to avoid the alleged deficiencies of the capitalistic economy. They aim at a system which, as they see it, is as far from socialism as it is from capitalism and which is better than either of those two. By direct intervention of the government, they want to remove what they consider unsatisfactory in the market economy.

Such a policy of government interference with the market phenomena was already recommended by Marx and Engels in the *Communist Manifesto*. But the authors of the *Communist Manifesto* considered the ten groups of interventionist measures they suggested as measures to bring about step-by-step full socialism. However, in our time the government spokesmen and the politicians of the left recommend the same measures as a method, even as the *only* method, to salvage capitalism.

The advocates of interventionism or government interference with the market protest that they do not want socialism, but rather to retain private ownership of the material factors of production, free enterprise, and market exchange. But they assert that these institutions of the market economy could be easily misused, and are often misused, by the propertied classes for an unfair exploitation of the poorer strata of the population. To prevent such an outcome they want to restrain the discretion of the individuals by governmental orders and prohibitions. The government should interfere with all those actions of the businessmen which it considers as detrimental to the public interest; in other respects, however, it should leave the market alone.

According to this interventionist doctrine the government alone is called upon to decide in every single case whether or not the "public interest" requires government intervention. The real meaning of the interventionist principle, therefore, amounts to the declaration: Business is free to act as long as what it does complies exactly with the plans and intentions of the government. Thus nothing is left to the market other than the right to execute meekly what the government wants it to do. Nothing remains of the market economy but some labels, although their meaning is radically altered.

The interventionist doctrine fails to comprehend that the two systems — the market economy of consumers' supremacy and the government directed economy — cannot be combined into a practicable composite. In the market economy the entrepreneurs are unconditionally subject to the supremacy of the consumers. They are forced to proceed in such a way that their operations are approved by the purchases of the consumers and thus become profitable. If they fail in these endeavors, they suffer losses and must, if they do not succeed in amending their methods, go out of business.

However, even if the government prevents the entrepreneurs from choosing those projects that the consumers wish them to execute, it does not attain the ends it wanted to attain by its order or prohibition. Both producers and consumers are forced to adjust their behavior to the new state of affairs brought about by the government's intervention. But it may happen that the way in which they, the producers and consumers, react appears as still less desirable, in the eyes of the government and the advocates of its interference, than the previous state of the unhampered market that the government wanted to alter. Then if the government does not want to abstain from any intervention and to repeal its first measure, it is forced to add to its first intervention a new one. The same story then repeats itself at another level. Again the outcome of the government's intervention appears to the government as even more unsatisfactory than the preceding state that it was designed to remedy.

In this way, the government is forced to add to its first intervention more and more decrees of interference until it has actually eliminated any influence of the market factors — entrepreneurs, capitalists, and employees as well as consumers — upon the determination of the ways of production and consumption.

12

The Agony of the Welfare State

For about a hundred years the Communists and interventionists of all shades have been indefatigable in predicting the impending final collapse of capitalism. While their prophecies have not come true, the world today has to face the agony of the much glorified policies of the Welfare State.

The Welfare State

The guiding principles of the Welfare State were best laid down by Ferdinand Lassalle (1825–64), both the friend and rival of Marx. Lassalle ridiculed the liberal doctrines. They assigned to the state, he remarked sneeringly, only the functions of a night watchman. In his eyes the state (with a capital S) was God and Santa Claus at the same time. The state had inexhaustible funds at its disposal, which could freely be used to make all citizens prosperous and happy. The state should nationalize big business, underwrite projects for the realization of which private capital was not available, redistribute national income, and provide for everyone security from the cradle to the grave.

For Bismarck and his professorial henchmen, deadly foes of "Anglo-Saxon" freedom as they were, this welfare state program was the consummation of the historical mission of Germany's ruling Hohenzollern dynasty as well as of the social gospel of a new Christianity. This *Sozialpolitik* provided a common ground for the cooperation of churchmen and atheists, of royalists and republicans, of nationalists and internationalists. Capitalism had multiplied population figures and raised the average standard of living to an unprecedented height. Yet all these groups were united in the fight against capitalism's alleged inhumanities.

Reprinted from *The Freeman*, May 4, 1953.

The new German policy was soon enthusiastically praised by British Fabianism, and later adopted by all European nations and by the United States.

The Welfare State school communicated to mankind the tidings that the philosophers' stone had finally been found. Self-styled "new economics" dismissed as palpable nonsense what "orthodox" economics had said about the alleged nature-given limitation of useful goods and resources and the consequent necessity of saving and progressive capital accumulation. There is, they shouted, abundance; poverty is merely the outcome of bad policies favoring the selfish interests of the few at the expense of the many.

Let the Rich Pay

If the interventionist says the state should do this or that (and pay for it) he is fully aware of the fact that the state does not own any funds but those which it collects as taxes from citizens. His idea is to let the government tax away the greater part of the income and capital of the wealthy citizens and spend this revenue for the benefit of the majority of the people. The riches of the nabobs are considered inexhaustible, and so, consequently, are the funds of the government. There is no need to be stingy in matters of public expenditure. What may appear as waste in the affairs of individual citizens, when we consider the nation's budget, is a means of creating jobs and promoting welfare.

Under the impact of such doctrines the system of progressive tax rates was carried to extremes. But then finally the myth of the inexhaustibleness of the wealth of the rich had to evaporate. The politicians were perplexed when they discovered that they had reached the limit. Several years ago, Mr. Hugh Gaitskell [1906–63], head of the British Treasury in the socialist cabinet of Mr. Clement Attlee [1883–1967], had to admit "that there is not enough money to take away from England's rich to raise the standard of living any further." The same is true for all other nations. In this country even if all taxable income of those earning more than $25,000 were confiscated, the additional income to the government would amount to much less than $1,000,000,000, a trifle when compared with a [1953] budget of roughly $78,000,000,000 and a threatened deficit of $10,000,000,000. The house of cards built by the "new economics" is crashing.

Politics seemed to be a very simple thing in these last decades. The main task of a politician was to induce the government to spend more and more. Subsidies, public works, new offices with hosts of employees, and many other costly things secured popularity and votes. Let "them," that is, the rich, pay. But now their funds are spent. Henceforth the funds of the beneficiaries themselves will have to be tapped if more handouts are to be made to them.

The statist philosophy considers the entrepreneur a useless idler who skims the cream from industry without performing any corresponding economic service. The nationalization of business it is said merely abolishes the unjustified privileges of parasitic drones. A salaried public servant does the jobs previously assigned to the businessman much more efficiently and much more cheaply. The expropriation of private ownership is especially urgent in the field of public utilities.

Guided by these principles, the governments of the various European countries long ago nationalized the railroads, the telephone and the telegraph, and many other branches of business. The result was catastrophic: scandalously poor service, high rates, yearly increasing deficits that have to be covered out of budgetary allowances.

Derailment of State Railroads

The financial embarrassment of the main European countries is predominantly caused by the bankruptcy of the nationalized public utilities. The deficit of these enterprises is incurable. A further rise in their rates would bring about a drop in total net proceeds. The traffic could not bear it. Daily experience proves clearly to everybody but the most bigoted fanatics of socialism that governmental management is inefficient and wasteful. But it is impossible to sell these enterprises back to private capital because the threat of a new expropriation by a later government would deter potential buyers.

In a capitalist country the railroads and the telegraph and telephone companies pay considerable taxes. In the countries of the mixed economy, the yearly losses of these public enterprises are a heavy drain upon the nation's purse. They are not taxpayers, but tax-eaters.

Under the conditions of today, the nationalized public utilities of Europe are not merely feasting on taxes paid by the citizens of their own country; they are also living at the expense of the American taxpayer. A considerable part of the foreign-aid billions is swallowed by the deficits of Europe's nationalization experiments. If the United States had nationalized the American railroads, and had not only to forgo the taxes that the companies pay, but, in addition, to cover every year a deficit of several billions, it would not have been in a position to indemnify the European countries for the foolishness of their own socialization policies. So what is postponing the obvious collapse of the Welfare State in Europe is merely the fact that the United States has been slow and "backward" in adopting the principles of the Welfare State's "new economics": it has not nationalized railroads, telephone, and telegraph.

Yet Americans who want to study the effects of public ownership of transit systems are not forced to visit Europe. Some of the nation's largest cities — among them Detroit, Baltimore, Boston, San Francisco — provide them with ample material. The most instructive case, however, is that of the New York City subways.

New York City subways are only a local transit system. In many technological and financial respects, however, they surpass by far the national railroad systems of many countries. As everybody knows, their operation results every year in a tremendous deficit. The financial management accumulates operating deficits, planning to fund them by the issuance of serial bonds. Only a municipality of the bigness, wealth, and prestige of New York could venture on such a policy. With a private corporation financial analysts would apply a rather ugly word to its procedures: bankruptcy. No sane investor would buy bonds of a private corporation run on such a basis.

Incorrigible socialists are, of course, not at all alarmed. "Why should a subway pay?" they are asking. "The schools, the hospitals, the police do not pay; there is no reason why it should be different with a transit system." This "why" is really remarkable. As if the problem were to find an answer to a *why*, and not to a wherefrom.

There is always this socialist prepossession with the idea that the "rich" can be endlessly soaked. The sad fact, however, is that there is not enough left to fill the bottomless barrels of the public treasury. Precisely because the schools, the hospitals, and the police are very expensive, the city cannot bear the subway deficit. If it wants to levy a special tax to subsidize the subway, it will have to tax the same people who are supposed to profit from the preservation of the low fare.

The other alternative is to raise the fare from the present [1953] level of ten cents to fifteen cents.* It will certainly be done. And it will certainly prove insufficient. After a while a rise to twenty cents will

---

* On January 1, 1990, the fare on the New York City subway was raised to $1.15.

follow—with the same unfavorable result. There is no remedy for the inefficiency of public management. Moreover there is a limit to the height at which raised rates will increase revenue. Beyond this point further rises are self-defeating. This is the dilemma facing every public enterprise.

Subways at a Dead End

How little the management of the New York City subways is touched by the spirit of business was proved a short time ago when it triumphantly announced economies made by cutting down services. While all private enterprises in the country compete with one another in improving and expanding services, the municipality of New York is proud of cutting them down!

When economists clearly demonstrated the reasons why socialism cannot work, the statists and interventionists arrogantly proclaimed their contempt for mere theory. "Let the facts speak for themselves; not economics books, only experience counts." Now the facts have spoken.

It is just a historical accident that transportation systems were nationalized while bakeries and automobile factories remained in the hands of private capital. If it had been the other way round, the socialists would perorate: "It is obvious that bakeries and automobile plants cannot pay like railroads. They are public utilities supplying the masses with vital necessities. They must show deficits, and the taxes paid by the extremely profitable railroads must provide the government with the funds required for making good these deficits."

It is paradoxical indeed that Washington is eager to spend the taxpayers' money for the benefit of European deficit railroads and does not bother about the transit deficits of large American cities. Marshall Plan aid* seems to differ from charity, at least in this respect — it does not begin at home.

History has been rather kind to the American voter. It has provided him with object lessons in socialism. If he looks behind the Iron Curtain, he can learn useful things about the one-party system of the classless and profitless "people's democracies." If he studies European budgets, he will be informed about the "blessings" of nationalization. Even if he

---

* The foreign aid plan sparked June 5, 1947, by General George C. Marshall, then Secretary of State, which became the European Recovery Program.

stays at home, he can extend his views by carefully reading what the newspapers report about the financial breakdown of New York City, the world's largest and richest urban agglomeration, the intellectual capital of Western civilization, the home of the United Nations. There is plenty of experience that can induce a man to analyze scrupulously what the progressive propaganda has taught him, and to think twice before again casting his vote for the apostles of socialization and advocates of public spending.

13

Wage Interference by Government

When in the nineteenth century the question was asked: What can be done in order to raise wage rates and thereby to improve the average standard of living of the most numerous class of the population, the economists answered: One has to accelerate the increase of capital as compared with population. This answer infuriated the reformers and socialists. Historian Thomas Carlyle called economics the dismal science, and Karl Marx smeared the economists as bourgeois idiots and sycophants of the exploiters. But such abusive language cannot change the facts. Today the statesmen of all underdeveloped countries realize very well that what is needed to improve the lot of the masses of their peoples is investment of additional capital. In spending dozens of billions of dollars for foreign aid the American Government implicitly admits the correctness of this thesis. And even the most fanatical foes of capitalism no longer venture to deny that the comparatively high standard of living of the manual workers in this country and in some parts of Europe is due to the increase in the amount of capital invested per head of the employees.

Thus at least in dealing with the economic problems of underdeveloped nations the President, Congress, and public opinion virtually acknowledge the doctrine of the much abused classical economists. But in dealing with domestic problems they are guided by very different ideas. They proceed as if the height of wage rates could be fixed *ad libitum* [at will] by government decree or by labor union pressure and compulsion. Our tax system — especially the way in which personal incomes, corporations, and estates and inheritances are taxed — not only reduces considerably the amount of savings, but in many regards directly results in capital decumulation. But the authorities and their

Reprinted from *Christian Economics*, April 28, 1964.

advisers are not concerned about these effects. They are intent upon raising wage rates either through decreeing minimum wage rates or through pro-union policies.

Labor Union Privileges

The laws have in the last decades granted to the unions many privileges. But these legal privileges also would not have given to unions and to the methods of collective bargaining the tremendous power that they enjoy today in this country and in almost all other noncommunist countries. What makes the unions formidable is the fact that the authorities — the federal government as well as the state and municipal governments — have designedly and wittingly abandoned for the benefit of the unions the essential power of political sovereignty, viz., the exclusive right to suppress disobedience by recourse to violent action. When striking workers resort to acts of violence against strikebreakers or against the persons or the property of those who employ strikebreakers, the authorities preserve a lofty neutrality. The police do not protect those attacked; the district attorneys do not prosecute the assailants and consequently no opportunity is given to the penal courts to try to punish them.

What is today euphemistically called the right to strike is in fact the right of striking workers, by recourse to violence, to prevent people who want to work from working. This means that the authorities have surrendered to the unions an essential attribute of their governmental functions. In matters of wage determination the voice of the unions has the power that in other matters the Constitution and the laws assign exclusively to orders of the authorities issued in conformity with the laws. You must obey such orders and prohibitions or else your obedience will be obtained by beating you into submission.

The statesmen and politicians who step-by-step — not only in this country but also in all other countries of Western industrialism — granted this quite exceptional, tremendous privilege to the unions were guided by the belief that raising wage rates above the height the unhampered market would have fixed them is beneficial to all those who want to make a living by earning wages. As they saw it, a rise in wage rates will reduce profits and interest rates and thus improve the lot of those toiling in factories and offices at the sole expense of a socially quite useless "leisure class."

These self-styled friends of the common man failed to see the fact that capitalism is essentially mass production for supplying the masses. In the precapitalistic ages the processing industries, the artisans organized in guilds and crafts, produced only for the wants of small groups of well-to-do. Under capitalism, however, the masses of the working people are the main consumers of the products. Big business always serves the many; the shops serving the fancies of the rich never attain bigness. If we refer to the consumers, we refer, by and large, to the same people we are talking about in referring to the wage earners.

Above-Market Wage Rates

The labor market fixes wage rates at the height at which all those intent upon hiring workers can hire as many as they want and all those anxious to find a job can find one. If wage rates, either by government decree or by union pressure and compulsion, are raised above this height, there are two alternatives. Either prices are raised concomitantly, so both demand and sales drop, production must be curtailed, and a part of the previously employed workers must be discharged. Or prices remain unchanged, although the cost of production is increased, so that firms that are producing under the least favorable conditions and, therefore, with the highest costs will suffer losses and be forced to go out of business or at least to restrict the quantity of their production. Again workers will have to be discharged. Thus, whatever is done to impose wage rates higher than those the free unhampered market would have determined results in unemployment of a part of the potential labor force.

If a union succeeds in forcing the employers to pay higher wage rates than those they were prepared to pay under the prevailing state of market conditions, this is not a victory for "labor," i.e., for all those who are anxious to earn wages. It is a boon only for those workers who will be employed at the new rates. It is a calamity for all those whom it condemns to lasting unemployment.

The effect of raising wage rates above the potential market rates, i.e., unemployment for some, is not denied by any economist. Even Lord Keynes did not question it. He realized very well that there is no other means to fight unemployment than to adjust wage rates to the height consonant with the state of the unhampered market. The characteristic mark of the Keynesian approach to the problem of unemployment is that, for practical and tactical reasons, he suggested bringing about this adjustment by inflation and its inevitable consequence, a rise in commodity prices. He thought that "a movement by employers to revise money-wage bargains downward will be much more strongly resisted than a gradual and automatic lowering of real wages as a result of rising prices." * As everybody knows today it is impossible to delude the unions and their members in this way. People are nowadays index conscious.

The outstanding fact is that it is impossible to raise wage rates by coercive measures, be it a direct government minimum wage decree, or labor union violence or threat of such violence, without bringing about lasting unemployment of a part of those looking for jobs. The exceptional powers the governments granted to the unions do not benefit all those anxious to earn wages, but only a part of them. The others are victimized. Experience with labor union policies and governmental minimum wage rates has confirmed what economic theory teaches: There is no other method of improving the well-being of the whole class of wage earners than by accelerating saving and the accumulation of new capital.

* *The General Theory of Employment, Interest and Money* (London, 1936), p. 264.

14

Unemployment and the Height of Wage Rates

Public opinion, misguided by the fanatical propaganda on the part of the deadly foes of freedom and prosperity, looks upon the disputes concerning the height of wage rates as if they were only conflicts between wage earners and employers. It ascribes to the employers the power to determine wage rates *ad libitum.* It fails to realize the fact that the entrepreneur is not sovereign in the conduct of his enterprise but entirely subject to the most rigid orders given by his customers, the public. It does not depend on the businessman's arbitrariness to determine what he produces and how. He is, by the instrumentality of the profit and loss system, forced to supply the buying public in the best possible and cheapest way with those commodities and services which they are asking for most urgently. All his measures are directed toward meeting the wishes of the public. The consumers are sovereign and the businessmen are their servants.

Consumer Sovereignty

It is the consumers that ultimately determine the prices of the products and thereby indirectly the prices their purveyors are able to pay for the material means of production and for the labor required for turning out the products. It is the consumers that determine that a movie star should get a much higher pay than a welder, a charwoman much less than a boxing champion.

Economics describes this state of affairs in formulating its marginal utility doctrine. It points out that the price paid for every factor of

Reprinted from *Christian Economics,* April 18, 1961.

production, whether material or human, depends on the value that the consumers ascribe to its contribution to the turning out of the product. If the businessman spends more for the purchase of a factor than the consumers are prepared to refund to him in buying the product, he suffers losses and, if he does not change his practice in time, he is forced to go out of business. In this way the market, i.e., all of the people, determine the prices of the material factors of production and the height of salaries and wage rates paid to all people working in the offices, shops, and farms.

This is what is meant by those who call the market economy a democracy in which every penny gives a right to vote. The whole of the nation is, as it were, a tribunal that assigns to everybody the prices which he can reap in selling his products or his labor. Everybody participates in this process in a double capacity. On the one hand he is, as a buyer and a consumer, a member of the tribunal that assigns to everybody his income and on the other hand he is, as a breadwinner, one of those to whom an income is assigned. In buying admission to a show, the man who makes a hundred dollars a week in his job in a factory assigns a salary of $10,000 a week to an actor. It is the same man's valuation that assigns a much lower pay to the work of a bus driver or a housepainter.

What Makes Wages Rise

In their capacity as earners of wages and salaries the immense majority of the nation are vitally interested in the establishment of conditions that cause wages and salaries to rise. There is but one way to attain this end, viz., to raise the marginal productivity of the individual job holder's contribution by increasing the amount of capital invested per capita. The height of wages depends on the height of the per head quota of capital invested. When the accumulation of capital outruns the increase in population, the marginal utility of the worker's contribution rises and makes wages go up concomitantly. Saving and capital accumulation are the very implements of improving the material conditions of the wage earners.

Wages and salaries are in present-day America much higher than they were in the past because the quantity of capital invested increased more rapidly than the number of people anxious to get jobs. The plight of the underdeveloped nations is due to their shortage of capital. It is not denied by anybody that what these countries need in order to improve the standard of living of their masses is more capital. A man working in India with the primitive tools that in the capitalistic countries have been discarded long since produces much less per unit of time than the American or British worker. Consequently the compensation he receives is much lower.

It is the most stupid of all communist lies that the considerable capital investments America and Western Europe made in Latin America, Asia, and Africa mean "exploitation" of the natives for the benefit of the foreign capitalists. What was wrong with these economically backward countries was that they did not develop spontaneously those legal and institutional conditions that make saving and capital accumulation safe against the arbitrariness and the greed of those in political office. Where the laws do not sufficiently protect private ownership of the means of production, there cannot be any indigenous development of modern industrial plants. Nature has endowed much better with natural resources most of those countries that are today looked upon as backward than it has the soil of the countries occupied by the capitalistic nations. The poverty of these underdeveloped nations is not due to natural conditions. It is a result of their bad policies. If the foreign capitalists had not provided them with capital, most of them would still even have to do without railroads and hydroelectric power plants. Every investment that foreigners made in their lands was immediately followed by an upward movement of wages, not only in the plants erected by the foreigners themselves, but also in other fields of business.

What Generates Unemployment

Public opinion believes that the improvement in the conditions of the wage earners is an achievement of the unions and of various legislative measures. Public opinion gives to unionism and to legislation credit for the rise in wage rates, the shortening of hours of work, the disappearance of child labor, and many other changes. The prevalence of this belief made unionism popular and is responsible for the trend in labor legislation of the last decades. As people think that they owe their high standard of living to unionism, they condone violence, coercion, and intimidation on the part of unionized labor and are indifferent to the curtailment of personal freedom inherent in the union-shop and closed-shop clauses.

But this popular doctrine misconstrues every aspect of economic reality. As has been pointed out, the height of wage rates at which all those eager to get jobs can be and are employed depends on the marginal productivity of their performance. If the employers are prevented, either by union pressure and compulsion or by government decree, from hiring help at this market rate, and are forced to pay more, the costs incurred by the employment of workers in the production of a number of articles rise above the prices the consumers are prepared to expend for the value added to the product by these workingmen's efforts. In order to avoid losses and bankruptcy, the businessmen are under the necessity to restrict their production activities and therefore to reduce the number of men employed.

At the wage rates established in a free labor market, i.e., in a market not manipulated — we may better say not sabotaged — by labor union or government compulsion, all those who are anxious to get jobs can find employment. But if wage rates are fixed above the potential market rates, unemployment of a part of the potential labor force develops. Mass unemployment becomes a lasting phenomenon.

It is not the operation of the market economy that generates unemployment with all its moral and material evils, but precisely the ill-contrived, although well-intentioned, actions of unions and governments. There is no other means to do away with unemployment than to abstain from any government and union meddling with the height of wage rates.

Inflation Not Fit to Fight Unemployment

The self-styled American "liberals" propose to do away with unemployment by inflation. They suggest an increase in the quantity of money in circulation through credit expansion.

Lord Keynes did not invent, but merely popularized this makeshift. He was well aware of the fact that inflation inevitably results in a rise in all commodity prices or, what is merely another way of describing the same effect, in a drop in the monetary unit's, the dollar's, purchasing power. But he argued that the wage earners will acquiesce in "a gradual and automatic lowering of real wages as a result of rising prices." * It is obvious that Keynes thus fully admitted that nothing but a lowering of real wage rates can do away with unemployment. The inflation which he recommended was designed as a clever trick to cheat the workers. He expected that they would not be shrewd enough to realize that real wages

---

* Keynes, *General Theory* (1936), p. 264.

had dropped and that, therefore, they would not ask for higher pay to compensate for the reduction in the monetary unit's purchasing power.

Keynes failed entirely to see that the decades of reckless inflation have made everybody — the newspapers, the average man, the house-wives, and the workers and union leaders — index conscious. His as-sumption underrates in an almost unbelievable way the intellectual powers of the masses. One cannot avoid the nefarious implications of the spurious union doctrine by deceiving the public. Moreover it must be remembered that inflation is not a policy that can last. If inflation and credit expansion are not stopped in time, they result in a more and more accelerated drop in the monetary unit's purchasing power, and in skyrocketing commodity prices until the inflated money becomes en-tirely worthless and the whole government-manipulated currency sys-tem collapses. In our age, this has happened to the monetary regime of various countries.

How Honest Workers Plan to Do Away with Unemployment

An analysis of the Keynesian prescription for doing away with unem-ployment clearly shows that Lord Keynes also never doubted that what causes unemployment is a policy that fixes wage rates above the level at which the free market would have fixed them. What he suggested to at-tain full employment was a peculiar, and as he believed, very cunning, method to reduce real wage rates. In fact all people who gave serious thought to the matter agree in pointing out that at the wage rates deter-mined on the unhampered labor market all those eager to find jobs are getting them. (Incidentally it may be mentioned also that Karl Marx and the doctrines of the Marxian parties admitted that unions as well as gov-ernments cannot, without creating unemployment, raise wage rates above the rates corresponding to the conditions of the market.)

The terrorism of the union bosses and the political parties fed by ample union subsidies have for many years succeeded in popularizing the myth that expects a betterment of the wage earners' material con-ditions, not from an increase in the per head quota of capital invested and the resulting technological advancement, but from government action and from union violence. But fortunately it is impossible for lies to remain unchallenged forever. There are signs that the truth about in-dustrial relations is beginning to spread in spite of all endeavors of the union bosses to conceal it.

While the Administration and Congress are embarrassed by the rising tide of unemployment and do not consider any other method to reduce it than by resorting to inflation, better schemes are recommended from the midst of the unemployed. In Wheeling, West Virginia, a community on the Ohio River, an unemployed steelworker named Thomas E. Elliott, who has worked only a month and a half in the past four years, advances an anti-unemployment plan that does not require any aid from Washington. His plan, as outlined in *U.S. News and World Report*,* is to offer to prospective employers better and cheaper labor. He and 1,400 other unemployed will promise any company coming in that they will do an honest day's work at a fair wage, but if the plant makes a profit they will expect to get additional pay. "Steel wages are too high today," Mr. Elliott said. "Some men who have been getting $3 an hour in the steel mills will have to be satisfied with $1.85 or $2 an hour." Better to have a job at lower wages, he decided, than to remain unemployed while asking for $3 an hour.

If this plan materializes, a plain citizen will have contributed to the welfare of the nation and its manual workers more than all the learned advisers of the Administration and all the members of the innumerable government agencies. Good luck to you, Mr. Elliott!

---

* January 9, 1961, pp. 101–3. Mr. Elliott's "Save-a-Plant Plan" could have helped his economically depressed area insofar as above-market wage rates were the cause of its problems. However, since 1961, traditional smokestack industries in the United States have been beset by other exorbitant and mandatory costs, notably for federally imposed pollution control and safety standards.

15

Wage Earners and Employers

To answer that question we must first look at a little history. In the pre-capitalistic ages a nation's social order and economic system were based upon the military superiority of an elite. The victorious conqueror appropriated to himself all the country's utilizable land, retained a part for himself, and distributed the rest among his retinue. Some got more, others less, and the great majority nothing. In the England of the early Plantagenets [the line of British kings, descended from French Normans, who reigned from 1154 to 1399], a Saxon was right when he thought: "I am poor because there are Normans to whom more was given than is needed for the support of their families." In those days the affluence of the rich was the cause of the poverty of the poor.

Conditions in the capitalist society are different. In the market economy the only way left to the more gifted individuals to take advantage of their superior abilities is to serve the masses of their fellowmen. Profits go to those who succeed in filling the most urgent of the not-yet-satisfied wants of the consumers in the best possible and cheapest way. The profits saved, accumulated, and plowed back into the plant benefit the common man twice. First, in his capacity as a wage earner, by raising the marginal productivity of labor and thereby real wage rates for all those eager to find jobs. Then later again, in his capacity as a consumer when the products manufactured with the aid of the additional capital flow into the market and become available at the lowest possible prices.

The characteristic principle of capitalism is that it is mass production to supply the masses. Big business serves the many. Those outfits

Transcript of radio broadcast made during intermission of the U.S. Steel Concert Hour, May 17, 1962; first published in *The Freeman*, May 1988. Mises had been asked to respond to the question: "Are the interests of the American wage earners in conflict with those of their employers, or are the two in agreement?"

that are producing for the special tastes of the rich never outgrow medium or even small size. Under such conditions those anxious to get jobs and to earn wages and salaries have a vital interest in the prosperity of the business enterprises. For only the prosperous firm or corporation has the opportunity to invest, that is, to expand and to improve its activities by the employment of ever better and more efficient tools and machines.

The better equipped the plant is the more can the individual worker produce within a unit of time, the higher is what the economists call the marginal productivity of his labor and, thereby, the real wages he gets. The fundamental difference between the conditions of an economically underdeveloped country like India and those of the United States is that in India the per head quota of capital invested and thereby the marginal productivity of labor and consequently wage rates are much lower than in this country. The capital of the capitalists benefits not only those who own it but also those who work in the plants and those who buy and consume the goods produced.

And then there is one very important fact to keep in mind. When one distinguishes, as we did in the preceding observations, between the concerns of the capitalists and those of the people employed in the plants owned by the capitalists, one must not forget that this is a simplification that does not correctly describe the real state of present-day American affairs. For the typical American wage earner is not penniless. He is a saver and investor. He owns savings accounts, United States Savings Bonds and other bonds, and first of all insurance policies. But he is also a stockholder. At the end of the last year [1961] the accumulated personal savings reached $338 billion. A considerable part of this sum is lent to business by the banks, savings banks, and insurance companies. Thus the average American household owns well over $6,000 that are invested in American business.

The typical family's stake in the flourishing of the nation's business enterprises consists not only in the fact that these firms and corporations are employing the head of the family. There is a second fact that counts for them, to wit that the principal and interest of their savings are safe only as far as the American free enterprise is in good shape and prospering. It is a myth that there prevails a conflict between the interests of the corporations and firms and those of the people employed by them. In fact, good profits and high real wages go hand in hand.

16

Full Employment and Monetary Policy

At the price determined in an unhampered market all those who consider it satisfactory can sell and all those who are prepared to pay it can buy. If commodities remain unsold, this is not due to their "unsalability" but to speculation on the part of their owners; they hold out because they expect that they will be able to sell later at a higher price.

It is different when the authorities try to influence the market by compulsion. If the government decrees and enforces minimum prices higher than the potential market prices, a part of the supply offered for sale at the official minimum price remains unsold. This fact is well known. Therefore, if a government wants to push the price of a commodity above the potential market price, it does not simply resort to the fixing of minimum prices. Rather it tries to reduce the quantity offered for sale on the market, for instance by purchasing and withholding a part of the supply available.

All this applies also to labor. At the wage rates determined in the labor market everybody who looks for a job can get it and everybody who wants to employ workers can hire them. In the unhampered labor market, wage rates always tend toward full employment.

Market wage rates rise when the marginal productivity of labor outruns the marginal productivity of capital goods; or, more simply, when the per-head quota of capital invested increases. This is effected either by accumulation of new capital or by a drop in the number of workers. An increase in the amount of capital is the result of saving and consequent investment. A reduction in the supply of labor on the market can be brought about by restricting immigration. In the age of liberalism, in the traditional classical meaning of the term, there were practically no migration barriers. In this age of welfarism and unionism, well-nigh all governments have either completely prohibited immigration or, as for instance the United States and other American republics, stipulated definite quotas. Beyond that, some American unions have tried to reduce still more the number of jobseekers in their segments of the labor market by excluding racial minorities from some kinds of employment and by rendering entrance into certain branches extremely difficult.

There is need to emphasize that only such "artificial" or "institutional" reduction of the labor supply makes it possible for the unions to raise their members' wage rates. Their success in raising the wages of their members is won at the expense of those whom they have excluded. These outsiders are forced to look for jobs in industries in which remuneration is lower than what they would have earned in the field that is closed to them.

Effects of Labor Unions

Labor unionism as we know it today is the outcome of a long evolution. In the beginning only a few branches were organized, mostly those with the best-paid skilled workers. At that time, those who could not find a job in a unionized industry because wages had been pushed above the potential market height and thereby the demand for labor had been reduced, were forced to go into the nonunionized branches of business. Their influx into these branches increased in them the number of jobseekers and thus tended to depress there the height of wage rates. Thus, the higher wages of unionized workers brought about pressures on the jobs and wages of nonunionized workers. The more unionization spread, the more difficult it became for those who had lost their jobs on account of union policy to find other jobs; they remained unemployed. Wherever and whenever the unions succeeded in raising wage rates above the potential market rate, i.e., above the amount the workers would have earned without union interference, "institutional" unemployment developed as a lasting phenomenon.

As the union leaders see it, the determination of wage rates is the outcome of a struggle for power between the employers and the employees. Their interpretation does not acknowledge that wages depend on the state of the market and that the workers who receive the wages form the immense majority of the consumers out of whose pockets the wages are ultimately paid. The average wage earner considers it unfair that the movie star and the boxing champion are paid a hundred times more than the welder and the charwoman. He fails to see that his own behavior, his own purchases on the market, and those of other wage earners like him contribute to this result. An entrepreneur cannot pay more to a worker than he expects to collect from the customers for this man's performance. Even the most infatuated supporters of the exploitation doctrine are finally forced to admit that, at a certain height of wage rates, lasting unemployment of a considerable part of the potential labor force becomes unavoidable.

The market economy is ultimately controlled by the conduct of the consumers, that is by the conduct of all the people. In buying or in desisting from buying, the consumers determine what ought to be produced, of what quality and in what quantity. They determine who should make profits and who should suffer losses. They make rich men poor and poor men rich. The consumers are continuously shifting control of the material factors of production into the hands of those entrepreneurs, capitalists, and landowners who are most successful in supplying them, the consumers, in the cheapest and best possible way. Thus, in the capitalistic economy control of the factors of production is, as it were, a revocable mandate granted by the public. The operation of the market, in a daily repeated plebiscite, assigns to everybody the place in which he is to contribute to the united effort of all. This daily plebiscite determines the height of everybody's income.

The Alternative — Socialism

The individual resents the fact that he is forced to adjust himself to the conditions of the market and must forgo many of his own wishes and inclinations. However, it is obvious that the immeasurable benefits that cooperation under the system of the social division of labor affords to everybody must be paid for by some sacrifices. Whatever society's economic organization may be, it must always prevent man from behaving without due concern for the existence of others. The alternative to the hegemony of the market under capitalism is not absolute freedom, but the unconditional surrender of all to the supremacy of the socialist planning authority.

Society cannot do without an institution that channels the available workers into those branches in which they are most urgently needed and withdraws them from those in which there is less need for them.

The labor market serves this purpose by raising wage rates in expanding industries and reducing them in shrinking industries. The alternative is to assign to each man a job by government order.

The tyranny of the labor market is milder than that of socialist regimentation. It grants to the individual a margin within which he is free to ignore the market's directives. If he is prepared to put up with a lower income, he can choose vocations in which he can either dedicate himself to his ideals or indulge his inclination for laziness. But the command of the socialist dictator does not brook contradiction.

There is only one method to abolish lasting mass unemployment, the return to the freedom of the labor market. Lasting mass unemployment is always institutional. It is the inevitable effect of the enforcement of wage rates that are higher than the potential market rates at which all jobseekers could find employment. It does not matter whether these minimum wage rates were decreed directly by the government or induced indirectly by the fact that the government is not willing to protect the enterprises and the strikebreakers against the violence of the unions.

The political power of the unions has succeeded in suppressing the dispassionate discussion of these problems. But it could not prevent the undesirable consequences of the unions' policies from wreaking havoc. In the twenties, in many European countries mass unemployment became the main political embarrassment. It was clear that these conditions could not continue indefinitely. Something had to be done. Smart politicians thought that they had found a solution. As it was deemed impermissible to antagonize the unions, and to tamper with the money wage rates dictated by them, they resorted to currency devaluation, reducing purchasing power and, thus, real wage rates. England took the lead in 1931. Very soon other countries followed.

For a while the nostrum worked. Some time passed before the unions began to pay full attention to the drop in the monetary unit's purchasing power. But when the index of the cost of living became the main issue in wage negotiations, the monetary method of eliminating mass unemployment had exhausted its serviceableness.

A New Messiah

It was precisely at this juncture that Lord Keynes entered the scene with his good tidings, the allegedly new economic doctrine designed to supersede all previous economic teachings, including those of the earlier writings of Keynes himself. Following in the wake of the politicians who in 1931 had demolished the British gold standard, and of their imitators, he pointed out that "a gradual and automatic lowering of real wages," that results from a lowering of the monetary unit's purchasing power, will be less strongly resisted than attempts to revise money wages downward. But in 1936, when Keynes's book was published, this no longer agreed with the facts.

Keynes's *General Theory* of 1936 and his later writings are hardly different from the bulk of inflationist literature which for more than a century has flooded the world. Like the authors of all these pamphlets, Keynes tries to dispose of all those who do not share his opinions by calling them "orthodox." He never tries to disprove their teachings rationally. He enriched the prosaic language of diplomatic correspondence by terms borrowed from the messianic jargon of the "monetary cranks." For instance, in the British document that inaugurated the events which finally led to the establishment of the International Monetary Fund, he declared that credit expansion performs the "miracle . . . of turning a stone into bread." But he did not add any new idea to the old, long since entirely refuted and discredited arguments of the inflationists. All Keynes accomplished was to coin a new slogan — "full employment" — which became the motto of present-day policies of inflation and credit expansion.

The full-employment doctrine underlying these inflation and credit expansion policies, in complete accord with the teachings of the *Communist Manifesto*, declares that the very operation of the capitalistic mode of production inevitably generates the emergence of mass unemployment. Unlike the creed of the more consistent Marxians it does not, however, contend that the return of periods of economic depression and large-scale unemployment is absolutely inevitable in the market economy. It attributes to the State (with a capital S) the power to create jobs for everybody. All that the State has to do is to put more money into the hands of the people and thereby to increase demand. It is wrong, this official full-employment doctrine goes on to assert, to call an increase in the quantity of money created for this purpose, inflation. It is just "full-employment" policy. Those "reactionaries" who ramble on about monetary stability and the return to gold are depicted as the worst enemies of civilization, public welfare, and the common man.

The climate of opinion of the United States is fully dominated by these ideas. The unions are in a position to succeed in what are euphemistically called wage negotiations because the laws are loaded in favor of the unions and because the Government is always prepared to use its power to their advantage. (In this regard it does not make much difference whether the Administration is Republican or Democratic.) From time to time the unions ask for raises; the employers are forced to yield; as soon as business begins to slacken and workers are discharged, public opinion vehemently asks for more "easy money." After a short period of hesitation the Administration gives in and puts pressure upon the Federal Reserve Board to reduce interest rates, so as to increase the quantity of money and make it "easier."

A Few Dissenters

Fortunately the inflationary policy is still seriously resisted by a group of critics who are not numerous but who are conspicuous by their competence and familiarity with the problems involved. Among these dissenters are several eminent writers, a few influential businessmen, and, what is worthy of notice, also some members of the Federal Reserve Board. This handful of men do not have the power to put an end to this nefarious monetary and credit policy. Yet their weighty reasoning has in the last years, especially under President Eisenhower's regime, succeeded in keeping the inflationary ventures within narrow limits. It is the merit of their warning voices that the world's richest country has up to now not embarked upon the pernicious policy of runaway inflation.

The full significance of this success can only be appreciated if one takes into account the vehemence of the pro-inflationist propaganda of university teachers and of "progressive" politicians and journalists. Some of the utterances of these people are really amazing. Thus several years ago the then chairman of the Federal Reserve Bank of New York declared: "Final freedom from the domestic money market exists for every sovereign national state where there exists an institution which functions in the manner of a modern central bank, and whose currency is not convertible into gold or into some other commodity." The lecture that contained this statement had the characteristic title: "Taxes For Revenue Are Obsolete."[*] In the same vein, a professor of economics[†] pointed out, in a voluminous work, that the government "can raise all the money it needs by printing it"; the purpose of taxation is "never to raise money" but "to leave less in the hands of the taxpayer."

[*] Beardsley Ruml in *American Affairs*, 8 (1946): pp. 45–46.
[†] Abba P. Lerner, *The Economics of Control* (1944; New York: Augustus M. Kelly, 1970), 307.

The weakness of the small group advocating sound monetary policy and fighting all inflationary measures is their disinclination to attack the "full employment" doctrine openly and directly. It is practically impossible to bring this issue up before the public. Certainly there are men with the courage to risk their careers or even their personal safety by criticizing the "full employment" doctrine. But there are neither newspapers nor publishers who would dare to spread doctrines that criticize and reject the institution of unionism in principle. Even those writers who occasionally expose blackmail and embezzlement on the part of individual union officers emphasize again and again that they consider the institution of unionism as such, and the policies of the unions, as beneficial to the welfare of the wage earners and the whole nation; they merely intend to free the unions from dishonest leaders. As long as such ideas about the effects of unionism prevail, even modest attempts at repealing the privileges granted to the unions by the New Deal are doomed to fail, and there cannot be any question of protecting enterprises and those willing to work against violence on the part of the unions.

At the most recent meeting of the International Monetary Fund there was much talk about the danger of inflation. In order to fight this danger, it is no longer enough to work for a better understanding of monetary problems. It is no less important to enlighten public opinion about the absurdity of the "full-employment" doctrine that guides the conduct of all governments and all political parties today.

17

Gold versus Paper

Most people take it for granted that the world will never return to the gold standard. The gold standard, they say, is as obsolete as the horse and buggy. The system of government-issued fiat money provides the treasury with the funds required for an open-handed spending policy that benefits everybody; it forces prices and wages up and the rate of interest down and thereby creates prosperity. It is a system that is here to stay.

Now whatever virtues one may ascribe — undeservedly — to the modern variety of the greenback standard, there is one thing that it certainly cannot achieve. It can never become a permanent, lasting system of monetary management. It can work only as long as people are not aware of the fact that the government plans to keep it.

The Alleged Blessings of Inflation

The alleged advantages that the champions of fiat money expect from the operation of the system they advocate are temporary only. An injection of a definite quantity of new money into the nation's economy starts a boom as it enhances prices. But once this new money has exhausted all its price-raising potentialities and all prices and wages are adjusted to the increased quantity of money in circulation, the stimulation it provided to business ceases. Thus even if we neglect dealing with the undesired and undesirable consequences and social costs of such inflationary measures and, for the sake of argument, even if we accept all that the harbingers of "expansionism" advance in favor of inflation, we must realize that the alleged blessings of these policies are short-lived. If one wants to perpetuate them, it is necessary to go on and on increasing the quantity of money in circulation and expanding credit

Reprinted from *The Freeman*, July 13, 1953.

at an ever-accelerated pace. But even then the ideal of the expansionists and inflationists, viz., an everlasting boom not upset by any reverse, could not materialize.

A fiat-money inflation can be carried on only as long as the masses do not become aware of the fact that the government is committed to such a policy. Once the common man finds out that the quantity of circulating money will be increased more and more, and that consequently its purchasing power will continually drop and prices will rise to ever higher peaks, he begins to realize that the money in his pocket is melting away. Then he adopts the conduct previously practiced only by those smeared as profiteers; he "flees into real values." He buys commodities, not for the sake of enjoying them, but in order to avoid the losses involved in holding cash. The knell of the inflated monetary system sounds. We have only to recall the many historical precedents beginning with the Continental Currency of the War of Independence.

Why Perpetual Inflation Is Impossible

The fiat-money system, as it operates today in this country and in some others, could avoid disaster only because a keen critique on the part of a few economists alerted public opinion and forced upon the government cautious restraint in their inflationary ventures. If it had not been for the opposition of these authors, usually labeled orthodox and reactionary, the dollar would long since have gone the way of the German mark of 1923. The catastrophe of the Reich's currency was brought about precisely because no such opposition was vocal in Weimar Germany.

Champions of the continuation of the easy money scheme are mistaken when they think that the policies they advocate could prevent altogether the adversities they complain about. It is certainly possible to go on for a while in the expansionist routine of deficit spending by borrowing from the commercial banks and supporting the government bond market. But after some time it will be imperative to stop. Otherwise the public will become alarmed about the future of the dollar's purchasing power and a panic will follow. As soon as one stops, however, all the unwelcome consequences of the aftermath of inflation will be experienced. The longer the preceding period of expansion has lasted, the more unpleasant those consequences will be.

The attitude of a great many people with regard to inflation is ambivalent. They are aware, on the one hand, of the dangers inherent in a continuation of the policy of pumping more and more money into the economic system. But as soon as anything substantial is done to stop increasing the amount of money, they begin to cry out about high interest rates and bearish conditions on the stock and commodity exchanges. They are loath to relinquish the cherished illusion which ascribes to government and central banks the magic power to make people happy by endless spending and inflation.

Full Employment and the Gold Standard

The main argument advanced today against the return to the gold standard is crystallized in the slogan "full-employment policy." It is said that the gold standard paralyzes efforts to make unemployment disappear.

On a free labor market the tendency prevails to fix wage rates for every kind of work at such a height that all employers ready to pay these wages find all the employees they want to hire, and all job-seekers ready to work for these wages find employment. But if compulsion or coercion on the part of the government or the labor unions is used to keep wage rates above the height of these market rates, unemployment of a part of the potential labor force inevitably results.

Neither governments nor labor unions have the power to raise wage rates for all those eager to find jobs. All they can achieve is to raise wage rates for the workers employed, while an increasing number of people who would like to work cannot get employment. A rise in the market wage rate — i.e., the rate at which all job-seekers finally find employment — can be brought about only by raising the marginal productivity of labor. Practically, this means by raising the per-capita quota of capital invested. Wage rates and standards of living are much higher today than they were in the past because under capitalism the increase in capital invested by far exceeds the increase in population. Wage rates in the United States are many times higher than in India because the American per-capita quota of capital invested is many times higher than the Indian per-capita quota of capital invested.

There is only one method for a successful "full-employment policy" — let the market determine the height of wage rates. The method that Lord Keynes has baptized "full-employment policy" also aimed at reestablishment of the rate which the free labor market tends to fix. The peculiarity of Keynes's proposal consisted in the fact that it proposed to eradicate the discrepancy between the decreed and enforced official wage rate and the potential rate of the free labor market by lowering the purchasing power of the monetary unit. It aimed at holding nominal wage rates, i.e., wage rates expressed in terms of the national fiat money, at the height fixed by the government's decree or by labor union pressure. But as the quantity of money in circulation was increased and consequently a trend toward a drop in the monetary unit's purchasing power developed, real wage rates, i.e., wage rates expressed in terms of commodities, would fall. Full employment would be reached when the difference between the official rate and the market rate of *real* wages disappeared.

There is no need to examine anew the question whether the Keynesian scheme could really work. Even if, for the sake of argument, we were to admit this, there would be no reason to adopt it. Its final effect upon the conditions of the labor market would not differ from that achieved by the operation of the market factors when left alone. But it attains this end only at the cost of a very serious disturbance in the whole price structure and thereby the entire economic system. The Keynesians refuse to call "inflation" any increase in the quantity of money in circulation that is designed to fight unemployment. But this is merely playing with words. For they themselves emphasize that the success of their plan depends on the emergence of a general rise in commodity prices.

It is, therefore, a fable that the Keynesian full-employment recipe could achieve anything for the benefit of the wage earners that could not be achieved under the gold standard. The full-employment argument is as illusory as all the other arguments advanced in favor of increasing the quantity of money in circulation.

The Specter of an Unfavorable International Balance

A popular doctrine maintains that the gold standard cannot be preserved by a country with what is called an "unfavorable balance of payments." It is obvious that this argument is of no use to the American opponents of the gold standard. The United States [1953] has a very considerable surplus of exports over imports. This is neither an act of God nor an effect of wicked isolationism. It is the consequence of the fact that this country, under various titles and pretexts, gives financial aid to many foreign nations. These grants alone enable the foreign recipients to buy more in this country than they are selling in its markets. In the absence of such subsidies it would be impossible for any country to buy anything abroad that it could not pay for, either by exporting commodities or by rendering some other service such as carrying foreign goods in its ships or entertaining foreign tourists. No artifices of monetary policy, however sophisticated and however ruthlessly enforced by the police, can in any way alter this fact.

It is not true that the so-called have-not countries have derived any advantage from their abandonment of the gold standard. The virtual repudiation of their foreign debts, and the virtual expropriation of foreign investments that it involved, brought them no more than a momentary respite. The main and lasting effect of abandoning the gold standard, the disintegration of the international capital market, hit these debtor countries much harder than it hit the creditor countries. The falling off of foreign investments is one of the main causes of the calamities they are suffering today.

The gold standard did not collapse. Governments, anxious to spend, even if this meant spending their countries into bankruptcy, intentionally aimed at destroying it. They are committed to an antigold policy, but they have lamentably failed in their endeavors to discredit gold. Although officially banned, gold in the eyes of the people is still money, even the only genuine money. The more prestige the legal-tender notes produced by the various government printing offices enjoy, the more stable their exchange ratio is against gold. But people do not hoard paper; they hoard gold. The citizens of this country, of course, are not free to hold, to buy, or to sell gold.* If they were allowed to do so, they certainly would.

No international agreements, no diplomats, and no supernational bureaucracies are needed in order to restore sound monetary conditions. If a country adopts a noninflationary policy and clings to it, then the condition required for the return to gold is already present. The return to gold does not depend on the fulfillment of some material condition. It is an ideological problem. It presupposes only one thing: the abandonment of the illusion that increasing the quantity of money creates prosperity.

* This right to own gold was restored to U.S. citizens as of January 1, 1975.

The excellence of the gold standard is to be seen in the fact that it makes the monetary unit's purchasing power independent of the arbitrary and vacillating policies of governments, political parties, and pressure groups. Historical experience, especially in the last decades, has clearly shown the evils inherent in a national currency system that lacks this independence.

18

Inflation and You

There has been so much learned talk about the threats and dire consequences of inflation that plain folks begin to be suspicious. Did not the
economists of the 1920s, except for a few outsiders whom the others
scorned as orthodox doctrinarians, forecast everlasting prosperity?
What if their present fears are no better founded than their optimism
fifteen years ago? The layman, therefore, has the right to ask the specialist to explain the matter and to do so in simple terms. We economists should not be exempt indefinitely from the obligation, which is
accepted by doctors, engineers, and other scientists, of making ourselves understood by the layman. The obligation is clear-cut in the matter of inflation, an economic problem which is as close to every American as his own skin.

Everybody knows that inflation consists of a large increase in the available quantity of money and money substitutes such as bank credits. In
a country like the United States, which transacts so much of its business by checks and through bank credits, the main vehicle of inflation
is not so much the printing of additional paper money as the increase
of deposit currency. Everybody also knows that a general rise of prices
and wages is the unavoidable and inescapable result of inflation. And
finally, most people realize that when inflation is going on price control
is a quite ineffective method of controlling prices and wages; at best, it
is a temporary expedient to break or postpone the force of inflationary
effects.

There is widespread ignorance, however, concerning the social implications of inflation. How will it affect you personally, if you are a professional man, a worker, a farmer? What will it do to your possessions,
your debts, your insurance policies?

Reprinted from *Mercury*, July 1942.

Social and Economic Effects of Inflation

The first fact that needs to be noted in answering such questions is that inflation is detrimental to all creditors. The higher prices rise, the lower will fall the purchasing power of the principal and interest payments due. The dollar which was loaned out had a higher purchasing ability, could provide more goods, than the dollar which is paid back.

And who is a creditor? Does inflation touch only businessmen and financiers? Nothing of the sort. You who read these lines are certainly a creditor. Every person who has a legal claim to deferred payments of any kind is a creditor. If you have a savings account with a bank, if you own bonds, if you are entitled to a pension, if you have paid for an insurance policy, you are a creditor, and are, hence, directly hit by inflation.

Professional men, civil servants, commissioned officers of the armed forces, teachers, most white-collar workers, salaried employees, skilled specialists, mechanics, and engineers normally provide for their own old age and for their dependents in ways that make them creditors, that is through savings, insurance, pensions, and annuities. Moreover, Social Security has brought the great masses of ordinary workers into the ranks of creditors. For all these millions of people, every further step toward inflation means a further decline in the real value of the claims or credits they have saved up by years of toil and sacrifice. They will collect the number of dollars to which they are entitled — but each of those dollars will be thinner than it used to be, capable of providing less food, clothing, and shelter.

The loss of the creditor, of course, is the profit of the debtor. The man who borrowed a thousand or a million full-sized dollars repays his lender with a thousand or a million depreciated dollars. The mortgages on farms and on real estate, the debts owed by industrial enterprises, all shrink as inflation proceeds. Thus, a comparatively small group of debtors is favored at the expense of the teeming groups of creditors.

The most fateful results of inflation derive from the fact that the rise of prices and wages which it causes occurs at different times and in a different measure for various kinds of commodities and labor. Some classes of prices and wages rise more quickly and rise higher than others. Not merely inflation itself, but its unevenness, works havoc.

While inflation is under way, some people enjoy the benefit of higher prices for the goods or services they *sell*, while the prices for goods and services they *buy* have not yet risen or have not risen to the same extent.

These people profit from their fortunate position. Inflation seems to them "good business," a "boom." But their gains are always derived from the losses of other sections of the population. The losers are those in the unhappy situation of selling services or commodities whose prices have not yet risen to the same degree as have prices of the things they buy for daily consumption.

These victims, by and large, are the same kind of people — roughly, the middle classes — who are injured as creditors through the depreciation of their bank savings, insurance policies, pensions, etc. The salaries of teachers and ministers, the fees of doctors, go up only slowly as compared to the tempo with which prices of food, rent, clothing, and so on, go up. There is always a considerable time lag between the increase in the money income of the white-collar workers and professional people and the increase in costs of food, clothing, and other necessities.

Hedging Against Inflation

Has the average man any means of evading the detrimental effects of inflation?

Those insured, or entitled to pensions or social security benefits, cannot avoid being victimized. And the picture is not much brighter for other groups of creditors. Of course, the bondholder may sell his bonds and the bank depositor may withdraw his balance. But if they keep the money, they are no less subject to the harmful effects of the fall in the money's purchasing power. In other words, the dollar continues to evaporate whether it is resting in a bank, a bond, or a strongbox at home.

For the Europeans, struck by the great inflations of World War I and its aftermath, there was a simple means of escape. They needed only to change their local currencies for the money of a country with a sound currency. They bought dollars or they bought gold. It might have been illegal, but it worked. For Americans, no such remedy is available. If the dollar goes bad, no foreign currency can conceivably prove better. At the same time, the U.S. government has closed the avenue of escape by forbidding its citizens to own gold coins or ingots.*

You may buy a farm. But that is a remedy only if you become a farmer and till the soil with your own hands. Otherwise, it is a remedy

---

* From 1933 to 1975, U.S. citizens were prohibited by law from owning monetary gold.

not for yourself but for the tenant who works the farm. It may reasonably be expected that, in the course of inflation, new laws will safeguard tenants — whether on farms or in residences — against rises in rent.* In European inflations, rents were always restricted by legislation.

You may buy a home for yourself and your family. But in a period of inflation, economic conditions change swiftly and in unexpected ways. You cannot foresee whether it will be necessary suddenly to change your place of residence and employment. Then you will have to sell the house — renting it is almost useless — and experience proves that such forced sales rarely bring the amounts laid out for acquiring the property.

You may buy common stock. But the experts are convinced that taxation will confiscate not only the profits but a good deal of the capital invested, too. While the prices of all commodities are rising, stock market quotations may still cling more or less to preinflation levels. This means that in owning common stock you are not much better protected than in owning bonds.

You may buy jewelry and other valuables. But you cannot always expect to sell these at a later date for what you paid for them. Nobody knows in advance how the market conditions for any given valuable will develop. Diamonds and rubies, for instance, may hold much of their value. But what if the owners of the largest hoards of precious stones should unload them because of changing political or social conditions?

Neither is it possible to escape the detrimental effects of the time lag between the rise of different prices and wages. Trade union policies are futile in this connection. As long as the war (World War II) is going on, labor may succeed in obtaining, at least for some groups, wages which correspond to the rise of commodity prices. But sooner or later if industry does not keep pace, they will face the choice between a sharp decline in wages and the maintenance of high wage levels with long-lasting unemployment for millions. In the long run, inflation hurts the interests of all groups of labor, as well as those of the middle classes.

There is only one class which, as a whole, derives profit from inflation: the indebted farmers. Their mortgages are wiped out and the

---

* In October of 1942, Congress "authorized and directed" President Roosevelt to control prices, wages, salaries, and rents. Nationwide price, wage, and rent controls continued throughout the war, but were ended shortly thereafter. However, some cities chose to continue rent controls thus distorting the market and prices, and producing persistent shortages of rental housing in those localities.

products of their own toil bring higher returns corresponding to the higher prices they must pay for things they purchase.

The owners of really large fortunes, too, may succeed in preserving a greater or smaller portion of their wealth, but inflation results in the consumption of a good deal of a nation's capital stock.

Even if some special groups profit, the whole country is poorer.

Moral and Political Effects of Inflation

Worse than the immediate economic consequences of inflation are its attendant moral and political dangers.

It has been asserted that Nazism is the fruit of the vast German inflation of 1923. That is not quite correct. It would be more correct to say that the great inflation and the Nazi scourge both derived from the mentalities and the doctrines that long dominated German public opinion. The State, which the German socialist Ferdinand Lassalle had already proclaimed as god, was supposed to be able to achieve anything. The omnipotent State was credited with the magic power of unlimited spending without any burden on the citizenry. Money, said the German "monetary cranks," is a creature of the State; there is no harm in issuing infinite quantities of paper currency.

Fortunately, such superstitions are strange to the healthy common sense of America. Inflation, therefore, will never go as far in this country as it did in Germany. Even a much more moderate inflation, however, shakes the foundations of a country's social structure. The millions who see themselves deprived of security and well-being become desperate. The realization that they have lost all or most all of what they had set aside for a rainy day radicalizes their entire outlook. They tend to fall easy prey to adventurers aiming at dictatorship, and to charlatans offering patent-medicine solutions. The sight of some people profiteering while the rest suffer infuriates them. The effect of such an experience is especially strong among the youth. They learn to live in the present and scorn those who try to teach them "old-fashioned" morality and thrift.

Inflation and Government Borrowing

The writer, having witnessed the course of inflations in one European nation after another, believes that it is not too late to stop further inflation in the United States by bold and painful measures. Inflation is not an act of God. It is a result of the methods used to provide a part of the means for the conduct of the war. One set of methods can still be replaced by another, less harmful set. It is still possible to keep down the amount of money and money substitutes *by financing the total amount necessary through taxation and loans.*

People sometimes call inflation a special way of "taxing" a country's citizens. This is a dangerous opinion. And it is wholly untrue. Inflation is not a method of taxation, but an alternative for taxation. When a government imposes taxes, it has full control. It can tax and distribute the burden any way it considers fair and desirable, allotting a larger share of the tax burden to those who are better able to carry it, reducing the burden on the less fortunate. But in the case of inflation, it sets in motion a mechanism that is beyond its control. It is not the government, but the operation of the price system, that decides how much this or that group will suffer.

And there is another important difference. All taxes collected flow into the vaults of the public treasury. But with inflation, the public treasury's gain is less than what it costs the individual citizen, since a considerable part of that cost is drained off by the profiteers, the minority that benefits from the inflation.

It is no less fallacious to consider inflation as a method of raising loans for public use. Technically, inflation does increase the total of the government's indebtedness to the banks. But the banks' intervention is only instrumental. If the government borrows from the banks, the banks do not grant loans out of their own funds, or out of money deposited with them by the public; the banks are not real lenders; they grant the loans out of their "excess reserves." They merely expand credit for the benefit of the government. In other words, they increase the quantity of money substitutes.

When you as an individual buy a government bond, you make a loan to the government; you put part of your cash holdings into the hands of the treasury. There is then no increase in the total quantity of currency or credits available and hence no inflation.

However, it is different when government borrows from the banks' "excess reserves." Their so-called "excess reserves" are not a tangible thing. The term is merely a phrase indicating the limits within which the law is prepared to tolerate credit expansion, that is to say further inflation. The effects of loans from available "excess reserves" are just as inflationary as the effects of issuing more paper money. It is a mistake, therefore, to confuse this government "borrowing" from the "excess re-serves" of the banks with genuine loans.

Popular education is absolutely essential. It is clear that the efforts of the U.S. government to collect the means necessary for the conduct of the war by taxation and by sale of government bonds represent sound measures for heading off inflation. Everybody should be made to un-derstand that the burden of high taxes and of making personal loans to the government are minor evils compared to the disastrous and inexo-rable consequences of inflation. Not only for the sake of the national welfare, but for the sake of your own interests—whether you are rich or poor, employer or wage earner—you should do your best to arrest the further progress of inflation.

19

Inflation

The government provides a part of the funds required for rearmament by inflation, that is, by increasing the quantity of money in circulation and the amount of bank balances subject to check.

The unavoidable consequence of inflation is the emergence of a general tendency of all prices to rise. If the government had procured all the money it needed for rearmament by taxing the citizens, the increased demand on its part would have been counteracted by a drop in the purchases of the taxpayers. The expanded military consumption would have been neutralized on the market by a restriction in civilian consumption. But with inflation the additional demand of the armed forces comes on top of the nondecreased demand of the public and makes prices soar.

What the bureaucrats have in mind when talking about "fighting" inflation is not *avoiding* inflation, but *suppressing* its inevitable consequences by price control. This is a hopeless venture. The attempt to fix prices at a lower rate than that which the unhampered market would determine renders unremunerative the business of some producers, that is, those operating at the highest costs. This forces them to discontinue production.

Wartime Experience

Inflation, in conjunction with price control, brings about scarcity. Housewives remember very well what happened in World War II with meat, butter, eggs, and many other articles under the regime of the

Reprinted from the *New York World Telegram & Sun*, May 7, 1951.

Office of Price Administration. Yet price control has been reestablished.* If Congress does not let the present price control law expire on June 30, as scheduled, the country will very soon experience anew not only all the hardships of inflation, but also all the evils created by the vain attempts to conceal these hardships by price control.

Economists know very well that there is only one means available to prevent a further rise in all commodity prices, namely, to end inflation entirely. If the government obtains all its funds from the public and stops increasing the quantity of money in circulation and borrowing from the commercial banks, prices will remain unchanged, by and large, and there will not be any need for the activities of a price dictator.

But the administration does not want to stop inflation. It does not want to endanger its popularity with the voters by collecting, through taxation, all it wants to spend. It prefers to mislead the people by resorting to the seemingly nononerous method of increasing the supply of money and credit. Yet, whatever system of financing may be adopted, whether taxation, borrowing, or inflation, the full incidence of the government's expenditures must fall upon the public.

With inflation as well as with taxation, it is the citizens who must foot the total bill. The distinguishing mark of inflation, when considered as a method of filling the vaults of the Treasury, is that it distributes the burden in a most unfair way, overcharging those who are least able to bear it.

A Semantic Trick

To avoid being blamed for the nefarious consequences of inflation, the government and its henchmen resort to a semantic trick. They try to change the meaning of the terms. They call "inflation" the inevitable *consequence* of inflation, namely, the rise in prices. They are anxious to relegate into oblivion the fact that this rise is produced by an increase in the amount of money and money substitutes. They never mention this increase.

---

* After the outbreak of the Korean conflict in June 1950, President Truman was authorized under the Defense Production Act (signed September 8, 1950) to "stabilize prices and wages." This price control law was revised several times and extended until April 30, 1953. Eisenhower, who had become president in January 1953, did not request a further extension and it was allowed to expire.

They put the responsibility for the rising cost of living on business. This is a classical case of the thief crying "catch the thief." The government, which produced the inflation by multiplying the supply of money, incriminates the manufacturers and merchants and glories in the role of being a champion of low prices. While the Office of Stabilization and Price Control is busy annoying sellers as well as consumers by a flood of decrees and regulations, the only effect of which is scarcity, the Treasury goes on with inflation.

20

Inflation: An Unworkable Fiscal Policy

In dealing with problems concerned with the economics of mobilization, it is first of all necessary to realize that fiscal policies have reached a turning point.

In recent decades all nations have looked upon the income and the wealth of the more prosperous citizens as an inexhaustible reserve which could be freely tapped. Whenever there was need for additional funds, one tried to collect them by raising the taxes to be paid by the upper-income brackets. There seemed to be enough money for any suggested expenditure because there seemed to be no harm in "soaking the rich" a bit more. As the votes of these rich do not count much in elections, the members of the legislative bodies were always ready to increase public spending at their expense. There is a French dictum: *Les affaires, c'est l'argent des autres.* "Business is other people's money." In these last sixty years political and fiscal affairs were virtually "other people's money." Let the rich pay, was the slogan.

End of an Era

Now this period of fiscal history has come to an end. With the exception of the United States and some of the British Dominions, what has been called the ability-to-pay of the wealthy citizens has been completely absorbed by taxes. No further funds of any significance can be collected from them. Henceforth all government spending will have to be financed by taxing the masses.

The European nations concerned are not yet fully aware of this fact because they have found a substitute. They are getting Marshall Plan aid; the U.S. taxpayer fills the gap.

Transcript of remarks before the Conference on the Economics of Mobilization, held at White Sulphur Springs, West Virginia, April 6–8, 1951, under the sponsorship of the University of Chicago Law School. Reprinted from *The Commercial and Financial Chronicle*, April 26, 1951.

In this country things have not yet gone as far as they have in other countries. It is still possible to raise an additional $2 or $3 billion, or perhaps even $4 billion, by increasing corporation taxes, and "excess profits" taxes, and by rendering the personal income tax more progressive. But under present conditions, even $4 billion would be only a fraction of what the Treasury needs. Thus, in this country we are also at the end of a period of fiscal policies. The whole philosophy of public finance must undergo a revision. In considering the pros and cons of a suggested expenditure the members of Congress will no longer be able to think: The rich have enough; let *them* pay. In the future, the voters on whose ballots the Congressmen depend will have to pay.

Inflation, an increase in money and credit, is certainly not a means to avoid or to postpone for more than a short time the need to resort to taxes levied on people other than those belonging to the rich minority. If, for the sake of argument, we leave aside all the objections which may be raised against any inflationary policy, we must take into account the fact that inflation can never be more than a temporary makeshift. Inflation cannot be continued over a long period of time without defeating its fiscal purpose and ending in a complete debacle as was the case in this country with the Continental currency, in France with the *mandats territoriaux*, and in Germany with the mark in 1923.

What makes it possible for a government to increase its funds by inflation is the ignorance of the public. The people must ignore the fact that the government has chosen inflation as a fiscal system and plans to go on with inflation endlessly. It must ascribe the general rise in prices to other causes than to the policy of the government and must assume that prices will drop again in a not-too-distant future. If this opinion fades away, inflation comes to a catastrophic breakdown.

The Housewife's Behavior

If the housewife who needs a new frying pan reasons: "Now prices are too high; I will postpone the purchase until they drop again," inflation can still fulfill its fiscal purpose. As long as people share this view, they increase their cash holdings and bank balances, and a part of the newly created money is absorbed by these additional cash holdings and bank balances; prices on the market do not rise in proportion to the inflation.

But then — sooner or later — comes a turning point. The housewife discovers that the government expects to go on inflating and that consequently prices will continue to rise more and more. Then she reasons: "I do not need a new frying pan today; I shall only need one next year. But I had better buy it now because next year the price will be much higher." If this insight spreads, inflation is done for. Then all people rush to buy. Everybody is anxious to reduce his holding of cash because he does not want to be hurt by the drop in the monetary unit's purchasing power. The phenomenon then appears which in Europe was called the "flight into real values." People rush to exchange their depreciating paper money for something tangible, something real. The knell sounds of the currency system involved.

In this country we have not yet reached this second and final stage of every protracted inflation. But if the authorities do not very soon abandon any further attempt to increase the amount of money in circulation and to expand credit, we shall one day come to the same unpleasant result.

It is not a matter of choosing between financing the increased government expenditure by collecting taxes and borrowing from the public on the one hand and financing it by inflation on the other hand. Inflation can never be an instrument of fiscal policy over a long period of time. Continued inflation inevitably leads to catastrophe.

Therefore, we should not waste our time in discussing methods of price control. Price control cannot prevent the rise in prices if inflation is going on. Even capital punishment could not make price control work in the days of Emperor Diocletian or during the French Revolution. Let us concentrate our efforts on the problem of how to avoid inflation, not upon useless schemes of how to conceal its inexorable consequences.

Taxation the Key

What is needed in wartime is to divert production and consumption from peacetime channels toward military goals. In order to achieve this, it is necessary for the government to tax the citizens, to take away from them the money which they would otherwise spend for things they must no longer buy and consume so the government can spend it for the conduct of the war.

At the breakfast table of every citizen in wartime sits an invisible guest, as it were, a GI who shares his meal. Parked in the citizen's garage is not only the family car, but also — invisibly — a tank or a plane. The important fact is that a GI needs more in food, clothing, and other things than he used to consume as a civilian. And military equipment wears out much more quickly than civilian equipment. The costs of a modern war are enormous.

The adequate method of providing the funds the government needs for war is, of course, taxation. Part of the funds may also be provided by borrowing from the public, the citizens. But if the Treasury increases the amount of money in circulation or borrows from the commercial banks, it inflates. Inflation can do the job for a limited time. But it is the most expensive method of financing a war; it is socially disruptive and should be avoided.

Inflation: A Convenient Makeshift

There is no need to dwell upon the disastrous consequences of inflation. All people agree in this regard. But inflation is a very convenient makeshift for those in power. It is a handy means to divert the resentment of the people from the government. In the eyes of the masses, big business, the "profiteers," the merchants — not the Administration — appear responsible for the rise in prices and the ensuing need to restrict consumption.

Perhaps somebody will consider what I am saying here as antidemocratic, reactionary, and economic royalism. But the truth is that inflation is a typically antidemocratic measure. It is a policy of governments that do not have the courage to tell the people honestly what the real costs of their conduct of affairs are.

A truly democratic government would have to tell the voters openly that they must pay higher taxes because expenses have risen considerably. But it is much more agreeable for a government to present only a part of the bill to the people and to resort to inflation for the rest of its expenditures. What a triumph if they can say: Everybody's income is rising, everybody has now more money in his pocket, business is booming.

Deficit spending is not a new invention. During the greater part of the nineteenth century it was the preferred fiscal method of precisely those governments that were not then considered democratic and progressive — Austria, Italy, and Russia. Austria's budget showed a deficit yearly from 1781 on, until the late '80s of the nineteenth century, when an orthodox professor of economics, Dunajewski, as minister of finance, restored the budgetary equilibrium. There is no reason to be proud of deficit spending, nor to call it progress.

Going After Lower Brackets

If one wants to collect more taxes, it will be necessary to lay a burden greater than hitherto on the lower income brackets, the strata of society whose members consume the much greater part of the total amount consumed in this country. Up to now it has been customary to tax predominantly corporations and individuals with higher incomes. But even the outright confiscation of these revenues would only cover a fraction of the additional funds the country needs today.

Some experts have declared that it is necessary to tax the people until it hurts. I disagree with these sadists. The purpose of taxation is not to hurt, but to raise the money the country needs to rearm and to fight in Korea. It is a sad fact that world affairs now make it necessary for the government to force people who used to buy nylon stockings and shirts to shift to other du Pont products, namely munitions.

In his book *Eternal Peace*, the German philosopher Immanuel Kant (1724–1804) suggested that government should be forbidden to finance wars by borrowing. He expected that the warlike spirit would dwindle if all countries had to pay cash for their wars. However, no serious objection can be raised against borrowing from the public, from people who have saved and are prepared to invest in government bonds. But borrowing from the commercial banks is tantamount to printing additional bank notes and expanding the amount of deposits subject to check. That is inflation.

Semantic Confusion

There is nowadays a very reprehensible, even dangerous, semantic confusion that makes it extremely difficult for the nonexpert to grasp the true state of affairs. Inflation, as this term was always used everywhere and especially in this country, means increasing the quantity of money and bank notes in circulation and the quantity of bank deposits subject to check. But people today use the term "inflation" to refer to the phenomenon that is an inevitable consequence of inflation, that is the tendency of all prices and wage rates to rise. The result of this deplorable confusion is that there is no term left to signify the cause of this rise in prices and wages. There is no longer any word available to signify the phenomenon that has been, up to now, called inflation. It follows that nobody cares about inflation in the traditional sense of the term. As you cannot talk about something that has no name, you cannot fight it. Those who pretend to fight inflation are in fact only fighting what is the inevitable consequence of inflation, rising prices. Their ventures are doomed to failure because they do not attack the root of the evil. They try to keep prices low while firmly committed to a policy of increasing the quantity of money that must necessarily make them soar. As long as this terminological confusion is not entirely wiped out, there cannot be any question of stopping inflation.

Look at the silly term, "inflationary pressures." There is no such thing as an "inflationary pressure." There is inflation or there is the absence of inflation. If there is no increase in the quantity of money and if there is no credit expansion, the average height of prices and wages will by and large remain unchanged. But if the quantity of money and credit is increased, prices and wages must rise, whatever the government may decree. If there is no inflation, price control is superfluous. If there is inflation, price control is a sham, a hopeless venture.

It is the government that makes our inflation. The policy of the Treasury, and nothing else.

We have been told a lot about the need for, and the virtues of, direct controls.

We have learned that they preserve the individual's liberty to choose the grocer he prefers. I do not want to examine what value may be attached to direct controls from a metaphysical point of view. I only want to stress *one* fact: As a means for preventing and fighting inflation or its consequences, direct controls are absolutely useless.

21

Socialism, Inflation, and the Thrifty Householder

The most serious dangers for American freedom and the American way of life do not come from without. They are not of a military character. Neither will socialism conquer this country — and, for that matter, the civilized nations of Western Europe — in the shape of an open surrender to the program of the Communist International. Whatever chances socialism may have in the United States are due to the economic policies of our own political parties that gradually undermine the economic and social foundations of American freedom and prosperity.

Both traditional parties, the Republicans as well as the Democrats, are sincere in protesting their abhorrence of totalitarianism. The voters in casting their ballots for either of these parties are fully convinced that they are voting for officeholders who are firmly committed to the preservation intact of the Constitution and all the freedoms it grants to the individual citizens. These politicians and their supporters would be seriously alarmed if they realized that they are virtually paving the way for a system that does not differ essentially from the totalitarian system they decidedly reject.

Socialism and Planning Not Different from Communism

The fundamental fallacy that leads contemporary political thinking astray is to be seen in the fictitious distinction between communism on the one side and socialism and planning on the other side.

The two terms socialism and communism are synonyms. Communism is a very old term, while the term socialism was first coined in

Reprinted from *Christian Economics*, October 18, 1960.

France at the end of the 1830s. Up to the year 1917 both were used indiscriminately. Thus Marx and Engels called the program they published in 1848 the *Communist Manifesto*, while the parties they organized for the realization of this program called themselves socialist parties.

Before 1917 no distinction was made between the two words. When Lenin called his party "communist," he meant that it was a party sincerely aiming at the realization of socialism as distinct from the parties that, according to Lenin, merely called themselves socialist parties while in fact they were "social traitors" and "servants" of the bourgeoisie. Lenin never pretended that his Communist party had any other goal than the realization of socialism. The official name he gave to his government was — and is — the Union of the Soviet *Socialist* Republics. If somebody says he is opposed to communism, but cherishes socialism, he is no more consistent or logical than a man who declares that he is opposed to murder but cherishes assassination.

The essential feature of the socialist, or communist conduct of affairs is the substitution of the government's unique plan for the plans of individual citizens. "Planning" is therefore nothing but one term more to signify what the terms socialism and communism are designed to signify.

Yet many leaders of our political parties are deluded by the idea that socialism and planning are something different from communism and that in fostering these schemes they are opposing communism, while in fact they are fully adopting the Communist program. Of course, these confused politicians pretend that what they are aiming at is a socialist system that preserves democracy and representative government. They say they want to abolish "only" *economic* freedom and to retain *political* freedom. They are at a loss to realize that economic control is not merely control of one sector of human life which can be separated from other sectors. If the government controls all material factors of production, it controls all aspects of the individuals' activities. If it controls all publishing facilities, all printing presses, radio, television, and all assembly halls, every political activity depends on the discretion of the authorities. If everybody is bound to work according to the orders of the government, only those whom the rulers trust are free to devote their time and their efforts to public affairs. It is not an accident that representative government and civil liberties developed step-by-step with the substitution of capitalism for feudalism and disappeared everywhere as soon as socialism — whether the "right" model (German Nazism and Italian

Fascism) or the "left" model (Russian Bolshevism) — supplanted the market economy. Despotism is the necessary political corollary of socialism just as representative government is the necessary constitutional corollary of capitalism.

Unwitting Support of Socialism by Inflationary Policies

Certainly there are many among the "left" wing leaders of both political parties who are consciously intent upon abolishing any trace of freedom and converting America into a full replica of the Soviet system. But most of our politicians and the rank and file of the voters are not guilty of such a betrayal. On the contrary, they are anxious to preserve the traditional system of government, the free institutions, established by the founding fathers, the institutions that were the foundations of this country's greatness, glory, and prosperity, as they were the essential features of the civilization of Western Europe. But even these sincere advocates of liberty are, unbeknown to themselves, undermining the "American way of life." They are lending a helping hand to allegedly beneficial economic policies that, on the one side, sabotage the operation of the market economy and, on the other side, restrict the individuals' self-determination by expanding the field of government control, euphemistically called "social" control.

The most detrimental of all varieties of economic policies is inflation, i.e., the policy of increasing the supply of money and money substitutes. If additional legal-tender banknotes are issued or if additional bank balances subject to check (checkbook money) are created, nothing is added to the material wealth of a country. But those persons into whose pockets these newly created means of payment are flowing are thereby in a position to expand their purchases. Thus an additional demand for commodities and services comes into being while the supply of such commodities and services has not been increased. The inevitable outcome is a tendency for prices to soar.

There is no need to depict in detail the unwelcome, nay the catastrophic effects of such a state of affairs. Everybody is familiar with them; everybody knows how he was hurt by them. Among reasonable men there is hardly anybody who would dare to advocate openly a policy of inflation. Nonetheless this country, and most other countries of the world, have for many decades been committed to inflationist measures.

The fault rests with a lack of responsibility and a fickleness of character on the part of statesmen and politicians as well as with the greed of powerful pressure groups who want to get handouts from the government, the notorious "something for nothing." A government cannot spend but at the expense of the people. As taxes have already long since overstepped the optimum of returns and there is hardly any sizeable increase to be expected from further raising the already levied taxes or devising new ones, the main way to finance additional government spending is with inflation.

It is a serious error to assume that a nation can win and can become richer by increasing the supply of money and money substitutes. What one group of people may gain, is lost by other groups.

Inflation and the Creditors

Let us look upon one important aspect of the problem, the nexus of creditor and debtor. One of inflation's main effects is the progressive dilution of debts. The more inflation progresses, the more is the debtor favored at the expense of the creditor. While the nominal value of a loan remains unchanged, its purchasing power shrinks more and more. Of course, some people believe that this is after all not too bad, or that it may even be desirable. The creditors, they think, are rich and will get over such losses. But the debtors are poor and will be benefited by a reduction in the burden of their debt.

Yet, this way of reasoning is entirely fallacious. It is based upon a fateful misconstruction of essential features of the capitalistic system, under which a continually increasing multitude of people with moderate means are becoming creditors.

One of the main achievements of the capitalistic system is to be seen in the opportunity it offers to the masses of citizens to save and thereby to improve their material well-being.

In the "good old days," effectual saving was possible only for the well-to-do. The farmer, the artisan, and the owner of urban real estate could fructify their thrift into improvement of their own farms, shops, and buildings. But the landless worker had only one method of saving, to hoard by burying a few coins or hiding them in some other way. This was a very unsatisfactory method of saving. Its main deficiency was that it did not bear any interest and did not give the saver an opportunity to acquire a share of the material factors of production. While new capital stock was added to the already previously available equipment, while new houses and workshops were built and were better equipped, the manual worker saw no way to contribute to this effort, nor to participate directly in its fruits. In this sense, he could feel that he was a "proletarian," a man who did not own any property and who was forever destined to live from hand to mouth.

The financial techniques of capitalism radically altered this state of affairs. Capitalism not only increased the marginal productivity of labor spectacularly and thereby raised wage rates and the employees' standard of living. It also made it possible for thrifty laborers to join in the endeavors of accumulating capital. It inaugurated institutions to fructify everybody's parsimony, first of all savings banks and insurance organizations. Even the smallest savings deposit bears interest. The success of these schemes was overwhelming. Billions were added to the capital working in the plants, farms, mines, and transportation facilities. A continually growing part of the nation's wealth is the counterpart of these holdings of the common man.

The Common Man a Creditor

These conditions manifest themselves in the fact that the average man is today a creditor rather than a debtor. The much talked-about rise in consumers' credit lending, originating from installment selling and buying must not deceive us. In the balance the common man is by far a creditor, not a debtor. The billions of dollars that big business and real estate owe to mortgage banks, commercial banks, savings banks, and insurance companies belong—virtually, although not formally—to the common man. He owns corporate bonds as well as bonds issued by the U.S. Treasury and by various subdivisions of the government. And finally familiarity with these types of investment provides him with a better understanding of the ways and practices of business and thus enables him also to venture on the acquisition of common stock. One of the most characteristic developments of present-day finance, the mutual funds and kindred schemes, shows the extent to which what is called risk capital also turns into a popular way of saving and investing.

Yet, however momentous these attempts to make the common man an owner of common stock may be, the main method of making employees, in their capacity as capitalists, participate in the well-being created by the free economy is by the acquisition of titles and claims payable in definite amounts of the nation's monetary unit. From this point too the masses acquire a lively interest in the stability of the nation's legal tender, for the value of all kinds of deposits, bonds, and insurance policies is inseparably linked to the purchasing power of the dollar. A policy of "creeping inflation" such as this country has now pursued for a long series of years — apart from all the other detrimental effects it produces — is in the strict meaning of the words antisocial and antidemocratic. It is a policy against the vital material interests of the common man. It hurts seriously those judicious and conscientious earners of wages and salaries who are intent upon improving their own and their families' lot by thrift.

Under a *sound* money policy these people would become more and more deproletarianized. They would acquire a continually rising share in the nation's wealth and become interested in the nation's economic effort, not only as employees, but also as owners of interest-bearing investments. But under inflationary policies they see how the purchasing power of their savings, their insurance policies, and their pensions is persistently dwindling. Their hopes for steady material improvement are dispelled. Their attempts to join those strata of the population who, by saving and capital accumulation, are cooperating in the improvement of economic conditions are thwarted. They become desperate and lose their confidence in the fairness and efficiency of the market economy.

The Communists Favor Inflation

The communist chiefs know very well how their cause is furthered by undermining the purchasing power of the dollar. They know they cannot succeed in a country in which the masses of the wage earners rely upon their savings and upon other income such as pensions and social security benefits determined in fixed amounts of the nation's legal tender. The main obstacle which their propaganda encounters in this country is the fact that the "common man" is more and more deproletarianized and sees his personal economic condition improved, not only by rising wages and salaries, but also by his claims to pensions and interest from savings. The 65 percent of the American population who hold life insurance policies are proof against the venom of the communist slogans and so are the 47 percent of the entire population who are time depositors in mutual savings and commercial banks. But when these people see the value of their thrift continually diminished by inflation, they lose their faith in the system and become an easy prey to the mendacious incitation of the subversive parties.

It is a really diabolic makeshift to egg various pressure groups on to ask for more and more government spending to be financed by credit expansion. The bill for such government extravagance is always footed by the most industrious and provident people. It is their claims that are shrinking with the dollar's purchasing power.

A sound monetary policy is one of the foremost means to thwart the insidious schemes of communism.

22

Inflation Must End in a Slump

This country, and with it most of the Western world, is presently going through a period of inflation and credit expansion. As the quantity of money in circulation and deposits subject to check increases, there prevails a general tendency for the prices of commodities and services to rise. Business is booming.

Yet such a boom, artificially engineered by monetary and credit expansion, cannot last forever. It must come to an end sooner or later. For paper money and bank deposits are not a proper substitute for nonexisting capital goods.

Economic theory has demonstrated in an irrefutable way that a prosperity created by an expansionist monetary and credit policy is illusory and must end in a slump, an economic crisis. It has happened again and again in the past, and it will happen in the future, too.

If one wants to avoid the recurrence of periods of economic depression, one must start by preventing the emergence of artificial booms. One must prevent the governments from embarking upon a policy of cheap interest rates, deficit spending, and borrowing from the commercial banks.

This is, of course, a very difficult task. Governments are in this regard very obstinate. They long for the popularity that booming business conditions seldom fail to win for the party in power. The unavoidable crash, they think, will appear only later; then the other party will be in power and will have to account to the voters for the evils which their predecessors have sown.

Thus there is no doubt that we shall one day have to face again an economic recession, although it is impossible to determine the date of its outbreak and the degree of its severity. It will be bad indeed. But

Reprinted from the *New York World Telegram & Sun*, August 28, 1951.

worse than the crisis itself could prove the psychological and ideological consequences of an erroneous *interpretation* of its causes.

For the spokesmen of the artificial expansionist policy are busy denying that economic crises are the inevitable effect of the preceding expansionist policy. They are anxious to exonerate the governments. As they see it, inherent shortcomings of the capitalist mode of production cause the periodical recurrence of bad business. There is no other means, they conclude, to avoid a crisis than to put the economic system under the full tutelage of a central planning board.

This is essentially the doctrine of Karl Marx. Those supporting it, those passionately attacking the insight that it is the policy of inflation and credit expansion which produces economic depressions, are — sometimes unwittingly — serving the cause of the Communists. When the slump comes, people indoctrinated by their teachings will argue precisely as Stalin expects them to. They will think: The efforts to preserve capitalism have proved vain; capitalism necessarily results in the recurrence of economic catastrophes; if we want stability, we must turn toward Communism.

In the antagonism between the doctrine of the economists who ascribe the emergence of economic crises to the policy of credit expansion and the official doctrine that ascribes them to alleged inherent defects of capitalism there is much more at stake than a merely doctrinal quarrel. The way in which people will react to the — unfortunately hardly avoidable — letdown of business that will follow the end of the present armament boom may decide the fate of our civilization.

People must learn in time what the inevitable consequences are of the monetary and credit policies adopted by the present administration. They must realize that what the collapse of the artificial boom will establish will not be any insufficiency of capitalism, private enterprise, and the market economy, but the failure of the methods of financing public expenditure as practiced by the New Deal and the Fair Deal.

A comprehension of the nature of the boom will also make people more cautious in their business dealings. They will not fall victim to the deception that the boom will go on forever.

23

The Plight of Business Forecasting

People by and large know today that a boom brought forth by a policy of credit expansion and "easy money" cannot last forever and must sooner or later lead to a slump. They do not want to be taken by surprise and ruined. They are anxious to learn *in time* when the turning point will come because they plan to arrange their affairs early enough so as not to be hurt by, or even to profit from, the crash. As they believe that economics is the art of predicting tomorrow's business conditions, they consult the economists.

"How will business be in the coming months?" asks the newspaperman when interviewing the economist. No convention of businessmen is held without the solicited presence of a professor of economics, or the head of a bank's research department, who in guarded language produces a cautiously qualified prediction about the nation's, or the world's business. Whenever and wherever a businessman catches sight of an economist, he tries to sound him out about the future state of the market.

What Brings About the Slump

Economics explains the phenomenon of the trade cycle (i.e., the repeated emergence of periods of unusually good business that are invariably followed after some time by a reversal into unusually bad business) as the necessary effect of the attempts to manipulate the rate of interest. Governments and political parties are committed to the idea that it is good policy to lower the rate of interest below the height it would attain on a free market. And they believe that the expansion of bank credit is the right means to produce this desired effect. They do

Reprinted from *National Review*, April 4, 1956; © 1956 by National Review, Inc., 215 Lexington Avenue, New York, N.Y. Reprinted by permission.

not realize that the boom which they artificially create by such credit expansion must finally result in the catastrophe of the depression.

Spokesmen of governments tried to disparage the economists' explanation of the recurrence of economic depressions. They tried in vain. This economic doctrine, the so-called monetary or circulation-credit theory of the business cycle, is irrefutable. The fanatical supporters of inflationism, unbalanced budgets, and reckless government spending have, it is true, succeeded in banning sound theory from universities and textbooks. And they have founded special research institutions whose main purpose it is to put the monetary theory into oblivion. But their triumph is always shortlived. Today people are fully aware of the fact that credit expansion is the ultimate cause of the slump. All public declarations on the state of business, even those uttered by bureaucrats, are based upon a full acknowledgment of the monetary doctrine of the trade cycle. It is precisely the cognition of this theory's correctness that in the present boom period alarms businessmen and prompts them to inquire nervously about the date of the turning point.

Economics: Not Quantitative

Economics predicts the outcome of definite modes of conduct, in our case, of a policy of credit expansion. But this prediction is *qualitative* only. Economic prediction can never disclose anything about the *quantitative* relations concerned. There is not, and there cannot be such a thing as *quantitative* economics.

In the field of the natural sciences there prevail constant relations between definite magnitudes. By means of laboratory experiments the scientists are in a position to determine these constants and to make practical use of them in predictions and in technological design. But in human action there are no such constant relations between magnitudes. There, all quantities are variables or, as a more appropriate term describes them, historical data. It is, therefore, not due to alleged backwardness, or to the much-talked-about "youth" of economic science, that it is not quantitative but, as people say, "merely" qualitative. No constant, fixed quantitative economic relationships exist, on which quantitative economic predictions would have to be based. And what does not exist cannot become a matter of scientific inquiry.

Economics can only tell us that a boom engendered by credit expansion will not last. It cannot tell us after what amount of credit expansion the slump will start or when this event will occur. All that economists and other people say about these quantitative and calendar problems partakes of neither economics nor any other science. What they say in the attempt to anticipate future events makes use of specific "understanding," the same method which is practiced by everybody in all dealings with his fellow man. Specific "understanding" has the same logical character as that which characterizes all anticipations of future events in human affairs — anticipations concerning the course of Russia's foreign policy, religious and racial conditions in India or Algeria, ladies' fashions in 1960, the political divisions in the U.S. Senate in 1970; and even such anticipations as the future marital relations between Mr. X and his wife, or the success in life of a boy who has just celebrated his tenth birthday. There are people who assert that psychology may provide some help in such prognostications. However that may be, it is not our task to examine this problem. We have merely to establish the fact that forecasts about the course of economic affairs cannot be considered scientific.

Statistics: Necessarily Retrospective

The usual method employed in business forecasts is statistical and, thereby, retrospective.

The statistician recites a mass of statistical information, which necessarily refers to the past only, and he works it into charts and curves. He is so preoccupied with arranging and rearranging the data available that he entirely fails to realize that they do not have any relevance to the problems in question. They refer to the past, not to the future. They depict trends that prevailed in the past and are, by and large, familiar to everybody. They in no way answer the questions that all people, and especially businessmen, are asking. People know that trends can change; they are afraid that they will change; and they would like to know when the change will occur. But the statistician knows only what everybody knows, namely, that they have not yet changed.

In the sphere of human action statistics are a special method of historical research. They record historical facts in quantitative terms. But history deals always with the past, never with the future. If the future were merely a continuation of the trends that prevailed in the past, it would not be uncertain and we would not then be in need of any forecasting. But as this is not the case, what is called economic forecasting is merely guesswork.

Professional forecasters blame their much talked about failures on the fact that the figures available are insufficient and reach them too late. This apology misses the point. However complete and recent statistical information may be, it always remains information about the past and does not assert anything about the future.

The Self-Contradiction of Forecasting

People's ideas about the possibility of business forecasting, and its practical value for the conduct of one's own affairs, are self-contradictory and unrealizable.

The businessman thinks: If I know the date of the boom's collapse some time in advance, I will be in a position to sell my stocks and reduce my inventories of both raw materials and products at boom prices. Then, at the critical moment, I will have cash and no debts. The man who entertains such ideas overlooks the fact that this knowledge could be helpful to him only if he alone has it, while all other people are still bullish. But how could this occur if, as popular opinion assumes, economic doctrine enables the economists to predict the day of the crisis? If economists really could predict when the crisis would occur, then all people would learn simultaneously the date of the impending crash. Consequently, they would all immediately try to adjust their transactions to this expectation. They would all stop buying forthwith and start selling. But then, as a consequence of this attitude, the catastrophic drop in prices, the slump, would appear at once; it would not wait for the distant day the economists had predicted. Nobody would derive any advantage from the economists' forecast; at the very instant this forecast was uttered and accepted as correct, the crisis would already be consummated.

From time immemorial people have known that the very act of predicting may change the actions of men and thus eliminate the forces that are required to bring about the predicted outcome. Obstinate fatalists have acquiesced in the illusion that all attempts to avoid a prognosticated evil are futile; and that frequently, in some mysterious way, against the intention of the actor, they even bring the prophecy about. No such subterfuge is permissible in our case. The very fact that people are putting faith in the forecast of a crash results in the annulment of the prediction: it instantly produces the crash. Thus, what the businessman wants to attain by asking the economist for information about the future of the market could not be realized, even if the economist were in a position to answer.

PART III

Mises as Critic

For Mises, books were important. They were the most effective means for transmitting ideas from generation to generation. He wrote many books himself, and he was constantly urging his students to write books. In almost every lecture he would suggest the titles of several books to read and several books to write.

Mises looked on the opportunity to review a book as more than a chance to discuss one book; it was an excuse for a short essay on economics. Although the books reviewed here may no longer be in print, his comments remain of interest.

Mises was a pessimist when he considered the conflicts and the violations of freedom throughout the world for which governments had been responsible in his lifetime. Yet, he was an optimist when he considered the potential of individuals to think, to reason, and to understand sound principles.

When Mises spoke to a Madison Square Garden rally of Young Americans for Freedom in 1962, he revealed his optimism. As quoted here, he said a "miracle" had happened. "Out of the ranks of the young boys and girls arose an opposition. There were on the campuses once again friends of freedom and they had the courage to speak their minds. Collectivism was challenged by individualism. . . . The idea of freedom made a comeback." He went on to say, "There are again young men and women eager to think over the fundamental problems of life and action. This is a genuine moral and intellectual resurrection, a movement that will prevent us from falling prey to the arbitrary tyranny of dictators."

Mises concluded, "As an old man I am greeting the young generation of liberators."

Mises's optimism appears now to have been somewhat justified. If the people throughout the world who are striving for freedom succeed in the future in establishing free markets and laissez faire, it will be due in large part to Mises's persistence throughout his life in teaching consistent economic principles.

24

Why Read Adam Smith Today?

A popular legend calls Adam Smith the Father of Political Economy and his two great books — *The Theory of Moral Sentiments*, first published in 1759, and *An Inquiry into the Nature and Causes of the Wealth of Nations*, first published in 1776 — epoch-making in economic history as well as in the evolution of economic thought. However, this is not quite correct. Smith did not inaugurate a new chapter in social philosophy and did not sow on land hitherto left uncultivated. His books were rather the consummation, summarization, and perfection of lines of thought developed by eminent authors — mostly British — over a period of more than a hundred years. Smith's books did not lay the foundation stone, but the keystone, of a marvelous system of ideas. Their eminence is to be seen precisely in the fact that they integrated the main body of these ideas into a systematic whole. They presented the essence of the ideology of freedom, individualism, and prosperity, with admirable logical clarity and in an impeccable literary form.

It was this ideology that blew up the institutional barriers to the display of the individual citizen's initiative and thereby to economic improvement. It paved the way for the unprecedented achievements of laissez-faire capitalism. The practical application of liberal principles multiplied population figures and, in the countries committed to the policies of economic freedom, secured even to less capable and less industrious people a standard of living higher than that of the well-to-do of the "good old" days. The average American wage-earner would not like to dwell in the dirty, badly lighted, and poorly heated palatial houses in which the members of the privileged English and French aristocracy lived two hundred years ago, or to do without those products of capitalist big business that render his life comfortable.

Introduction to the Henry Regnery Co. edition (1953) of Adam Smith, *An Inquiry into the Nature and Causes of The Wealth of Nations: Selections*.

The ideas that found their classical expression in the two books of Adam Smith demolished the traditional philosophy of mercantilism and opened the way for capitalist mass production for the needs of the masses. Under capitalism the common man is the much-talked-about customer who "is always right." His buying makes efficient entrepreneurs rich, and his abstention from buying forces inefficient entrepreneurs to go out of business. Consumers' sovereignty, which is the characteristic mark of business in a free world, is the signature of production activities in the countries of Western civilization.

The civilization is today furiously attacked by Eastern barbarians from without and by domestic self-styled Progressives from within. Their aim is, as one of their intellectual leaders, the Frenchman Georges Sorel,* put it, to destroy what exists. They want to substitute central planning by the government for the autonomy of the individual citizens, and totalitarianism for democracy. As their muddy and unwarranted schemes cannot stand the criticism leveled by sound economics, they exult in smearing and calumniating all their opponents.

Adam Smith too is a target of these smear campaigns. One of the most passionate advocates of destructionism had the nerve to call him, in the Introduction to an inexpensive edition of the *Wealth of Nations*, "an unconscious mercenary in the service of a rising capitalist class" and to add that "he gave a new dignity to greed and a new sanctification to the predatory impulses."[1] Other leftists resort to even still ruder insults.

As against such shallow opinions it may be appropriate to quote the verdict of wiser judges. The British historian Henry Thomas Buckle (1821–62) declared "that this solitary Scotchman has, by the publication of one single work, contributed more toward the happiness of man than has been effected by the united abilities of all the statesmen and legislators of whom history has presented an authentic record." The English economist Walter Bagehot (1826–77) said about the *Wealth of Nations*: "The life of almost everyone in England—perhaps of everyone—is different and better in consequence of it."

A work that has been praised in such a way by eminent authors must not be left on the shelves of libraries for the perusal of specialists and historians only. At least its most important chapters should be read by

1. Max Lerner in the Modern Library edition of the *Wealth of Nations* (New York: Random House, 1937), p. ix.
* Georges Sorel (1847–1922), a French political thinker, advocated at various times in his life violence, Marxism, revolutionary syndicalism, and Bolshevism.

all those who are eager to learn something about the past. There can hardly be found another book that could initiate a man better into the study of the history of modern ideas and the prosperity created by industrialization. Its publication date —1776, the year of the American Declaration of Independence — marks the dawn of freedom both political and economic. There is no Western nation that was not benefited by policies inspired by the ideas that received their classical formulation in this unique treatise.

However, a warning must be given. Nobody should believe that he will find in Smith's *Wealth of Nations* information about present-day economics or about present-day problems of economic policy. Reading Smith is no more a substitute for studying economics than reading Euclid is a substitute for the study of mathematics. It is at best a historical introduction into the study of modern ideas and policies. Neither will the reader find in the *Wealth of Nations* a refutation of the teachings of Marx, Veblen, Keynes, and their followers. It is one of the tricks of the socialists to make people believe that there are no other writings recommending economic freedom than those of eighteenth-century authors and that in their, of course unsuccessful, attempts to refute Smith they have done all that is needed to prove the correctness of their own point of view. Socialist professors — not only in the countries behind the Iron Curtain — withheld from their students any knowledge about the existence of contemporary economists who deal with the problems concerned in an unbiased scientific way and who have devastatingly exploded the spurious schemes of all brands of socialism and interventionism. If they are blamed for their partiality, they protest their innocence. "Did we not read in class some chapters of Adam Smith?" they retort. In their pedagogy the reading of Smith serves as a blind for ignoring all sound contemporary economics.

Read the great book of Smith. But don't think that this may save you the trouble of seriously studying modern economics books. Smith sapped the prestige of eighteenth-century government controls. He does not say anything about the controls of 1952 or the Communist challenge.

25

The Marxian Class Conflict Doctrine

The most popular of the Marxian teachings is the doctrine of the ir-reconcilable conflict of social classes.

Status or Caste in Precapitalistic Society

In the precapitalistic ages the characteristic mark of society's organiza-tion was status. In the status or caste society there prevail legal differ-ences among individuals. The individual's station in life was fixed by his status. He inherited from his parents at birth his caste membership and his position in life was rigidly determined by the laws and customs that assigned to each member of his rank definite privileges, duties, and disabilities. Exceptional good or bad luck might in some rare cases el-evate an individual into a higher rank or debase him into a lower rank. But as a rule, the conditions of the individual members of a definite or-der or rank could improve or deteriorate only with a change in the con-ditions of the whole membership. The individual was primarily not a citizen of a nation; he was a member of an estate (*Stand* in German, *état* in French).

This system, that in England had already been substantially tem-pered and humanized in the Middle Ages, is incompatible with the capitalistic methods of the market economy. It was finally abolished in the countries of the European continent by the French Revolution and by the revolutions and reforms which the French Revolution called forth. Its last vestiges in the capitalistic part of the world disappeared when slavery was abolished step-by-step in the Americas and in the overseas colonies of the European powers.

Reprinted from *Christian Economics*, October 3, 1961.

In the status society there prevails, on the one hand, a solidarity of interests of all members of the same caste and, on the other hand, an irreconcilable conflict of interests between the members of different castes. All slaves, for instance, are united in having a stake in the abolition of slavery while their masters are opposed. All members of the European nobility were opposed to the abolition of their tax exemption, from which the Third Estate people expected a relaxation of their own burden. But no such conflicts are present in a society in which all citizens are equal before the law. No logical objection can be advanced against distinguishing various classes among the members of such a society; any classification is logically permissible, however arbitrarily the mark of distinction may be chosen. But it is nonsensical to classify the members of a capitalistic society according to their position in the framework of the social division of labor and then to identify these "classes" with the castes of a status society. It is precisely this that the Marxian doctrine of the irreconcilable struggle of classes does.

Marxian "Classes"

The "classes" that Marx distinguishes within a capitalistic society have a continually fluctuating membership. Class affiliation under capitalism is not a hereditary quality. It is assigned to each individual by a daily repeated plebiscite, as it were, of all the people. The buying public, the consumers, by their buying and abstention from buying, determine who should own and run the plants, who should work in the factories and mines, who should play the parts in the theater performances, and who should write the newspaper articles. They do it in a similar way in which they determine in their capacity as voters who should act as president, governor, or judge. In order to get rich in a capitalistic society and to preserve one's once-acquired wealth one must satisfy the wishes of the public. Those who have acquired wealth as well as their heirs must try to keep it by defending their assets against the competition of already established firms and of ambitious newcomers. In the unhampered market economy, not sabotaged by concessions and exemptions accorded to powerful pressure groups, there are no privileges, no protection of vested interests, no barriers preventing anybody from striving after any prize. Access to the Marxian-designated classes is free to everybody. The members of each class compete with one another. They are not united by a common class interest and not opposed to the members of other classes by being allied either in the defense of a common privilege, which those wronged by it want to see abolished, or in the attempt to abolish a legal disability which those deriving advantage from it want to preserve.

The champions of modern political freedom and laissez faire asserted: If the old laws establishing status privileges and disabilities are abolished and no new practices of the same character — such as subsidies, discriminatory taxation, indulgence granted to nongovernmental agencies like unions to use coercion and intimidation — are introduced, there is equality of all citizens under the law. Nobody is hampered in his aspirations and ambitions by any legal obstacles. Everybody is free to compete for any social position or function for which his personal abilities qualify him.

But Marx saw things in a different light. He maintained that capitalism did not abolish bondage and did not do away with the servitude of the working and toiling masses. It did not emancipate the common man. The people merely changed their masters. Formerly they were forced to drudge for the princes and aristocrats; now they are exploited by the bourgeoisie. The division of society into "social classes" is, in the eyes of Marx, sociologically and economically not different from its division into the castes of the status society. The bourgeois of the modern age is no less a predatory extortioner than were the noblemen and slaveholders of ages gone by.

But what characterizes the "social class" as such, and what entitles us to equate it with the castes of the status society? To this question Marx never gave an answer. All his books, pamphlets, and writings turn around the concept of the social class and the essence of his political and economic program is the abolition of "social classes" and the establishment of what he styles a classless society. But he never told us what he had in mind when employing the term "social class" and what justifies ascribing to the division of society into "social classes" the same effects as its division into castes had.

The main treatise of Karl Marx is *Das Kapital.* It was designed to provide a scientific justification of the ideas Marx had expressed in his numerous pamphlets and manifestos. Only the first volume of this book was published by Marx himself in 1867. Two years after the death of Marx his friend Engels published the second volume and finally, in 1894, eleven years after the death of Marx, the third volume, which consists of two parts, 870 pages altogether. Yet, the book remained unfinished. The third volume contains fifty-one chapters; then follows a fifty-second one-page chapter that is headed "The Classes." There Marx declares that the first question to be answered is what constitutes a class. But he does not provide an answer. Instead we read a note by the editor, Engels, saying: Here the manuscript breaks off.

One could be tempted to say: It is really tragic. Here is an author to whom fate denied the opportunity to define and to explain the fundamental concept of his philosophy, the concept on which all he said, argued, and planned depended. At the hour in which he was to write down the most important thing he had to tell mankind, death took him off. How lamentable!

But a closer inspection reveals a different aspect of the case. The abundant biographical material about Marx collected and published by his followers and the Marx-Engels-Lenin Institute in Moscow evinces the fact that Marx had ceased to work on his book many years before his death. There cannot be any doubt about the reason. When faced with the task of telling in precise words what he had in mind when perorating about "social classes" and giving reasons for his doctrine of the irreconcilable conflict of interests between the "social classes," Marx failed thoroughly. He had to acknowledge to himself that he was perplexed and was at his wit's end. He did not know what to say in the planned fifty-second chapter of the third volume and this embarrassment induced him to desist from finishing his great treatise. The essential dogma of the Marxian philosophy, the class conflict doctrine which he and his friend Engels had propagated for many decades, was unmasked as a flop.

Marxian Ideology Doctrine

The only retort that Marx, Engels, and all their followers down to the Russian Bolshevists and the European and American professorial admirers of Marx knew to advance against their critics was the notorious ideology doctrine. According to this makeshift a man's intellectual horizon is fully determined by his class affiliation. The individual is constitutionally unfit to reach out and to grasp any other doctrine than one that furthers the interests of his own "class" at the expense of other "classes." It is, therefore, unnecessary for a proletarian to pay any attention to whatever bourgeois authors may say and to waste time refuting their statements. All that is needed is to unmask their bourgeois background. That settles the matter.

This is the method to which Marx and Engels and later Marxians resorted in dealing with all dissenters. They never embarked upon the hopeless task of defending their self-contradictory system against devastating criticism. All they did was to call their opponents stupid bourgeois and to ascribe their opposition to their bourgeois class affiliation.

But Marx and Engels also contradicted their own doctrine in this regard. They both were scions of bourgeois families, brought up and living in a typical middle-class milieu. Marx was the son of a well-to-do member of the bar and married the daughter of a Prussian nobleman. His brother-in-law was Cabinet Minister of the Interior and as such the Chief of the Royal Prussian Police. Engels was the son of a wealthy manufacturer and a rich businessman himself; he indulged in the amusements of the British gentry such as riding to hounds in a red coat, and snobbishly refused to marry his mistress because she was of low origin. From the very Marxian point of view one would have to qualify Marxism as a doctrine of bourgeois origin.

The Destruction of Marxian Ideas Demands Vigorous Criticism

The enormous power that the Marxian ideas and the political parties guided by them enjoy in the present is not due to any inherent merits of the doctrine. It is an outgrowth of the moral and intellectual indifference and apathy of those whose duty it ought to be to offer unswerving resistance to false doctrines and to disclose their untruth. Some eminent philosophers and economists have provided irrefutable arguments to show the perversion, the misrepresentation of facts, and the self-contradictions of the Marxian creed. But their books are not read by those whose responsibility it is to enlighten the public. Thus the masses today indolently endorse all the socialist slogans and look upon every step forward on the way toward totalitarianism as progress toward the establishment of an earthly paradise. It is the inertness and sloth on the part of many of our most eminent fellow citizens that make the impetuous advance of the communist power possible.

The task of fighting Marxian dialectical materialism and all the various epistemological, philosophical, economic, and political doctrines emanating from it can only be accomplished by well-informed people. Those who want to contribute seriously to the defense of Western civilization against the onslaught of the dictators must acquaint themselves with the doctrines they plan to fight and must with full vigor study the writings of those authors who have long since entirely demolished all the Marxian fables and distortions. One has to admit that this is not an easy matter. Yet, there are in this world no great things that can be accomplished but by moral resolution and strenuous exertion.

26

The Marxian Theory of Wage Rates

The most powerful force in the policies of our age is Karl Marx. The rulers of the many hundreds of millions of comrades in the Communist countries behind the Iron Curtain pretend to put into effect the teachings of Marx; they consider themselves as the executors of the testament of Marx. In the noncommunist countries there is more restraint in the appreciation of Marx's achievements, but still he is praised at all universities as one of the greatest intellectual leaders of mankind, as the giant who has demolished inveterate prejudices and errors and has radically reformed philosophy and the sciences of man. Little attention is paid to the few dissenters who do not join in the chorus of commendation of Marx. They are boycotted as reactionaries.

The most remarkable fact about this unprecedented prestige of an author is that even his most enthusiastic admirers do not read his main writings and are not familiar with their content. A few passages and sentences from his books, always the same, are quoted again and again in political speeches and pamphlets. But the voluminous books and the scores of articles and pamphlets turned out by Marx are, as can be easily shown, not perused even by politicians and authors who proudly call themselves Marxians. Many people buy or borrow from a library reprints of Marx's writings and start reading them. But, bored to death, they usually stop after a few pages, if they had not already stopped on the first page.

Doctrines of Marx

If people were familiar with the doctrines of Marx, they would never talk, as they often do, about socialism "according to the designs and precepts

Reprinted from *Christian Economics*, May 30, 1961.

of Marx." For Marx neither devised the concept of socialism nor did he ever say anything about the organization and operation of a socialist commonwealth except that it would be a blissful realm of unlimited abundance in which everybody would get all he needed. The idea of socialism — the abolition of private control of the material means of production and of free enterprise and the exclusive management of all economic affairs by the government — had been fully elaborated by French and British authors before Marx embarked upon his career as an author and propagandist. There was nothing left to be added to it and Marx did not add anything. Nor did he ever attempt to refute what economists had already brought forward in his time to show the illusiveness and absurdity of the socialist schemes. He derided as vain utopianism any occupation with the problems of a socialist economic system. As he himself viewed his own contribution, it consisted in the discovery of the alleged fact that the coming of socialism was inevitable and that socialism, precisely because it is bound to come "with the inexorability of a law of nature" and was the final goal to which mankind's history must necessarily lead, would be the fulfillment of all human wishes and desires, a state of everlasting joy and happiness.

The writings of Marx, first of all the ponderous volumes of his main treatise, *Das Kapital*, do not deal with socialism. Rather they deal with the market economy, with capitalism. They depict capitalism as a system of unspeakable horrors and utmost detestableness in which the immense majority of people, the proletarians, are ruthlessly oppressed and exploited by a class of felonious capitalists. Everything in this nefarious system is hopelessly bad, and no reform, however well intentioned, can alleviate, still less remove, the abominable suffering of the proletarians. Nothing else can be said in favor of capitalism than that precisely on account of its monstrosity and atrocity it will one day, when the evils it produces become intolerable, result in the great social revolution that will generate the socialist millennium.

The "Iron Law" of Wages

The pith of Marx's economic teachings is his "law" of wages. This alleged law that is at the bottom of his entire criticism of the capitalistic system is, of course, not of Marxian make. It was devised by earlier authors, had long since been known under the label of the "iron law of wages," and had already been thoroughly refuted before Marx employed it as the foundation of his doctrine. Marx chose to ignore all that had been said to show the viciousness of the reasoning implied in this alleged law. He made some sarcastic remarks about the German translation of the English term "iron law," as suggested by his main rival for the leadership of the German socialist party, Ferdinand Lassalle (1825–64). But he built his entire economic reasoning, all his prognostication of the future course of economic affairs, and his whole political program upon the illusory basis of this fallacious theorem.

This so-called "iron law" declares that wage rates are determined by the cost of the means of subsistence required for the bare maintenance of the labor force. The wage earner cannot get more than is physiologically needed to preserve his capacity to work and to enable him to raise the number of children required to replace him when he dies. If wages rise above this level, the wage earners will rear more progeny and the competition of these additional seekers for employment will reduce wage rates again to what this doctrine considers the *natural* level. If, on the other hand, wages drop below this alleged natural level, the workers will not be able to feed the number of offspring needed to fill the ranks of the labor force. There will then develop a shortage of laborers and competition among the employers will bring wage rates back to the natural level.

From the point of view of this alleged "iron law" the fate of the wage earners under capitalism appears hopeless. They can never lift themselves above the level of bare subsistence. No reforms, no governmental minimum wage enactments, no activities of labor unions can prove effectual against this "iron law." Under capitalism, the proletarians are doomed to remain forever on the verge of starvation. All the advantages derived from the improvement of technological methods of production are pocketed exclusively by the capitalists. This is what the Marxian category of exploitation means. By right, Marx implies, all the products ought to benefit those who are producing them, the manual workers. The mere existence of the bourgeoisie is parasitic. While the proletarians suffer, the bourgeois exploit, feast, and revel.

Capitalist Production

Now one has only to look around in order to detect that something must be entirely wrong with this description of capitalism's economic functioning. The great innovation brought about by the transformation of the precapitalistic mode of production into the capitalistic system, the historical event that is called the Industrial Revolution, was precisely the inauguration of a new principle of marketing. The processing industries of the good old days catered almost exclusively to the wants of the well-to-do. But what characterizes capitalism as such is that it is mass production for the satisfaction of the needs of the masses. The much greater part of all the products turned out by the factories is consumed, directly or indirectly, by the same people who are working in the factories. Big business is big precisely because it produces the goods asked for, and bought by, the masses. If you go into the household of the average common man of a capitalistic country, you will find products manufactured in the plants of big business. It is fantastic nonsense to assert that all the wage earner gets are the bare necessities to sustain himself and to rear enough children to fill the jobs in the factories. While businesses that produce for the masses grow big, those that are turning out luxury goods for the few never grow above the size of medium, or even small, businesses.

The essential shortcoming of the "iron law of wages" was that it denied to the wage earner his human character and dealt with him as if he were a nonhuman creature. In all nonhuman living beings the urge is inwrought to proliferate up to the limits drawn by the available supply of the means of subsistence. Nothing but the quantity of attainable nourishment checks the boundless multiplication of elephants and rodents, of bugs and germs. Their number keeps pace with the available aliments. But this biological law does not apply to man. Man aims also at other ends than those involving the physiological needs of his body. The "iron law" assumed that the wage earner, the common man, is no better than a rabbit, that he craves no other satisfactions than feeding and proliferation and does not know of any other employment for his earnings than the procurement of those animal satisfactions. It is obvious that this is the most absurd assumption ever made. What characterizes man as man and elevates him above the level of the animals is that he aims also at specifically human ends which we may call "higher ends." Man is not like other living beings that are driven exclusively by the appetites of their bellies and their sex glands. The wage earner is also a man, that is a moral and intellectual person. If he earns more than the absolutely required minimum, he spends it upon the satisfaction of his specifically human wants; he tries to render his life and that of his dependents more civilized.

At the time Marx and Engels adopted this spurious "iron law" and asserted in the *Communist Manifesto* (1848) that the average wage is "that quantum of the means of nourishment (*Lebensmittel*) which is absolutely requisite (*notwendig*) to keep the laborer in bare existence as a laborer," judicious economists had already exposed the fallaciousness of this syllogism. But Marx did not heed their criticism. His whole economic doctrine set forth in his main treatise, *Das Kapital*, is based upon the "iron law." The falseness of this presumed law, the falseness of which has not been questioned by anybody for about a hundred years, cuts the ground from under all his economic reasoning. And it demolishes entirely the main demagogy of the Marxian system, the doctrine that contends that the recipients of wages and salaries are exploited by the employers.

The Inevitability of Socialism

In the elaboration of his system of philosophy and economics Marx was blinded to such an extent by his passionate hatred of Western civilization that he did not become aware of the blatant contradictions in his own reasoning. One of the most essential dogmas of the Marxian message, perhaps its very core and substance, is the doctrine of the inevitability of the coming of socialism. In *Das Kapital* (1867), Marx proclaims that capitalism "begets, with the inexorability of a law of nature, its own negation," that is, it produces socialism. It is this prophecy that accounts for the obstinate fanaticism of the various communist and socialist factions of our age.

Marx tried to prove this cardinal dogma of his creed by the famous prognostication that capitalism generates necessarily and unavoidably, a progressive impoverishment of the masses of the wage earners. The more capitalism develops, he says, the more "grows the mass of misery, oppressions, slavery, degradation and exploitation." With "the progress of industry" the worker "sinks deeper and deeper," until finally, when his sufferings have become unbearable, the exploited masses revolt and establish the everlasting bliss of socialism.

It is well known that this prognostication of Marx was no less disproved by the facts of social evolution than all other Marxian prophecies. Since Marx wrote the lines quoted in 1848 and 1867, the standard of living of the wage earners has in all capitalistic countries improved in a way unprecedented and undreamt of.

But there is still something more to say about this piece of Marx's argumentation. It contradicts the whole Marxian theory of the determination of wage rates. As has been pointed out, this theory asserts that *wage rates under capitalism are always and necessarily so low that for physiological reasons they cannot drop any further without wiping out the whole class of wage earners.* How is it then possible that capitalism brings forth a *progressing impoverishment* of the wage earners? Marx in his prediction of the progressive impoverishment of the masses contradicted not only all the facts of historical experience. He also contradicted the essential teachings of his own theory based on the "iron law of wages," namely that capitalist wage rates are so low that they cannot drop any further without wiping out the workers.

The Marxian economic system, so much praised by hosts of self-styled intellectuals, is a hodge-podge of arbitrary statements conflicting with one another.

27

The Soviet System's Economic Failure

It seems that in the heated polemics of the Cold War people have lost sight of the issue in dispute between socialism and capitalism. The objective of socialism and communism is neither to "bury" us, nor to occupy the whole of the city of Berlin, nor the conquest of any of the remaining free countries.

Socialism, as all its harbingers announced in the past and as its professorial, journalistic, and political advocates repeat again and again in their books, speeches, and platforms, aims at a spectacular improvement in the average man's standard of living.

The Marxians and all other friends of socialism declare that capitalism inevitably results in progressing impoverishment of the masses. While the rich are getting richer, they say, the poor are getting poorer. This is especially true of "mature" capitalism, the present-day American system of what they call "imperialistic monopoly and finance capitalism." They claim that all schemes, such as labor unionism or social security designed to ward off or to assuage the sinister effects of the free enterprise system, are in vain.

There is only one way, they say, open to prevent the eclipse of civilization. That is to substitute socialism for capitalism. Socialism will pour a horn of plenty on the masses whom the capitalistic "exploiters" have reduced to utmost penury.

This is what the socialist message promised the world and what the U.S.S.R., the Union of Soviet Socialist Republics, was resolved to achieve. "Have a little patience and wait until our Five-Year Plan takes effect; then you will see what socialism can do. Don't trust the theorists who claim that they have demonstrated the inferiority and absurdity of the socialist methods. We will show you what miracles government all-

Reprinted from the *New York World Telegram & Sun*, October 5, 1959.

round planning can accomplish. Do not cry over spilt milk. One cannot make an omelet without breaking eggs. But our omelet will be a marvel."

Now, where are these much-glorified blessings of the socialist methods of production? We have today, forty-two years after the "ten days that shook the world" and after a succession of half a dozen five- and seven-year plans and bloody purges, the opportunity to compare the operation of the two systems, capitalism and socialism. Nobody would have the courage to deny that the average man's standard of living is incomparably higher in capitalistic Western Europe — not to speak of the United States, the paragon of capitalism — than it is in communist Russia. Leaving aside everything else that may be said about the dictatorship of the proletariat, there is need to emphasize that socialism failed lamentably in the very point that, according to its own doctrine, is the only one that counts.

The Communists try to divert attention from this essential fact by a barrage of doctored statistics and by telling us that at some later date — in 1965, 1984, or 2050 — Russia's production will equal or even outstrip present-day American production. Up to now all such predictions have been disproved by reality. Experience has belied all this empty boasting. And whenever another free country has been incorporated into the socialist orbit, its industrial and agricultural output has immediately declined.

The socialists have entirely misrepresented the working of the market economy, the system popularly called capitalism. Capitalism is essentially mass production for the satisfaction of the needs of the masses. While the processing industries in the precapitalistic ages catered almost exclusively to the wants of a minority of well-to-do, modern business serves the much talked about common man.

All that big business turns out serves, directly or indirectly, but inevitably, the average citizen. There is no other means for business to prosper and to grow into bigness than to render its products and services accessible to the many.

The shops that produce luxury goods for the few remain small or at least medium sized. Thus capitalism resulted in an unprecedented improvement of the masses' standard of living and in a no less unprecedented increase in population figures. Capitalism deproletarianizes the proletarians and raises them to the "bourgeois" level. The average American wage-earner enjoys amenities of which the richest princes and lords of the precapitalistic ages did not even dream.

The rulers of Russia know very well why they prevent their people, by means of a rigid system of censorship, from learning about true conditions in the capitalistic West. The communist power is based upon keeping the masses behind the Iron Curtain in crass ignorance. The Soviet system would collapse if its victims were to get reliable information about the normal life of the common man in Western Europe and in this country.

28

On Some Atavistic Economic Ideas

The social and economic meaning of institutions may change in the course of history while their legal definition and character remain unaltered. Whenever this is the case, serious misunderstandings originate that lead astray the reasoning not only of the masses but also that of economists and politicians.

Let us deal with two outstanding examples.

Land Reform

The reformers and revolutionaries of the precapitalistic ages aimed at a radical transformation of land ownership. As they saw it, God had given the land as an endowment to all men. As far as any man's estate exceeds the size needed for the support of his family, he deprives others of what by rights is their due. Nobody has from the point of view of natural law the right to keep as his own more than his legitimate share. In order to establish a fair social order, all land has to be confiscated and redistributed in equal portions to all heads of families. Then the most blatant inequalities of social and economic conditions will disappear. There will no longer be any poverty. All men will be equal.

Such was, still in the twentieth century, the program of the Social Revolutionaries, the most popular party of Imperial Russia and the early years of Lenin's dictatorship. Many politicians of Latin America and of some nations of the Old World still today warmly recommend the same policies and their endeavors meet with sympathetic approval in the United States and in other Western countries.

Mises wrote this short essay on primitive economic ideas for inclusion in the 1966 Festschrift for Jacques Rueff published on the occasion of his seventieth birthday. It has previously appeared only in French.

It can easily be understood how such a program originated in a milieu of feudal conditions. Under feudalism and kindred systems the inequality in the size of the individual inhabitants' land holdings was an outcome of the political and military order of governmental affairs. A rigid caste system assigned to everybody a definite place in the social hierarchy and a definite position in the economic organization. The individual was born and died in the rank and circumstances inherited from his ancestors. The villein, the peasant, bemoaning his poverty and servile peasant status, could not think of any other way of betterment than that of confiscation of all land holdings and a fair redistribution.

But under the conditions of the capitalistic market society this program of land reform no longer makes any sense. In the market economy the consumers daily decide anew who should own the material factors of production and how much anybody should own. By their buying or abstention from buying the consumers allot control of the material factors of production to those who know how to use them in the best and cheapest way for the satisfaction of the most urgent wants of the consumers. Ownership of land means in the market economy the sovereignty of the consumers. The owners are mandataries of the consumers as it were, bound to employ their property as if it were entrusted to them by the people. When they fail in this regard, they suffer losses. Then they are forced to improve their management or, finally, they go bankrupt. Others who know better how to serve the consumers replace them.

Ownership of land, as of all other material factors of production, is an asset in the market economy only for those who use it in the best possible way for the satisfaction of the consumers. The idea that inspired the plans for so-called agrarian reform is nonsensical in the market economy. Under the conditions of modern methods of agricultural management, a more or less equal distribution of the soil among the farming population is merely a scheme for granting privileges to a group of less efficient producers at the expense of the immense majority of consumers. The operation of the market tends to eliminate all those farmers whose cost of production is higher than the marginal costs needed for the production of that amount of farm products the consumers are ready to buy. It determines not only the size of the farms as well as the methods of production applied; it determines no less what fields should be tilled and what fields should be left fallow.

Favoritism for Debtors

Another example of the survival of atavistic reform ideas is provided by the popularity of government interference to favor debtors at the expense of creditors.

When more than twenty-five hundred years ago Solon in Athens resorted to such a policy and when more than four hundred years later in Rome the Gracchi brothers adopted a similar course, they could consider their policies as a method of favoring poor people at the expense of richer ones. Before the nineteenth century only the well-to-do could lend money and reap interest on funds lent. But capitalism has radically changed these conditions too. Under the modern credit organization the more opulent strata are more often debtors than creditors. They own mortgaged real estate, business firms that are indebted to the banks and insurance companies, common stock of corporations that have issued corporate bonds. On the other hand the common man is a creditor insofar as he has taken out insurance policies, has savings deposits with commercial banks and savings banks, owns bonds whether government issued or corporate, and is entitled to receive retirement and old age pensions.

The most spectacular manifestation of the misinterpretation of the economic meaning of the present-day creditor-debtor nexus was provided by the program of the National-Socialist-German-Labor-Party, the Nazis. Their economic expert, Gottfried Feder, coined the slogan *"Brechung der Zinsknechtschaft"* that can by and large be translated as "Destruction of Interest Slavery." It was adopted as Point II of the "unalterable" Party Program that aimed at the "Abolition of any Income acquired without Labor and Pain." The popularity of this slogan was irresistible in Germany in the 1920s and early 1930s. In vain did some economists criticize it. One of the few newspapers that tried to block the Nazis' way to power once published a headline, "Do you, average reader, know that you are a creditor?" The German voters who practically unanimously voted for Hitler certainly did not know it.

Neither do the average men in other countries. The governments can embark upon the inflationary policies they style "deficit spending" and "an easy money policy" because there is no opposition on the part of the masses of people whose endeavors to provide for their old age and for the future of their children are frustrated. In spite of all the unfavorable experiences they had with the monetary policies of the past, the voters look with indifference upon the effort to preserve sound money.

The most momentous virtue of the gold standard is precisely the fact that it makes the determination of money's purchasing power independent of the ambitions and machinations of political parties and pressure groups. It thus prevents inflationary policies and thereby protects the savings of the common man. But unfortunately this fact is ignored by the millions of Americans who are the owners of many billions of savings accounts, bonds, and insurance policies. Thus the deficit spending and easy money policy of the American government does not find any opposition on the part of the parties that dominate the political life of the nation.

29

Capital and Interest:
Eugen von Böhm-Bawerk and the Discriminating Reader

The publication of a new English-language translation of Böhm-Bawerk's monumental work on *Capital and Interest** raises an important question. There is no doubt that Böhm-Bawerk's book is the most eminent contribution to modern economic theory. For every economist it is a must to study it most carefully and to scrutinize its content with the utmost care. A man not perfectly familiar with all the ideas advanced in these three volumes has no claim whatever to the appellation of an economist. But what about the general reader, the man who does not plan to specialize in economics because his strenuous involvement in his business or in his profession does not leave him the leisure to plunge into detailed economic analysis? What does this book mean to him?

To answer this question we have to take into account the role that economic problems play in present-day politics. All the political antagonisms and conflicts of our age turn on economic issues.

It has not always been so. In the sixteenth and seventeenth centuries the controversies that split the peoples of Western civilization into feuding parties were religious. Protestantism stood against Catholicism, and within the Protestant camp various interpretations of the Gospels begot discord. In the eighteenth century and in a great part of the nineteenth century constitutional conflicts prevailed in politics. The principles of royal absolutism and oligarchic government were resisted by liberalism

Reprinted from *The Freeman*, August 1959.

* *Capital and Interest* (3 vols.): I. *History and Critique of Interest Theories*, II. *Positive Theory of Capital*, III. *Further Essays on Capital and Interest* (South Holland, Ill.: Libertarian Press, 1959).

(in the classical European meaning of the term) that advocated representative government. In those days a man who wanted to take an active part in the great issues of his age had to study seriously the matter of these controversies. The sermons and the books of the theologians of the age of the Reformation were not reserved to esoteric circles of specialists. They were eagerly absorbed by the whole educated public. Later the writings of the foremost advocates of freedom were read by all those who were not fully engrossed in the petty affairs of their daily routine. Only boors neglected to inform themselves about the great problems that agitated the minds of their contemporaries.

In our age the conflict between economic freedom, as represented in the market economy, and totalitarian government omnipotence, as realized by socialism, is the paramount matter. All political controversies refer to these economic problems. Only the study of economics can tell a man what all these conflicts mean. Nothing can be known about such matters as inflation, economic crises, unemployment, unionism, protectionism, taxation, economic controls, and all similar issues, that does not involve and presuppose economic analysis. All the arguments advanced in favor of or against the market economy and its opposites, interventionism or socialism (communism), are of an economic character. A man who talks about these problems without having acquainted himself with the fundamental ideas of economic theory is simply a babbler who repeats parrotlike what he has picked up incidentally from other fellows who are not better informed than he himself. A citizen who casts his ballot without having studied to the best of his abilities as much economics as he can fails in his civic duties. He neglects using in the appropriate way the power that his citizenship has conferred upon him in giving him the right to vote.

Now there is no better method to introduce a man to economic problems than that provided by the books of the great economists. And certainly Böhm-Bawerk is one of the greatest of them. His voluminous treatise is the royal road to an understanding of the fundamental political issues of our age.

The general reader should start with the second volume in which Böhm analyzes the essence of saving and capital accumulation and the role capital goods play in the process of production. Especially important is the third book of this second volume; it deals with the determination of value and prices. Only then should the reader turn to the first volume that gives a critical history of all the doctrines advanced on the source of interest and profit by earlier authors. In this historical review the most important part is the chapter that analyzes the so-called exploitation doctrines, first of all the doctrine that Karl Marx developed in his *Das Kapital*, the Koran of all Marxians. The refutation of Marx's labor theory of value is perhaps the most interesting, at any rate the politically most momentous chapter of Böhm's contribution.

The third volume consists of fourteen brilliant essays in which Böhm-Bawerk deals with various objections raised against the validity of his theory.

The new translation was made by Professor Hans Sennholz, the chairman of the Department of Economics at Grove City College, and by Mr. George D. Huncke. Mr. Frederick Nymeyer is to be credited with the initiative of making the whole work of Böhm-Bawerk accessible to the English-reading public. The hitherto only available translation is obsolete as it was made from the first edition of the treatise which consisted only of two volumes. The new translation gives the full text of the revised and considerably enlarged third edition which Böhm-Bawerk completed a few weeks before his premature death in 1914.

A book of the size and profundity of *Capital and Interest* is not easy reading. But the effort expended pays very well. It will stimulate the reader to look upon political problems, not from the point of view of the superficial slogans resorted to in electoral campaigns, but with full awareness of their meaning and their consequences for the survival of our civilization.

Although Böhm-Bawerk's great opus is "mere theory" and abstains from any practical application, theory is the most powerful intellectual weapon in the great struggle of the Western way of life against the destructionism of Soviet barbarism.

30

The Symptomatic Keynes

As is customary with biographies, Professor R. F. Harrod's *The Life of John Maynard Keynes* (Harcourt, Brace, 1951) provides an abundance of information about insignificant happenings and uninteresting people who crossed the path of his subject. The whole of page 171, for instance, is devoted to the description of a lady who happened to be the niece of an authentic duke. We are told how she dressed, how and where she lived, what her eccentricities were, and many other things. Perhaps the lady was really a very eminent woman, perhaps no less remarkable than the author Mathilde Wesendonck, who had an affair with the composer Richard Wagner. But the duke's niece missed her Richard Wagner, and her only claim to fame is that on July 2, 1914, she entertained the Prime Minister and John Maynard Keynes at a small dinner party.

Not only is the social side of eating and drinking amply dealt with in this book by Harrod, but also the business side. Keynes founded a theater in Cambridge and paid attention to the detail of its management. "Nothing was too trivial for him," says Professor Harrod.

> By a happy and successful idea, a restaurant was attached to the theater, and I recall receiving a letter from him asking me to write a testimonial for a chef. . . . He was anxious to encourage expenditure upon wine in the restaurant rather than upon cocktails and spirits. . . . He gave an instruction that, instead of the usual addition of 50 per cent to the cost price, only 2s. 6d. should be added in the case of champagne, with the consequence that profits on that item actually rose!

Such small talk would do for the many things Lord Keynes was and did besides being Keynes. He belonged to many groups and circles, to the University of Cambridge, to the Bloomsbury Bohemia of the last

Reprinted from *The Freeman*, June 18, 1951.

years preceding World War I, to the active friends of the theater and the ballet. He was a "society" man and a collector. He wrote a noteworthy book, *A Treatise on Probability*. He played a role in the Liberal Party. He spent a good many of his years as a government economist. As such he cooperated in the drafting of many ordinances and international conventions, the vast paper work that accompanies the decline of Western civilization, freedom, and prosperity. None of these activities elevated him above the rank of the hosts registered in *Who's Who* and daily mentioned in the newspapers. But other questions remain: Was Keynes not perhaps more? Was he not a man who shaped the ideas and policies of his age? Was he not a historical character? Such are the problems a biography of Lord Keynes ought to deal with.

There are people who believe that the two books of Keynes that became best sellers—*The Economic Consequences of the Peace* (1920), and *The General Theory of Employment, Interest and Money* (1936)— decisively influenced the course of British policies and of world affairs. It is said that the first of these books inaugurated the anti-French and pro-German tendencies of Great Britain's "appeasement" policy which virtually encouraged the rise of Nazism, permitted Hitler to defy the essential clauses of the Treaty of Versailles, and finally resulted in the outbreak of the Second World War. It is furthermore asserted that the second book generated the "Keynesian revolution" of economic policies. The abandonment of the gold standard and the adoption of outright inflationary or "expansionist" fiscal methods, the New Deal and the Fair Deal, the full-employment policy, the intensification of anti-importation measures and many other kindred ventures are ascribed to the "unorthodox" ideas propagated by Keynes. If these assertions are correct, Keynes appears as the most influential personality of our age, whether the effects of these policies are to be considered as beneficial or disastrous.

Keynes's Appeal to "Progressives"

Because of limitations of space we must set aside the first of these two questions and concentrate upon the second. Keynes was definitely not the inaugurator of a new economic policy. The governments did not have to wait for his advice in order to learn that inflation is a handy means to fill the empty vaults of the treasury. The Keynesian policies were practiced by governments and powerful political parties long before they were advocated by Keynes. Keynes's writings were enthusiastically received by people who found in them an apparently scientific justification for what they had already done for a long time in defying the teachings of economics.

Nothing was more contemptible in the eyes of the post-Victorian English than the ideas of laissez faire that had multiplied England's population and secured to the average Englishman the highest standard of living in Europe. Lords and commoners, divines and atheists, manufacturers and union members, Fabians and Colonel Blimps — all agreed in rejecting the "dismal science." They hated the theory according to which there was but one means toward the general improvement of people's material well-being, viz., to increase the per head quota of capital invested. They longed for short cuts to an earthly paradise: a protective tariff, a cheap money policy, the closed shop, doles, and social security. They did not want to be told by the economists that it is the policy of the unions that creates unemployment as a lasting mass phenomenon and that the periodical recurrence of crises is the inevitable outcome of the easy money policy. They knew better; all evils were caused by capitalism.

To such people the Keynesian slogans appealed strongly. Here they found what they were looking for. If demand lags, create "effective" demand by expanding credit! If there is unemployment, print more money! If you want to increase "the real national dividend of useful goods and service," then "dig holes in the ground paid for out of savings!" And, first of all, do not save, spend!

The triumph of Lord Keynes's last book, the *General Theory*, was instantaneous. Although reasonable economists refuted his doctrines, it has become the gospel of the self-styled progressives all over the world. Today many universities simply teach Keynesianism. It is really paradoxical. Nobody can any longer fail to realize that what is needed most is more saving and capital accumulation and that the inflationary and expansionist policies are on the verge of complete breakdown. But the students are still taught the dangers of saving and the blessings of expansionism.

Lord Keynes had, as his biographer points out, "a very rare combination of gifts; his endowment in any one of them would by itself have made him a notable person." But politics and history are not concerned with the virtues Professor Harrod registers in his detailed catalogue. They ask: Did he enrich mankind's treasure of ideas and did he influence the course of events? The answer to both questions is in the negative. The ideas he professed were untenable and, even so, not original. The books he wrote supported firmly established policies which would have gone on without this support. He was highly renowned, famous, and popular in an age of decay and disintegration, but his writings were not the cause of these disasters; they were only symptoms.

31

Professor Hutt on Keynesianism

The Keynesian doctrine, as developed by 1936 in *The General Theory of Unemployment, Interest, and Money*, tries to prove the soundness of the two most popular but least tenable components of contemporary economic policies: inflationism and labor unionism. At the time of its publication the spectacular failure of these two methods of interfering with the market phenomena could no longer be concealed. Yet the governments and the political parties were firmly resolved not to abandon "deficit spending" and the support of labor union violence and intimidation. Their official wisdom explained the progressive rise in prices — which they misnamed inflation — as caused by machinations on the part of bad people, the profiteers, and they considered that unemployment was one of the unavoidable shortcomings of a "free," i.e., not regimented, economy.

But from day to day it became more obvious that it was not enough to find a lame excuse for the current policies. What the noncommunist West seemed to need was a comprehensive doctrine that could be adopted as the economic philosophy of these governments that, while ostensibly proclaiming their anticommunism, step-by-step approached a system of all-round government control of business. *The General Theory*'s success was due to the fact that it tried to provide such a justification of the American New Deal and the devaluation practices of the various European nations.

The enthusiastic praise that Keynes's doctrine received on the part of professors and authors propagating government omnipotence could for a while divert attention from the fact that from the beginning all discriminating economists rejected it and unmasked its inherent fallacies. Some of the most important of these critical essays were collected and

Reprinted from *The Freeman*, January 1964.

republished by Henry Hazlitt under the title *The Critics of Keynesian Economics* (Van Nostrand, 1960). Hazlitt himself has in a voluminous brilliantly written study, *The Failure of the "New Economics"* (Van Nostrand, 1959), clearly demonstrated the shortcomings, contradictions, and other failings of Keynesianism.

To Clear the Air

As an economic doctrine, Keynesianism is now dead. But the serious errors and misunderstandings of fundamental issues of economics that made its emergence and its fleeting success possible still prevail. There remain with us many empty slogans and illusory concepts that easily mislead those seeking a satisfactory interpretation of phenomena. It is necessary to clear away the debris of the Keynesian structure in order to open the way for a correct grasp of the principles of the market and the functioning of price flexibility.

This is the task that the new book of Professor W. H. Hutt, *Keynesianism — Retrospect and Prospect* (Chicago: Regnery, 1963, 447 pp.), wants to accomplish. Hutt calls his work *A Critical Restatement of Basic Economic Principles.* Such a restatement was badly needed indeed. The main failure of Keynes and all his disciples and admirers is to be seen in the fact that they simply do not know what prices are, how they originate, and what they bring about.

Prices come into existence by the eagerness of people to exchange one commodity or service against another commodity or service. They are the outcome of various individuals' readiness to buy or to sell. Every price is the outgrowth of a definite constellation of demand and supply. No price could ever be different from what it really was, because people failed to appear on the market at that time who were ready to bid a higher price, or who were ready to ask a lower price. The structure of prices reflects the state of the material conditions determining people's existence and the success of the endeavors made to satisfy the most urgent needs, as far as these material conditions make it feasible.

Prices cannot be manipulated *ad libitum* [at will] by the social apparatus of coercion and compulsion, the police power. All the government — or a labor union to which the government has virtually delegated its power of enforcing orders by violent action — can achieve is to substitute coercion for voluntary action. Where there is coercion, the market economy no longer functions; disorder results in the production and the marketing of the articles subject to the governmental decree. Then the spokesmen of the authorities point to the inefficiency of the market system and ask for more government meddling with the price system.

The Market Economy

Professor Hutt analyzes point by point all the alleged shortcomings of the free market about which people complain. He presents a comprehensive analysis of all aspects of the Keynesian interpretation of the market economy. Most of the rising generation of economists were taught Keynesianism and therefore ignore all that economic theory has brought forward for an elucidation of what is going on in production and in the marketing of the products. A careful study of Professor Hutt's new volume will lead them back to a correct grasp of the problems of the market economy.

Professor Hutt's contributions to economic science were long since highly appreciated by all serious students of social problems. His rank among the outstanding economists of our age is not contested by any competent critic. Yet, what he has written up to now has appealed only to those specializing in the study of economics. This new volume on Keynesianism is addressed not only to specialists, but to all those who want to form a well-grounded opinion concerning the most burning problems of social policies. It is not only a refutation of erroneous doctrines. It is also an exposition of the fundamental principles and ideas of up-to-date economic theory. It is not merely a treatise for the specialist. It is also a book for all those eager to learn what sound economic doctrine has to say about the great problems of our age.

32

The Trade Cycle

The interpretation of the trade cycle — the recurrence of periods of feverishly booming business invariably followed by periods of depression — as first developed by the British Currency School and later perfected by modern economics runs this way:

There prevails on the part of public opinion a reluctance to look upon interest as a phenomenon uniquely dependent upon the general state of economic conditions. People are loath to comprehend that the discount of future goods as against present goods is not a specific characteristic of the market economy, but an inexorable category of human valuation which would direct the decisions of the planning board of a socialist system no less than it determines the conduct of every individual in a capitalistic system. People believe that artificially lowering the rate of interest by expansion of bank credit is a blessing for everybody except idle capitalists. They fail to realize that it is impossible to substitute additional bank credit for nonexisting capital goods and that therefore an artificially created boom must collapse and turn into a slump. They hail the illusory prosperity which such credit expansion brings about in its initial stages, and are bigoted enough not to recognize that the following depression is the inevitable consequence of the preceding orgy of speculation.

Against this theory, which is commonly called the monetary or circulation credit theory of the business cycle, there have never been raised any tenable objections. Even the report of the League of Nations, *Prosperity and Depression*, prepared by Professor Gottfried Haberler, admits that an author who wants to explain the business cycle in a different way "often tacitly assumes — or ought logically to assume — the willingness and ability of the banking system to expand credit on existing terms"

Reprinted from *The Freeman*, September 24, 1951.

(p. 7 of the new edition, 1939). Nonetheless, governments stubbornly cling to the policy of artificially lowering interest rates by credit expansion. Scores of authors try to defend this policy by producing spurious explanations of the trade cycle and by passing over in silence the monetary theory. As they see it, the recurrence of economic crises is inherent in the very nature of the unhampered market economy.

The originator of this fallacy was Karl Marx. It is one of the main dogmas of his teachings that the periodical return of commercial crises is an inherent feature of the "anarchy of production" under capitalism. Marx made various lame and contradictory attempts to prove his dogma; even Marxian authors admit that these ventures were utterly futile. Yet Marx and Engels and all their disciples down to Stalin and his henchmen have built their hopes upon the expectation that the crises will return again and again, each time more threateningly, and will finally induce people to abolish economic freedom and establish socialism. Hosts of pseudo-economists, while emphatically protesting their anticommunism, have unreservedly adopted this fundamental thesis of the Marxian creed. They are intent upon demonstrating its correctness, and design programs for what they call a "positive countercyclical policy." In effect all these programs aim at the substitution for private initiative of all-round planning by the government. In order to remedy the disastrous consequences of the government's policies of credit expansion and inflation, they suggest more and more government interference until any trace of the individual's freedom will have disappeared.

Professor Alvin H. Hansen's book, *Business Cycles and National Income* (Norton, 1951), is the latest product of this daily swelling literature. It does not add any new idea to those advanced by its predecessors. It merely repeats what has been said again and again and has been irrefutably exploded a hundred times. It tries to revive all the specters of confused economic thinking such as general overproduction, general overinvestment, acceleration principle, and so on. It presents an inadequate account of the opinions of previous authors, omitting the most important contributions. It includes ample historical and statistical material, badly assembled and poorly interpreted.

Professor Hansen's endeavors to discredit those who contend that the only efficient means for preventing the reappearance of crises is to abstain from any kind of credit expansion and inflation would not deserve any special attention if they were not symptomatic of the prevailing tendency in academic and official circles. The views held and propagated by these circles are even more fateful than the policies they try to vindicate.

The methods of reckless inflation and credit expansion engineered by the present Administration will inevitably, sooner or later, result in an economic debacle. Then people, indoctrinated by the official tenets, will argue: "The last desperate attempts to salvage capitalism, the New Deal and the Fair Deal, have entirely failed. It is obvious that capitalism must lead to a depression. No other remedy is left than to adopt full socialism." The teachings handed down in most of our schools as well as the passionate utterances of the communists on each side of the Iron Curtain will not allow any other interpretation.

As against all this talk it is imperative to instruct people in time that the trade cycle is not a phenomenon inherent in the unhampered operation of the market economy but, on the contrary, the inevitable effect of manipulation of the money market. People must learn that the only means to avoid the recurrence of economic catastrophes is to let the market — and not the government — determine interest rates. There is but one pattern of positive countercyclical policies, viz., *not* to increase the quantity of money in circulation and bank deposits subject to check. Deficit spending by borrowing from the commercial banks is the surest way toward economic disaster.

33

How Can Europe Survive?

In his book, *How Can Europe Survive?* (Van Nostrand, 1955), Dr. Hans F. Sennholz explodes one of the main fallacies underlying present-day economic policies.

The spurious doctrine, advanced by the majority of contemporary pseudo-economists and endorsed by almost all contemporary statesmen and politicians, runs this way: The operation of the market economy (capitalism, laissez faire) results in progressing poverty of the masses, in unemployment of an ever-increasing part of the potential labor force, in the regular recurrence of periods of economic depression. It disintegrates the international exchange of commodities and services and thereby hurts vital interests of all nations that cannot produce within the boundaries of their own countries all the food and raw material they need. In order to prevent a complete collapse of Western civilization, the governments must interfere. They must, in domestic policies, substitute government planning for the "anarchy of production" (a term employed by Karl Marx) and, in the international field, they must try to establish some sort of supernational government.

Main Points of Argument

Dr. Sennholz examines the issue in analyzing a special case, viz., the endeavors to "unify" Europe. The main points of his argument are:

1. The economic disintegration of Europe is not an outcome of the unhampered operation of the capitalist system. It is, on the contrary, the result of the various governments' interference with the business of their own countries. If a government "regulates" business conditions of its own country, it must prevent foreign business from nullifying this

Reprinted from *Christian Economics*, November 15, 1955.

regimentation by imports. It must adopt a policy of national isolation and thereby contribute to the economic disintegration of Europe.

2. Mere talking and drafting of international conventions will never reestablish European economic unity. As long as there is domestic interventionism, the present unsatisfactory state will last. The funds spent by the U.S. taxpayer for the economic unification of Europe were wasted.

Dr. Sennholz thus attacks and explodes a doctrine supported by all government economists, a doctrine that guides the official policy of the Administration. His book will certainly be unfavorably reviewed by the "Progressive" newspapers and magazines. But its ideas will, sooner or later, bring about a change both in ideologies and policies. The book is certainly the most important case study in the field of economic policies written in the last few years. Some minor points of it may be open to objections. But the general line of its reasoning cannot be questioned.

34

The Economic Point of View

The inauguration of a systematic science of economics, an achievement of the social philosophy of the Enlightenment that also begot the doctrine of popular sovereignty, was a challenge to the powers that be. Economics shows that there prevails in the succession and interdependence of the market phenomena an inescapable regularity that man must take into full account if he wants to attain ends aimed at. Even the most mighty government, operating with the utmost severity, cannot succeed in endeavors that are contrary to what has been called "economic law." It is obvious why despotic rulers as well as leaders of revolutionary masses disliked such doctrines. For them economics was the "dismal science" and they fought it indefatigably.

However, it was not the hostility of governments and powerful political parties that fomented the protracted discussions about the epistemological character and the logical method of economics in which the very existence and significance of this branch of knowledge were again and again questioned. What generated these debates was the vagueness that the early economists evinced in defining the field of their studies. It would be absurd to blame them for this want of clearness. They had sufficient reasons for concentrating upon those problems which they were trying to deal with and for neglecting others. What had stimulated their inquiry was definite issues of contemporary political controversies. Their great accomplishment was the discovery of the uniform order prevailing in the emergence of events previously considered chaotic. Only the later generations of economists were puzzled with the epistemological problems involved.

Dr. Kirzner's book provides a historical account of all the solutions suggested in this debate. It is a very valuable contribution to the history

Reprinted from the foreword to *The Economic Point of View* by Israel M. Kirzner (Van Nostrand, 1960).

of ideas, describing the march of economics from a science of wealth to a science of human action. The author does not, in the fashion adopted by some recent histories of economic doctrines, indulge in value judgments and paradoxical observations. He prefers to follow the sober methods of the best historians of economic theories, Böhm-Bawerk and Edwin Cannan. Every economist — and for that matter everybody interested in problems of general epistemology — will read with great profit Dr. Kirzner's analyses, especially his treatment of the famous discussion between Benedetto Croce and Vilfredo Pareto or the critical examination of the ideas of Max Weber and Lionel Robbins.

Essays on the history of economic thought are to be appreciated not only purely as history. No less important is the fact that they enable us to reexamine the present state of economic theory in the light of all attempts earlier generations made for their solution. In comparing our point of view with past achievements and errors we may either detect flaws in our own theories or find new and better reasons for their confirmation. Dr. Kirzner's thoughtful essay is a real aid in such a reexamination and in this consists its great value.

35

Liberty and Its Antithesis

As the harbingers of socialism tell us again and again, socialism will not only make all people rich but it will also bring perfect freedom to everybody. The transition to socialism, declares Frederick Engels, the friend and collaborator of Marx, is the leap of mankind from the realm of necessity into the realm of freedom. Under capitalism, say the communists, there is bondage for the immense majority; in the Soviet Union alone is there genuine liberty for all.

The treatment of this problem of freedom and bondage has been muddled by confounding it with the issues of the nature-given conditions of man's existence. In nature there is nothing that could be called freedom. Nature is inexorable necessity. It is the state of affairs into which all created beings are placed and with which they have to cope. Man has to adjust his conduct to the world as it is. He lacks the power to rise in rebellion against the "laws of nature." If he wants to substitute more satisfactory conditions for less satisfactory, he has to comply with them.

Freedom and Western Civilization

The concept of freedom and its antithesis make sense only in referring to the conditions of social cooperation among men. Social cooperation, the basis of any really human and civilized existence, can be achieved by two different methods. It can be cooperation by virtue of contract and voluntary coordination on the part of all individuals, or it can be cooperation by virtue of command on the part of a Führer and compulsory subordination of the many. The latter system is authoritarian. In the libertarian system every individual is a moral person, that is, he is free to

Reprinted from *Christian Economics*, August 1, 1960.

choose and to act and is responsible for his conduct. In the authoritarian system the supreme chief alone is a free agent while all the others are bondsmen subject to his discretion. Where the authoritarian system is fully established, as was for instance the case in the Incan empire of pre-Columbian America, the subjects are human merely in a zoological sense; they are virtually deprived of their specifically human faculty of choosing and acting, and are not accountable for their conduct. It was in accordance with this degradation of man's moral dignity that the Nazi criminals declined any responsibility for their deeds by pointing out that all they did was to obey the orders of their superiors.

Western civilization is based upon the libertarian principle and all its achievements are the result of the actions of free men. Only in the frame of a free society is it meaningful to distinguish between what is good and ought to be done and what is bad and ought to be avoided. Only in such a free society has the individual the power to choose between morally commendable and morally reprehensible conduct.

Man is not a perfect being and there is no perfection in human affairs. Conditions in the free society are certainly in many regards unsatisfactory. There is still ample room for the endeavors of those who are intent upon fighting evil and raising the moral, intellectual, and material level of mankind.

Authoritarianism

The designs of the communists, socialists, and all their allies aim at something else. They want to establish the authoritarian system. What they mean in extolling the benefits to be derived from what they call planning is a society in which all of the people should be prevented from planning their own conduct and from arranging their lives according to their own moral convictions. One plan alone should prevail, the plan of the great idol State (with a capital S), the plan of the supreme chief of the government, enforced by the police. Every individual should be forced to renounce his autonomy and to obey, without asking questions, the orders issued from the Politburo, the Führer's secretariat. This is the kind of freedom that Engels had in mind. It is precisely the opposite of what the term freedom used to signify up to our age.

It was the great merit of Professor Friedrich von Hayek to have directed attention to the authoritarian character of the socialist schemes whether they are advocated by international or by nationalist socialists, by atheists or by misguided believers, by white-skinned or by dark-skinned fanatics. Although there have always been authors who exposed the authoritarianism of the socialist designs, the main criticism of socialism centered around its economic inadequacy and did not sufficiently deal with its effects upon the lives of the citizens. Because of this neglect of the human angle of the issue, the great majority of those supporting socialist policies vaguely assumed that the restriction of individual freedom by a socialist regime will apply "only" to economic affairs. But as Hayek clearly pointed out in 1944 in his book *The Road to Serfdom*, economic control is not merely control of a sector of human life that can be separated from the rest; it is the control of the means for all our ends. As the socialist state has sole control of the means, it has the power to determine which ends are to be served and which ends men are to strive for. It is not an accident that Marxian socialism in Russia and nationalist socialism in Germany resulted in the complete abolition of all civil liberties and the establishment of the most rigid despotism. Tyranny is the political corollary of socialism, as representative government is the political corollary of the market economy.

Now Professor Hayek has enlarged and substantiated his ideas in a comprehensive treatise, *The Constitution of Liberty* (University of Chicago Press, 1960). In the first two parts of this book the author provides a brilliant exposition of the meaning of liberty and the creative powers of a free civilization. Endorsing the famous definition that describes liberty as the rule of laws and not of men, he analyzes the constitutional and legal foundations of a commonwealth of free citizens. He contrasts the two schemes of society's social and political organization, government by the people (representative government), based upon legality, and government by the discretionary power of an authoritarian ruler or ruling clique, an *Obrigkeit* as the Germans used to call it. Fully appreciating the moral, practical, and material superiority of the former, he shows in detail what the legal requirements of such a state of affairs are, and what has to be done in order to make it work and to defend it against the machinations of its foes.

The Welfare State

Unfortunately, the third part of Professor Hayek's book is rather disappointing. Here the author tries to distinguish between socialism and the Welfare State. Socialism, he alleges, is on the decline; the Welfare

State is supplanting it. And he thinks the Welfare State is, under certain conditions, compatible with liberty.

In fact, the Welfare State is merely a method for transforming the market economy step-by-step into socialism. The original plan of socialist action, as developed by Karl Marx in 1848 in the *Communist Manifesto*, aimed at a gradual realization of socialism by a series of governmental measures. The ten most powerful of such measures were enumerated in the *Manifesto*. They are well known to everybody because they are the very measures that form the essence of the activities of the Welfare State, of Bismarck's and the Kaiser Wilhelm's German *Sozialpolitik* as well as of the American New Deal and British Fabian Socialism. The *Communist Manifesto* calls the measures it suggests "economically insufficient and untenable," but it stresses the fact that "in the course of the movement" they outstrip themselves, necessitate further inroads upon the old social order, and are unavoidable as a means of entirely revolutionizing the mode of production."

Later, Marx adopted a different method for the policies of his party. He abandoned the tactics of a gradual approach to the total state of socialism and advocated instead a violent revolutionary overthrow of the "bourgeois" system that at one stroke should "liquidate" the "exploiters" and establish "the dictatorship of the proletariat." This is what Lenin did in 1917 in Russia and this is what the Communist International plans to achieve everywhere. What separates the communists from the advocates of the Welfare State is not the ultimate goal of their endeavors, but the methods by means of which they want to attain a goal that is common to both of them. The difference of opinions that divides them is the same as that which distinguished the Marx of 1848 from the Marx of 1867, the year of the first publication of the first volume of *Das Kapital*.

However, the fact that Professor Hayek has misjudged the character of the Welfare State does not seriously detract from the value of his great book. His searching analysis of the policies and concerns of the Welfare State shows to every thoughtful reader why and how these much praised welfare policies inevitably always fail. These policies never attain those, allegedly beneficial, ends which the government and the self-styled progressives who advocated them wanted to attain, but, on the contrary, bring about a state of affairs which—from the very point of view of the government and its supporters—is even more unsatisfactory than the previous state of affairs they wanted to "improve." If the government does not repeal its first intervention, it is induced to supplement it by further acts of intervention. As these fail again, still more meddling with business is resorted to until all economic freedom has been virtually abolished. What emerges is the system of all-round planning, i.e., socialism of the type which the German Hindenburg plan was aiming at in the first World War and which was later put into effect by Hitler after his seizure of power and by the British Coalition Cabinet in the second World War.

The main error that prevents many of our contemporaries from adequately comprehending the significance of various party programs and the trend of the welfare policies is their failure to recognize that there is, apart from outright nationalization of all plants and farms as effected in Russia and China, a second method for the full realization of socialism. Under this system, that is commonly called "planning" or, in war time, "war socialism," the various plants and farms remain outwardly and seemingly separate units, but they become entirely and unconditionally subject to the orders of the supreme planning authority. Every citizen, whatever his nominal position in the economic system may be, is bound to toil in strict compliance with the orders of the planning board, and his income, the amount he is permitted to spend for his consumption, is exclusively determined by these orders. Some labels and terms of the capitalistic system may be preserved, but under the altered conditions they signify something entirely different from what they used to signify in the market economy. Other terms may be changed. Thus in Hitler's Germany the head of an outfit who supplanted the entrepreneur or the corporation president of the market economy was styled the "shop manager" (*Betriebsführer*) and the labor force the "retinue" (*Gefolgschaft*). As the theoretical pacemakers of this system, for instance, the late Professor Othmar Spann (1878–1950), a collectivist, has pointed out again and again, it retains only the *name* of private ownership, while in fact there is exclusively public — state — ownership.

Only by paying full attention to these fundamental issues can one form a correct appreciation of the political controversies in the nations of Western civilization. If socialism and communism should succeed in these countries, it will be the socialism of the planning scheme and not the socialism of the nationalization scheme. The latter is a method applicable to predominantly agricultural countries like those of Eastern Europe and Asia. In the industrial countries of the West the planning scheme is more popular because even the most fanatical statolatrists shrink from directly nationalizing the intricate apparatus of modern manufacturing. Yet, the "planning scheme" is just as destructive of freedom as the "nationalization scheme" and both lead on to the authoritarian state.

36

Man, Economy and State:
A New Treatise on Economics

Most of what goes today under the label of the social sciences is poorly disguised apologetics for the policies of governments. What the philosopher George Santayana (1863–1952) once said about a teacher of philosophy of the, then Royal Prussian, University of Berlin, that it seemed to this man "that a professor's business was to trudge along a governmental towpath with a legal cargo," is today everywhere true for the majority of those appointed to teach economics. As these doctors see it, all the evils that plague mankind are caused by the acquisitiveness of greedy exploiters, speculators, and monopolists, who are supreme in the conduct of affairs in the market economy. The foremost task of good government is to curb these scoundrels by suppressing their "economic freedom" and subjecting all affairs to the decisions of the central authority. Full government control of everybody's activities — whether called planning, socialism, communism, or any other name — is praised as the panacea.

To make these ideas plausible one had to proscribe as orthodox, classical, neoclassical, and reactionary all that economics had brought forward before the emergence of the New Deal, the Fair Deal, and the New Frontier. Any acquaintance with pre-Keynesian economics is considered as rather unsuitable and unseemly for an up-to-date economist. It could easily raise in his mind some critical thoughts. It could encourage him to reflect, instead of meekly endorsing the empty slogans of governments and powerful pressure groups. There is, in fact, in the writings and teaching of those who nowadays call themselves "economists," no longer any comprehension of the operation of the economic system as such. Their books and articles do not describe, analyze, or explain the eco-

Reprinted from *New Individualist Review*, Autumn 1962.

nomic phenomena. They do not pay attention to the interdependence and mutuality of the various individuals' and groups' activities. In their view, there exist different economic spheres that have to be treated by and large as isolated domains. They dissolve economics into a number of special fields, such as economics of labor, agriculture, insurance, foreign trade, domestic trade, and so on. These books and articles deal with the height of wage rates, for example, as if it were possible to treat this subject independently of the problems of commodity prices, interest, profit and loss, and all the other issues of economics. They assemble, without any idea for what purpose they are doing it, a vast array of statistical and other historical data about the recent past, which they choose to style the "present." They entirely fail to comprehend the interconnectedness and mutual determination of the actions of the various individuals whose behavior results in the emergence of the market economy.

The economic writings of the last decades provide a pitiful story of progressing deterioration and degradation. Even a comparison of the recent publications of many older authors with their previous writings shows an advancing decline. The few, very few, good contributions that came out in our age were smeared as old-fashioned and reactionary by the government economists, boycotted by the universities, the academic magazines, and the newspapers, and ignored by the public.

Let us hope that the fate of Murray N. Rothbard's book *Man, Economy, and State* (Princeton: D. Van Nostrand, 1962) will be different. Dr. Rothbard is already well known as the author of several excellent monographs. Now, as the result of many years of sagacious and discerning meditation, he joins the ranks of eminent economists by publishing a voluminous work, a systematic treatise on economics.

The main virtue of this book is that it is a comprehensive and methodical analysis of all activities commonly called economic. It looks upon these activities as human action, i.e., as conscious striving after chosen ends by resorting to appropriate means. This cognition exposes the fateful errors of the mathematical treatment of economic problems. The mathematical economist attempts to ignore the difference between physical phenomena, on the one hand, the emergence and consummation of which man is unable to see the operation of any final causes and which can be studied scientifically only because there prevails a perceptible regularity in their concatenation and succession, and praxeological phenomena, on the other hand, that lack such a regularity but are conceivable to the human mind as the outcomes of purposeful aiming at definite ends chosen. Mathematical equations, says Rothbard, are appropriate and useful where there are constant quantitative relations among *unmotivated* variables; they are inappropriate in the field of conscious behavior. In a few brilliant lines he demolishes the main device of mathematical economists, viz., the fallacious idea of substituting the concepts of mutual determination and equilibrium for the allegedly outdated concept of cause and effect. And he shows that the concepts of equilibrium and the evenly rotating economy do not refer to reality; although indispensable for any economic inquiry, they are merely auxiliary mental tools to aid us in the analysis of real action.

The equations of physics describe a process through time, while those of economics do not describe a process at all, but merely the final equilibrium point, a hypothetical situation that is outside of time and will never be reached in reality. Furthermore, they cannot say anything about the path by which the economy moves in the direction of the final equilibrium position. As there are no constant relations between any of the elements which the science of action studies, there is no measurement possible and all numerical data available have merely a historical character; they belong to economic history and not to economics as such. The positivist slogan, "science is measurement," in no way refers to the sciences of human action; the claims of "econometrics" are vain.

In every chapter of his treatise, Dr. Rothbard, adopting the best of the teachings of his predecessors, and adding to them highly important observations, not only develops the correct theory but is no less anxious to refute all objections ever raised against these doctrines. He exposes the fallacies and contradictions of the popular interpretation of economic affairs. Thus, for instance, in dealing with the problem of unemployment he points out: in the whole modern and Keynesian discussion of this subject the missing link is precisely the wage rate. It is meaningless to talk of unemployment or employment without reference to a wage rate. Whatever supply of labor service is brought to market can be sold, but only if wages are set at whatever rate will clear the market. If a man wishes to be employed, he will be, provided the wage rate is adjusted according to what Rothbard calls his discounted marginal value product, i.e., the present height of the value which the consumers — at the time of the final sale of the product — will ascribe to his contribution to its production. Whenever the job-seeker insists on a higher wage, he will remain unemployed. If people refuse to be employed except at places, in occupations, or at wage rates they would like, then they are likely to be choosing unemployment for substantial periods. The full import of this state of affairs becomes manifest if one gives attention to the fact that, under present conditions, those offering their services on the labor market themselves represent the immense majority of the consumers whose buying or abstention from buying ultimately determines the height of wage rates.

Less successful than his investigations in the fields of general praxeology and economics are the author's occasional observations concerning the philosophy of law and some problems of the penal code. But disagreement with his opinions concerning these matters cannot prevent me from qualifying Rothbard's work as an epochal contribution to the general science of human action, praxeology, and its practically most important and up-to-now best elaborated part, economics. Henceforth all essential studies in these branches of knowledge will have to take full account of the theories and criticisms expounded by Dr. Rothbard.

The publication of a standard book on economics raises again an important question, viz., for whom are essays of this consequence written: only for specialists, the students of economics, or for all of the people?

To answer this question we have to keep in mind that the citizens in their capacity as voters are called upon to determine ultimately all issues of economic policies. The fact that the masses are ignorant of physics and do not know anything substantial about electricity does not obstruct the endeavors of experts who utilize the teachings of science for the satisfaction of the wants of the consumers. From various points of view one may deplore the intellectual insufficiency and indolence of the multitude. But their ignorance regarding the achievements of the natural sciences does not endanger our spiritual and material welfare.

It is quite different in the field of economics. The fact that the majority of our contemporaries, the masses of semibarbarians led by self-styled intellectuals, entirely ignore everything that economics has brought forward, is the main political problem of our age. There is no use in deceiving ourselves. American public opinion rejects the market economy, the capitalistic free enterprise system that provided the nation with the highest standard of living ever attained. Full government control of all activities of the individual is virtually the goal of both national parties. The individual is to be deprived of his moral, political, and economic responsibility and autonomy and to be converted into a pawn in the schemes of a supreme authority aiming at a "national" purpose. His "affluence" is to be cut down for the benefit of what is called the "public sector," i.e., the machine operated by the party in power. Hosts of authors, writers, and professors are busy denouncing alleged shortcomings of capitalism and exalting the virtues of "planning." Full of a quasireligious ardor, the immense majority is advocating measures that step by step lead to the methods of administration practiced in Moscow and in Peking.

If we want to avoid the destruction of Western civilization and the relapse into primitive wretchedness, we must change the mentality of our fellow citizens. We must make them realize what they owe to the much vilified "economic freedom," the system of free enterprise and capitalism. The intellectuals and those who call themselves educated must use their superior cognitive faculties and power of reasoning for the refutation of erroneous ideas about social, political, and economic problems and for the dissemination of a correct grasp of the operation of the market economy. They must start by familiarizing themselves with all the issues involved in order to teach those who are blinded by ignorance and emotions. They must learn in order to acquire the ability to enlighten the misguided many.

It is a fateful error on the part of our most valuable contemporaries to believe that economics can be left to specialists in the same way in which various fields of technology can be safely left to those who have chosen to make any one of them their vocation. The issues of society's economic organization are every citizen's business. To master them to the best of one's ability is the duty of everyone.

Now such a book as *Man, Economy, and State* offers to every intelligent man an opportunity to obtain reliable information concerning the great controversies and conflicts of our age. It is certainly not easy reading and asks for the utmost exertion of one's attention. But there are no shortcuts to wisdom.

37

Understanding the Dollar Crisis

The seven lectures that Professor Percy L. Greaves, Jr., delivered in June 1969 before the *Centro de Estudios sobre la Libertad* in Buenos Aires deal with the fundamental economic problems; they are about "human life," about "the ideas that motivate human beings," about "the most important and interesting drama of all — human action."

To us, mortal human beings as we are, the universe appears as consisting of two different fields or regions: the field of events human action is able to influence to some extent and the field of events that are beyond the reach of any human action. The line that separates these two regions from one another is not rigidly fixed forever. We know that in the course of history man has acquired the knowledge and the power to achieve things that to earlier generations had appeared as simply impossible. But we know also that certain things can never and will never be achieved by any human action, that man can and will never become omnipotent.

The history of mankind appears to us as the history of the progressive expansion of man's knowledge of what we call the laws that determine the course of all changes going on in the universe. But we do not affirm or assume or believe that this expansion of our knowledge will give to man one day something that could be called omniscience.

Man tries to learn as much as he can learn about the operation of the powers and factors that determine the mutual relations between the various elements that constitute the world, and he tries to employ this knowledge in attempts to influence the course of affairs. Man acts; that means, he tries to bring about definite effects. He aims at ends chosen. He is not, like the inanimate things and like the nonhuman animals,

Reprinted from the foreword to *Understanding the Dollar Crisis* by Percy L. Greaves, Jr. (Western Islands, 1973).

merely a puppet of the forces that have produced him and determine his environment. His endeavors to attain definite ends chosen are a factor cooperating in the emergence of the future state of world affairs.

The Gold Standard

The historical evolution of mankind's economic cooperation, which culminated in attempts — by and large successful — at establishing a world-embracing system of the division of labor and the international exchange of commodities and services, gave to the metal gold the function of a generally employed medium of exchange. It is idle to raise the question of what would have happened if such a thing as gold had not been available for use as a generally employed medium of exchange.

The gold standard made the marvelous evolution of modern capitalism technically possible. It led to the establishment of the modern methods of banking. But the businessmen who had developed them lacked the intellectual power to resist successfully the attacks upon the operation of the monetary and banking principles, the strict observance of which is absolutely necessary to make the system work and to prevent its catastrophic breakdown. If the determination of the quantity of money — the generally employed medium of exchange in transactions — were subject to actions on the part of any individuals or groups of individuals whose material interests would be affected by changes in the purchasing power of the monetary unit, the system would not have been able to avoid a complete collapse. Neither inflation nor deflation is a policy that can last.

The eminence of the gold standard consists in the fact that geological conditions strictly limit the amount of gold available. This has up to now made the operation of a gold currency system possible.

These seven lectures are not merely a substitute for a textbook on economics. They are much more. They are an attempt to analyze and to explain the meaning and the effects of the various systems, methods, and measures of economic policies.

38

The Secret of American Prosperity

The United States is today the world's most prosperous nation. There is no need to dwell upon this fact. Nobody contests it.

But, in the present-day political and ideological climate, riches are held in evil repute. By and large, people look upon the more prosperous with unconcealed envy and hatred. The New Deal philosophy assures that an individual's fortune which exceeds that of the much talked-about common man is ill-gotten and that it is the task of government to equalize wealth and incomes by confiscatory taxation.

Foreigners View American Prosperity

Most Americans fail to realize that the same ideas that shape the anti-capitalistic bias of American domestic policies also determine foreign nations' attitudes toward the United States. The average European — not to speak of the Asiatics and Africans — looks upon the United States with the same envy and hatred which the American "progressive" displays toward American business. He finds fault with the United States because it is more prosperous than his own country. In his opinion all Americans are bad for the simple reason that they enjoy a higher standard of living than he does. And just as the American "progressive" disparages as bribed "sycophants" of the exploiting bourgeoisie those few economists who have the courage to raise their voices against the New Deal, so the European "progressive" condemns as traitors all statesmen and writers supporting his government's pro-American policy in the Cold War.

The many billions of dollars that the United States government has distributed all over the world have not tempered these anti-American

Reprinted from *The Freeman*, November 1955.

sentiments. This aid, say the socialists, is a mere pittance, a quite in-sufficient payment on the immense debt that America owes to the rest of mankind. By rights, all the wealth of the United States ought to be equally distributed among all nations. In the opinion of foreign radicals it is an infringement of divine and natural law that the average Ameri-can lives in a nice gadget-equipped home and drives a car, while mil-lions abroad lack the necessities of a decent existence. It is a shame, they say, that the scions of the peoples who have created Western civi-lization are living in straitened conditions, while the Americans, mere money makers, lead a luxurious life.

In the opinion of the typical foreign "intellectuals" mankind is di-vided into two classes: the exploiting Americans on the one side and the exploited have-nots on the other side. The communist "intellectu-als" put all their hopes on "liberation" by the Soviets. The moderates expect that the United Nations will one day evolve into an effective world government that by means of a progressive world income tax will try to bring about more equality in the distribution of incomes all over the world, just as national income tax laws try to do within their re-spective countries. Both groups agree in rejecting what they call a pro-American policy on the part of their nation and favor neutralism as the first step toward the worldwide establishment of a fair social order.

This blend of anti-capitalistic and anti-American sentiments plays an ominous role in present-day world affairs. It excites sympathies for the cause of the Soviets and jeopardizes the best designed attempts to block the further advance of Russian power. It threatens to overthrow Europe's civilization from within.

Rappard Views American Prosperity

Sober-minded European patriots are worried. They are aware of the dangers that the neutralist ideology generates. They would like to unmask its fallacies. But they are checked by the fact that the essen-tial content of the anti-American doctrine fully agrees with the eco-nomic — or rather, pseudo-economic — theories that are taught at uni-versities in their own countries and are accepted by all political parties. From the point of view of the ideas that determine the domestic poli-cies of most European nations — and, for that matter, also those of the United States — a man's penury is due to the fact that some people have appropriated too much to themselves. Hence the only efficacious remedy is to bring about by government interference a more equal distribution of what is called the national income. No argument whatever can be discovered to show that this doctrine and the practical conclusions derived from it ought to be limited to conditions within a nation and should not also be applied in international relations in order to equalize the distribution of world income.

The ideological obstacles that stand in the way of a European who wants to attack the prevailing anti-American mentality seem therefore almost insurmountable. The more remarkable is the fact that an eminent author, braving all these difficulties, has published an essay that goes to the heart of the matter.

Professor William E. Rappard [1883–1958] is not unknown to the American public. An outstanding historian and economist, this Genevese was born in New York, graduated from an American university, and taught at Harvard. He is the world's foremost expert in the field of international political and economic relations. His contributions to political philosophy, first of all those expounded in 1938 in his book *The Crisis of Democracy*, will be remembered in the history of ideas as the most powerful refutation of the doctrines of Communism and Nazism. There are but few authors whose judgment, competence, and impartiality enjoy a prestige equal to that of Rappard.

In his new book* Professor Rappard is neither pro-American nor anti-American. With cool detachment he tries to bring out in full relief the factors that account for the economic superiority of the United States. He starts by marshaling the statistical data and proceeds with a critical examination of the explanations provided by some older and newer authors. Then comes his own analysis of the causes of American prosperity. As Professor Rappard sees it, these causes can be put together under four broad headings: mass production, the application of science to production, the passion for productivity, and the spirit of competition.

The political importance of Professor Rappard's conclusions is to be seen in the fact that they ascribe American prosperity fully to factors operating within the United States. America's present-day economic superiority is a purely American phenomenon. It is an achievement of

---

* William E. Rappard, *The Secret of American Prosperity*, trans. Kenneth A. J. Dickson, with a foreword by Henry Hazlitt (New York: Greenberg, 1955).

Americans. It is in no way caused or furthered by anything that would harm foreign nations. There is no question of exploitation of the "have-nots." No non-American is needy because there is well-being in America. Professor Rappard carefully avoids any allusion to the heated controversy concerning the European nations' attitudes toward the United States. He does not even mention the exploitation doctrine and the complaints of the self-styled have-nots. But his book demolishes these counterfeit doctrines and, by implication, the political programs derived from them.

It can hardly be disputed, says Professor Rappard, "that the wealth of a country very largely depends on the will of the nation. Other things being equal, then, a country will be richer and its economy will be more productive in proportion as its inhabitants want it to be." America is prosperous because its people wanted prosperity and resorted to policies fitted to the purpose.

Prosperity and Capital

The operation of the four factors to which Professor Rappard attributes the superior productivity of labor in the United States is certainly not confined to the United States. They are characteristic features of the capitalist mode of production that originated in Western Europe and only later came to the United States. Mass production was the essential innovation of the Industrial Revolution. In earlier ages craftsmen produced with primitive tools in small workshops almost exclusively for the needs of a limited number of well-to-do. The factory system inaugurated new methods of production as well as of marketing. Cheap goods for the many were and are its objective. It is this principle that, combined with the principle of competition, accounts for the expansion of the most efficient enterprises and the disappearance of inefficient ones.

It is true that these tendencies are today more powerful in the United States than in European countries this side of the Iron Curtain. But this is principally due to the fact that political antagonism to big business and its superior competitive power set in earlier and is more drastic in Europe than in the United States, and has therefore more vigorously curbed the "rugged individualism" of business. The difference which in this regard exists between Europe and the United States is a difference of degree, not of kind.

With regard to the application of science to production and the passion for productivity, there is little, if any, difference between America and Europe. There is no need to stress the fact that the passion to make his outfit as productive as possible is strong in every businessman. Concerning the application of science to production, Professor Rappard observes that the most knowledgeable and sincere American writers recognize "that the most fruitful investigations of recent years have nearly all been carried out by Europeans working either in their own countries or in American laboratories." The industrial lead of the United States is explained, Monsieur Rappard goes on to say, not by the discovery of new theoretical truth but by the rapid and constantly improved application of discoveries of any origin whatsoever.

In enunciating this fact, Professor Rappard gives us the decisive answer to the problem he has investigated. America's industrial superiority is due to the circumstance that its plants, workshops, farms, and mines are equipped with better and more efficient tools and machines. Therefore, the marginal productivity of labor and, consequently, wage rates are higher there than anywhere else. As the average quantity and quality of goods produced in the same period of time by the same number of hands is greater and better, more and better goods are available for consumption. Here we have the "secret" of American prosperity.

With some insignificant exceptions, there is no secrecy whatever about the best modern methods of production. They are taught at numerous technological universities and described in textbooks and technological magazines. Thousands of highly gifted youths from economically backward countries have acquired full knowledge of them at the educational institutions and in the workshops of the United States, Great Britain, France, Germany, and other Western countries. Besides, a great many American engineers, chemists, and agriculturists are prepared to offer their expert services to the businesses of the so-called under-developed nations.

Every intelligent businessman — not only in Western Europe, but no less in all other countries — is obsessed by the urge to furnish his enterprise with the most efficient modern equipment. How is it then that, in spite of all these facts, the American (and Canadian) firms alone make full use of modern technological achievements and by far outstrip the industries of all other countries?

It is the insufficient supply of capital that prevents the rest of the world from adjusting its industries to the most efficient ways of production. Technological "know-how" and the "passion for productivity" are useless if the capital required for the acquisition of new equipment and the inauguration of new methods is lacking.

What made modern capitalism possible and enabled the nations, first of Western Europe and later of Central Europe and North America, to eclipse the rest of mankind in productivity was the fact that they created the political, legal, and institutional conditions that made capital accumulation safe. What prevents India, for example, from replacing its host of inefficient cobblers with shoe factories is only the lack of capital. As the Indian government virtually expropriates foreign capitalists and obstructs capital formation by natives, there is no way to remedy this situation. The result is that millions are barefoot in India while the average American buys several pairs of shoes every year.[*]

America's present economic supremacy is due to the plentiful supply of capital. The allegedly "progressive" policies that slow down saving and capital accumulation, or even bring about dissaving and capital decumulation, came later to the United States than to most European countries. While Europe was being impoverished by excessive armaments, colonial adventures, anti-capitalistic policies, and finally by wars and revolutions, the United States was committed to a free enterprise policy. At that time Europeans used to stigmatize American economic policies as socially backward. But it was precisely this alleged social backwardness that accounted for an amount of capital accumulation that surpassed by far the amount of capital available in other countries. When later the New Deal began to imitate the anti-capitalistic policies of Europe, America had already acquired an advantage that it still retains today.

Wealth does not consist, as Marx said, in a collection of commodities, but in a collection of capital goods. Such a collection is the result of previous saving. The antisaving doctrines of what is, paradoxically enough, called New Economics, first developed by Messrs. Foster and Catchings[†] and then reshaped by Lord Keynes, are untenable.

---

[*] A more favorable attitude toward capital investment has developed in India since 1955, and new laws have been enacted so that both domestic and foreign entrepreneurs have invested more in India.

[†] College Professor William T. Foster (1879–1950) and businessman Waddill Catchings (1879–1967) joined forces to establish the Pollak Foundation for Economic Research and to coauthor several books in the 1920s that considered saving harmful and advocated contracyclical public works and "a constant flow of new money" to encourage consumer spending.

If one wants to improve economic conditions, to raise the productivity of labor, wage rates, and the people's standard of living, one must accumulate more capital goods in order to invest more and more. There is no other way to increase the amount of capital available than to expand saving by doing away with all ideological and institutional factors that hinder saving or even directly make for dissaving and capital decumulation. This is what the "underdeveloped nations" need to learn.

39

A Dangerous Recommendation for High School Economics

It is admitted by everybody that the understanding of the American economy developed in most high schools today is not adequate for effective citizenship. In cognizance of this fact, the Committee for Economic Development, and the American Economic Association, a body that includes in its ranks almost all American teachers of economics, cooperated in entrusting a task force of professors and educational administrators with the study of the problems involved.

Task Force Report

The report of this task force, published in September 1961, is one of the most interesting and characteristic documents of our age. It shows what is taught under the label of economics at most of the American colleges and universities. And it shows, as the distinguished authors of the report believe, what ought to be handed down also to the high school students. It provides virtually a résumé of the ideas held by "progressives" — men who have been most influential in this country's movement away from the free market economy.

As the report sees it, there are various economic systems — "capitalist, communist, or any other" — and the task of economics is to describe and to compare the good and the bad aspects of each of them. In drafting a scheme for this pursuit, the authors are in some respects anxious to belittle the differences between capitalism and Communism and in other respects to find some reason to praise the Communist treatment of various problems as against that effected in the market economy.

Reprinted from *Christian Economics*, April 3, 1962.

Thus the report correctly contends that American production is "guided by the demands of millions of individual consumers," although it tries to qualify this statement by adding to the verb "guided" the adverb "largely." It would have been accurate to continue that in Russia "the decisions on what shall be produced are made by the Communist leaders." But such a frank expression would have appeared too "reactionary" for a "progressive" document. So the report only says that the "major" decisions are made by the leaders. Could any of the authors tell us what the "minor" decisions are, as distinguished from the "major" ones, and who the people are to whom these minor decisions are entrusted?

It would have been logical to go on pointing out—in full agreement with fact—that for the money he has earned a Russian can get only what the Communist leaders deign to give him. But such a plain declaration, too, was repugnant to the authors of the report. Instead they chose to say that the Russians "are generally free to buy what they wish," modifying this manifestly false statement only by the stilted proviso "subject to the over-all availability of goods set by the central planners."

While in this matter of the direction of production activities and in many other regards the report sees but little difference between the market economy and the Communist method of central planning, in other respects it lays stress on the divergence of the two and finds that the Communist methods work better than the capitalistic. Thus it proclaims in italics, *"Communist societies have not suffered from economic instability (booms and depressions) to the same extent that private enterprise economies have."* And it goes on in Roman type: "This is partly because of the extent to which all communist activities are controlled by central planning, but especially because decisions on capital investment are made directly by the state, thus avoiding the instability of profit-motivated investment which characterizes private enterprise economies." We may pass over the fact that the return of periods of economic depression is not a phenomenon originating from the operation of a free market economy, an economy not sabotaged by the interference of the state. The returning periods of economic depression are precisely the effect of the reiterated attempts of governments to create artificial booms by "cheap money" policy, that is, by lowering the market rate of interest through an increase in the quantity of money and fiduciary media.

But let us ask the authors of the report: How do you learn whether business in a country is good or bad? In the free countries people publicly complain as soon as they think that they do not earn as much as they would like. You cannot open an American newspaper without getting information about the state of business. But in Russia a man who would dare to say that something is unsatisfactory with the course of Russian economic affairs would pronounce his own death sentence. Years ago many millions died from starvation in the Ukraine, and no Russian newspaper or book ever mentioned this "minor" incident. It is well known that agricultural output has dropped considerably wherever socialist management has replaced private farming. What kind of stability does China, the most populous of all Communist countries, enjoy? It seems that the task force credulously based its judgments about Russia's conditions upon the statistics published by the Russian offices without paying attention to the fact that statistics, if not controlled by a free press and by writers who are not on the government's payroll, can prove anything in favor of the government whose agencies compiled it.

Communist Bias

If the report had not been biased in favor of Communism, it would have had to say this about the controversy of capitalism and Communism: The Communist doctrine as expounded by Marx and endorsed by Lenin emphatically declared that capitalism must and will inevitably result in progressing impoverishment and enslavement of all workingmen, while Communism will bring to all people unprecedented affluence and perfect freedom. Events have entirely belied this prognostication. In the capitalistic countries of Western Europe and North America, the standard of living of the average common man is continually improving and is much more satisfactory today than in any previous epoch of history, while in the Communist countries the masses are extremely poor and utterly deprived of any civil liberties.

In order to demonstrate the inferiority of the market economy as against government action, the report takes pleasure in affirming repeatedly that there are things that private enterprise cannot achieve, e.g., police protection and provision of national defense. This observation is entirely irrelevant. No reasonable man ever suggested that the essential function of state and government, protection of the smooth operation of the social system against domestic gangsters and foreign aggressors, should be entrusted to private business. The anarchists who wanted to abolish any governmental institution, as well as Marx and Engels who muttered about the "withering away" of the state, were not champions of free enterprise. Resorting to violent suppression of antisocial activities, and producing things that can be used and consumed and thus satisfy human wants, are two entirely different matters.

In defending the report against criticism leveled in the *Wall Street Journal*, the chairman of the task force, Dean G. L. Bach, asserted that "careful definition of terms is essential to economic understanding." Everybody will agree. But did the report comply with this rule?

Without attempting any definition it ascribes to big business "extensive power" over its customers. What in this instance it calls power is the fact that an enterprise has succeeded in serving its customers better, or cheaper, or better *and* cheaper than its competitors do. Then again it speaks of the power of labor unions and mentions "strikes supported by union picketing" as "the most powerful union weapon," modifying this statement by appending the rather questionable proposition "but strikes occur infrequently." Nothing is said about what Harvard Law School Dean Roscoe Pound [1870–1964] called "the substantially general privileges and immunities of labor unions and their members and officials to commit wrongs to person and property" and to commit many other acts that are considered and punished as criminal offenses when committed by other people. The authors did not find it worthwhile to react to these words of the nation's most eminent legal expert. Nor to the books of law by Professor Sylvester Petro. All they did was to declare that such issues as the "closed shop" and "right-to-work laws" are worth "brief" (!) student attention.

Implementing the Task Force Report

One thing must be acknowledged concerning this report: It unblushingly provides a faithful exposition of the ambivalent economic philosophy of the present-day system of American government. All the evils that are plaguing the people of this country are the inevitable effect of policies that, under the misleading name of a "middle-of-the-road" program, are, step by step, substituting government compulsion and coercion for the initiative of individual citizens. These ideologies and policies make the "public sector" of the economy grow more and more within the nation at the expense of "the private sector." And they make the totalitarian "Communist sector" expand within the sphere of world politics and the free "capitalistic sector" shrink. Hitherto in this country the propagation of these policies and ideas was the concern of leftist parties and their press. Now it is suggested to indoctrinate the high school students with them. This will certainly provide jobs for thousands and thousands of staunch supporters of the allegedly "progressive" doctrines that in present-day America are expounded under the misleading labels "liberal" and "democratic." However, the ambitious expectations entertained by the sponsors and the authors of the report and by their political friends will hardly be realized.

The greater part of the pupils, preoccupied with other things, will not take any interest in the subject. And the judicious students will not meekly acquiesce in the official dogmas of the textbooks and will be shrewd enough to ask questions that will embarrass their teachers. They may ask for instance: Why does the government spend billions of the taxpayers' money in order to make the most important foodstuffs more expensive for the consumer? Or, Did any government ever improve the methods of production or embark upon supplying the consumers with new articles never produced before? Or, Why do the Communist governments prohibit their citizens from visiting foreign countries and from reading books and newspapers published abroad?

A sensible boy or girl will certainly not put up with the confused and contradictory observations that a teacher, imbued with the philosophy of the report, may bring forward.

The modern American high school, reformed according to the principles of John Dewey, has failed lamentably, as all competent experts agree, in the teaching of mathematics, physics, languages, and history. If the plans of the authors of this report materialize, it will add the teaching of economics to its other failings, and will also add to the curriculum indoctrination in very bad economics.

40

Foreign Spokesmen for Freedom

The great catastrophes that befell Germany in the first part of our century were the inevitable effect of its political and economic policies. They would not have happened at all or they would have been much less pernicious if there had been in the country any noticeable resistance to the fatal drift in official policies. But the characteristic mark of Germany in the age of Bismarck as well as later in that of World War I General Erich Ludendorff and of Hitler was strict conformity. There was practically no criticism of the interventionist economic policies and still less of inflationism. The great British economist Edwin Cannan (1861–1935) wrote that if anyone had the impertinence to ask him what he did in the Great War, he would answer, "I protested." Germany's plight consisted in the fact that it did not have, either before the armistice of 1918 or later, anybody to protest against the follies of its monetary and financial management. Before 1923 no German newspaper or magazine, in dealing with the rapidly progressing fall in the mark's purchasing power, ever mentioned the boundless increase in the quantity of banknotes printed. It was viewed as un-German not to accept one of the "loyal" interpretations of this phenomenon that put all the blame upon the policies of the Allies and the Treaty of Versailles.

In this regard conditions in Germany have certainly changed. There is in Germany today at least one monthly magazine that has both the courage and the insight to form an independent judgment on the economic and social policies of the government and the aims of the various parties and pressure groups. It is the *Monatsblätter für freiheitliche Wirtschaftspolitik*, edited now already for six years by Doctor Volkmar Muthesius. It is published by the Fritz Knapp Verlag in Frankfurt. Excellent articles written by the editor and a carefully selected group of

Reprinted from *The Freeman*, March 1961.

external contributors analyze every aspect of contemporary economic and social conditions.

Doctor Muthesius and his friends are unswerving supporters of free trade both in domestic and in foreign affairs. They reject the lavish bounties doled out to agriculture at the expense of the immense majority, the urban population. They are keen critics of the cheap demagogy of the government's alleged antimonopoly campaign. They unmask the dangers inherent in the privileges granted to the labor unions. In matters of taxation, a balanced budget, sound money, and "social" policies, they follow a line of thought similar to that of the American Goldwater-Republicans. They prefer the Adenauer* regime to the only possible alternative, a cabinet of Social-Democrats, but they do not close their eyes to the shortcomings of the Chancellor's policies. And they are not afraid of repeating again and again that it is only thanks to the United States that West Berlin is still free from Soviet rule.

A periodical that openly and without any reservations endorses the free enterprise system and the market economy is certainly a remarkable achievement in the classical land of socialism whether imperial or social-democrat or nationalist.

---

* Konrad Adenauer (1876–1967) was chancellor of West Germany from 1949 until 1963.

41

Freedom Has Made a Comeback

One of the characteristic marks of the age that witnessed more blood-shed, war, and destruction than any preceding era of history was the credulous appreciation of quasi-prophetic prognostications about the course of future history and about the final goals of mankind's evolution. In the wake of Hegel's philosophy, Marx had proclaimed that a mysterious, never-defined or clearly described agency called the "material productive forces" was inevitably leading the peoples toward the bliss of everlasting earthly paradise, socialism. Socialism, he contended, would radically transform all human and earthly affairs. In its frame there would no longer be any want or suffering. To work would not cause pain but pleasure and everybody would get all he needed. What a comfort to know that the coming of this perfect state of things was inevitable!

Seen from the point of view of these fables, which paradoxically were called scientific socialism, the foremost duty of every decent fellow was to fight unto death the dissenters who did not believe in the Marxian message and to prepare himself for life in utopia. The task of progressive education, heralded the pundits, is to adjust the rising generation to the conditions of their future socialist environment.

Only a few years ago the harbingers of these dogmas could assume that they had succeeded in this educational effort. Their semantic innovations were accepted by almost everybody. Progress meant progress on the road toward socialism, reaction any attempt to preserve freedom. "No enemies on the left" was a battle cry which very soon was followed by the still more shameful slogan: "Better Red than dead."

But then a miracle happened, the awakening of the common sense of sound, decent people. Out of the ranks of the young boys and girls

Statement at Young Americans for Freedom rally, Madison Square Garden, March 7, 1962. Reprinted from *The New Guard*, March 1962.

arose an opposition. There were on the campuses once again friends of freedom and they had the courage to speak their minds. Collectivism was challenged by individualism. No longer was liberty condemned as a bourgeois prejudice; no longer were constitutional, representative government and the rule of law smeared as clever make-shifts invented by the privileged few for the oppression of the many. The idea of freedom made a comeback.

There are overcautious skeptics who admonish us not to attach too much importance to these academic affairs. I think these critics are wrong. The fact that, out of the midst of the college youth, a new movement in favor of the great old ideals of individualism and freedom originated, is certainly of paramount importance. The spell of the dreadful conformity that threatened to convert our country into a spiritual desert is broken. There are again young men and women eager to think over the fundamental problems of life and action. This is a genuine moral and intellectual resurrection, a movement that will prevent us from falling prey to the arbitrary tyranny of dictators. As an old man I am greeting the young generation of liberators.

Economics and Ideas

In the first essay in this section Mises wrote, "The struggle between the two systems of social organization, freedom and totalitarianism . . . depends on ideological factors. The champions of freedom can win only if they are supported by a citizenry fully and unconditionally committed to the ideal of freedom."

The major economic fallacies of post–World War II Marxism and Progressivism have been demolished by economists of the Austrian, subjective value, marginal-utility school. Yet much still remains to be done to "unmask" these fallacies in the field of public opinion. For freedom to triumph, people must come to understand the importance of protecting private property and free markets. It is a tragedy for the world that now, just as the peoples in many lands are seeking to break the chains that bind them to Communism, they are looking to interventionist United States as their model.

In the final essay in this section Mises wrote:

"One of the main paradoxes of the modern world is this: The achievements of laissez-faire liberalism and the capitalistic market economy have finally instilled in all Eastern peoples the conviction that what the Western ideologies recommend and the Western policies practice is the right thing to be done. But by the time the East got this confidence in Western ways, the ideologies and policies of socialism and interventionism had supplanted liberalism in Europe and America. . . . Therefore, nothing is more important today than to enlighten public opinion about the basic differences between genuine liberalism, which advocates the free market economy, and the various interventionist parties which are advocating government interference with prices, wages, the rate of interest, profits and investment, confiscatory taxation, tariffs and other protectionist measures, huge government spending and finally inflation."

42

The Objectives of Economic Education

The struggle between the two systems of social organization, freedom and totalitarianism, will be decided in the democratic nations at the polls. As things are today, the outcome in the United States will determine the outcome for all other peoples too. As long as this country does not go socialist, socialist victories in other parts of the world are of minor relevance.

Some people — among them very keen minds — expect either a revolutionary upheaval of the communists, a war with Russia and its satellites, or a combination of both events.

However this may be, it is obvious that the final result depends on ideological factors. The champions of freedom can win only if they are supported by a citizenry fully and unconditionally committed to the ideals of freedom. They will be defeated if those molding public opinion in their own camp are infected with sympathies for the totalitarian program. Men fight unto death for their convictions. But nobody is ready to dedicate himself seriously to a cause which in his eyes is only 50 percent right. Those who say: "I am not a Communist, but . . ." cannot be counted upon to fight rigorously for freedom and against Communism.

In Russia, in 1917, the Bolsheviks numbered only a few thousand men. From the arithmetical point of view their forces were negligible. Yet, they were able to seize power and beat into submission the whole nation because they did not encounter any ideological opposition. In the vast empire of the Tsars there was no group or party advocating economic freedom. There was no author or teacher, no book, magazine, or newspaper that would have declared that freedom from bureaucratic

Extracts from a memorandum (1948) to Leonard E. Read, founder and president of the then newly established Foundation for Economic Education; previously published only in Spanish translation.

regimentation is the only method to make the Russian people as prosperous as possible.

All people agree that in France and in Italy [1948] the Communist
danger is very great. Yet, it is a fact that the majorities in both countries
are hostile to Communism. However, the resistance of these majorities
is weak, as they have espoused essential parts of socialism and of the
Marxian criticism of capitalism. Thanks to this ideological penetration
of Communist adversaries in France and Italy, the chances of the
Communists are much better than the numbers of Communist Party
members warrant.

The Philosophical Problem Implied

Those engaged in the conduct of business, the professions, politics, and
the editing and writing of newspapers and magazines are so fully absorbed by the sundry problems they have to face that they neglect to pay
attention to the great ideological conflicts of our age. The urgent tasks of
the daily routine impose on them an enormous quantity of pressing
work, and no time is left for a thoroughgoing examination of the principles and doctrines implied. Perplexed by the vast amount of detail and
trivia, the practical man looks only at the short-run consequences of the
alternatives between which he has to choose at the moment, and does
not bother about long-run consequences. He falls prey to the illusion
that this attitude alone is worthy of an active citizen successfully con-
tributing to progress and welfare; preoccupation with fundamental
questions is just a pastime for authors and readers of useless highbrow
books and magazines. In democratic America the men most distinguished in business, the professions, and politics have today the same
attitude toward "theories" and "abstractions" that Napoleon Bonaparte
displayed in ridiculing and abusing the "ideologues."

The disdain of theories and philosophies is mainly caused by the
mistaken belief that the facts of experience speak for themselves, that
facts by themselves can explode erroneous interpretations. The idea
prevails that no serious harm can be done by a fallacious philosophy,
an "ism," however vitriolic and insidious; reality is stronger than fables
and myths; truth automatically dispels lies; there is no reason to worry
about the propaganda of the apostles of untruth.

There is no need to enter into an investigation of the epistemological issues implied in this widely held opinion. It may be enough to

quote a few lines of John Stuart Mill. "Man," says Mill, ". . . is capable of rectifying his mistakes, by discussion and experience. Not by experience alone. There must be discussion, to show how experience is to be interpreted. Wrong opinions and practices gradually yield to fact and argument; but facts and arguments, to produce any effect on the mind, must be brought before it. Very few facts are able to tell their own story, without comments to bring out their meaning."[1]

Those people who believe that the mere record of the American achievements of economic individualism makes the youth of the United States safe from indoctrination with the ideas of Karl Marx, Thorstein Veblen, John Dewey, Bertrand Russell, and Harold Laski are badly mistaken. They fail to discern the role that Marxian polylogism plays in the living philosophy of our age.

According to the doctrine of Marxian polylogism, a man's ideas necessarily reflect his class position; they are nothing but a disguise for the selfish interest of his class and are irreconcilably opposed to the interests of all other social classes. The "material productive forces" that determine the course of human history have chosen the working "class," the proletariat, to abolish all class antagonisms and to bring lasting salvation to the whole of mankind. The interests of the proletarians, who are already the immense majority today, will finally coincide with the interests of all. Thus from the point of view of the inevitable destiny of man, the Marxians say, the proletarians are right and the bourgeois are wrong. There is no need, therefore, to refute an author who disagrees with the "progressive" teachings of Marx, Engels, and Lenin; all that is needed is to unmask his bourgeois background and show that he is wrong because he is either a bourgeois or a "sycophant" of the bourgeoisie.

In its consistent and radical form polylogism is accepted only by the Russian Bolsheviks. They distinguish between "bourgeois" and "proletarian" doctrines even in mathematics, physics, biology, and medicine. But the more moderate brand of polylogism, which applies the "bourgeois" or "proletarian" yardstick only to the social and historical branches of knowledge, is endorsed by and large even by many of those schools and authors who emphatically call themselves anti-Marxian. Even at universities, which radical Marxians vilify as strongholds of bourgeois mentality, general history as well as the history of

1. Mill, *On Liberty*, 3d ed. (London, 1864), pp. 38–39.

philosophy, literature, and art are often taught from the point of Marxian materialistic philosophy.

The tenets of people committed to Marxian polylogism cannot be shaken by any argument advanced by an author, politician, or other citizen suspected of bourgeois affiliation. As long as a considerable part of the nation is imbued — many of them unwittingly — with the polylogistic doctrine, it is useless to argue with them about special theories of various branches of science or about the interpretation of concrete facts. These men are immune to thought, ideas, and factual information that stem from the sordid source of the bourgeois mind. Hence it is obvious that the attempts to free the people, especially the intellectual youth, from the fetters of "unorthodox" indoctrination must begin on the philosophical and epistemological level.

The disinclination to deal with "theory" is tantamount to yielding submissively to Marx's dialectical materialism. The intellectual conflict between freedom and totalitarianism will not be decided in discussions about the meaning of concrete statistical figures and historical events, but in a thorough examination of the fundamental issues of epistemology and the theory of knowledge.

It is true that the masses have only a very crude and simplified cognition of dialectical materialism and its offshoot, the so-called sociology of knowledge. But all knowledge of the many is crude and simplified. What matters is not to change the ideology of the masses, but to change first the ideology of the intellectual strata, the "highbrows," whose mentality determines the content of the simplifications which are held by the "lowbrows."

Marxism and "Progressivism"

The social and economic teachings of the self-styled "un-orthodox Progressives" are a garbled mixture of divers particles of heterogeneous doctrines incompatible with one another. The main components of this body of opinion were taken from Marxism, British Fabianism, and the Prussian Historical School. Essential elements were also borrowed from the teachings of those monetary reformers, inflationists who were long known only as "monetary cranks." And the legacy of Mercantilism is important too.

All Progressives loathe the nineteenth century, its ideas and its policies. However, the principal ingredients of Progressivism, except for mercantilism which stems from the seventeenth century, were formed in that much-defamed nineteenth century. But, of course, Progressivism is different from every one of these doctrines, parts of each of which were synthesized to make Progressivism what it is. . . . Among those who call themselves Progressives there are certainly a number of consistent Marxians. . . . The great majority of the Progressives, however, are moderate and eclectic in their appraisal of Marx. Although sympathizing by and large with the material objectives of the Bolsheviks, they criticize certain attending phenomena of the revolutionary movement, for instance, the Soviet regime's dictatorial methods, its anti-Christianism and its "Iron Curtain."

Many outstanding champions of Progressivism openly declare that they aim ultimately at a substitution of socialism for free enterprise. But other Progressives announce again and again that by the suggested reforms they want to *save* capitalism, which would be doomed if not reformed and improved. They advocate interventionism as a permanent system of society's economic organization, not, as do the moderate Marxian groups, as a method for the gradual realization of socialism.

There is no need to enter here into an analysis of interventionism. It has been shown in an irrefutable way that all measures of interventionism bring about consequences which — from the point of view of the governments and parties resorting to them — are less satisfactory than the previous state of affairs which they were devised to alter. If the government and the politicians do not learn the lesson which these failures teach and do not want to abstain from all meddling with commodity prices, wages, and interest rates, they must add more and more regimentation to their first measures until the whole system of market economy has been replaced by all-round planning and socialism.

However, my purpose here is not to deal with the policies recommended by the champions of interventionism. These practical policies differ from group to group. It is merely a slight exaggeration to say that not only does each pressure group have its own brand of interventionism, but so does every professor. Each is keenly intent upon exploding the shortcomings of all rival brands. But the doctrine which is at the bottom of interventionist ventures, the assumption that contradictions and evils are allegedly inherent in capitalism, is by and large uniform with all varieties of Progressivism and generally accepted with hardly any opposition. Theories which are at variance are virtually outlawed. Anti-progressive ideas are represented in caricature in university lectures, books, pamphlets, articles, and newspapers. The rising generation does not hear anything about them except that they are the doctrines of the economic Bourbons, the ruthless exploiters and "robber barons" whose supremacy is gone forever.

The Main Thesis of Progressivism

The doctrines which are taught today under the appellation "Progressive economics" can be condensed in the following ten points.

1. The fundamental economic thesis common to all socialist groups is that there is a potential plenty, thanks to the technological achievements of the last two hundred years. The insufficient supply of useful things is due merely, as Marx and Engels repeated again and again, to the inherent contradictions and shortcomings of the capitalist mode of production. Once socialism is adopted, once socialism has reached its "higher stage," and after the last vestiges of capitalism have been eradicated, there will be abundance. To work then will no longer cause pain, but pleasure. Society will be in a position to give "to each according to his needs." Marx and Engels never noticed that there is an inexorable scarcity of the material factors of production.

The academic Progressives are more cautious in the choice of terms, but virtually all of them adopt the socialist thesis.

2. The inflationist wing of Progressivism agrees with the most bigoted Marxians in ignoring the fact of the scarcity of the material factors of production. It draws from this error the conclusion that the rate of interest and entrepreneurial profit can be eliminated by credit expansion. As they see it, only the selfish class interests of bankers and usurers are opposed to credit expansion.

The overwhelming success of the inflationist party manifests itself in the monetary and credit policies of all countries. The doctrinal and semantic changes that preceded this victory, which made this victory possible and which now prevent the adoption of sound monetary policies, are the following:

a. Until a few years ago, the term *inflation* meant a substantial increase in the quantity of money and money-substitutes. Such an increase necessarily tends to bring about a general rise in commodity prices. But today the term *inflation* is used to signify the inevitable *consequences* of what was previously called inflation. It is implied that an increase in the quantity of money and money-substitutes does not affect prices, and that the general rise in prices which we have witnessed in these last years was not caused by the government's monetary policy, but by the insatiable greed of business.

b. It is assumed that the rise of foreign exchange rates in those countries, where the magnitude of the inflationary increment to the quantity of money and money-substitutes in circulation exceeded that of other countries, is not a consequence of this monetary excess but a product of other agents, such as: the unfavorable balance of payments, the sinister machinations of speculators, the "scarcity" of foreign exchange, and the trade barriers erected by foreign governments, not by one's own.

c. It is assumed that a government, which is not on the gold standard and which has control of a central bank system, has the power to manipulate the rate of interest downward *ad libitum* without bringing about any undesired effects. It is vehemently denied that such an "easy money" policy inevitably leads to an economic crisis. The theory, which explains the recurrence of periods of economic depression as the necessary outcome of the repeated attempts to reduce interest rates artificially and expand credit, is either intentionally passed over in silence or distorted in order to ridicule it and to abuse its authors.

3. Thus the way is free to describe the recurrence of periods of economic depression as an evil inherent in capitalism. The capitalist society, it is asserted, lacks the power to control its own destiny.

4. The most disastrous consequence of the economic crisis is mass unemployment prolonged year after year. People are starving, it is claimed, because free enterprise is unable to provide enough jobs. Under capitalism technological improvement which could be a blessing for all is a scourge for the most numerous class.

5. The improvement in the material conditions of labor, the rise in real wage rates, the shortening of the hours of work, the abolition of child labor, and all other "social gains" are achievements of government pro-labor legislation and labor unions. But for the interference of the government and the unions, the conditions of the laboring class would be as bad as they were in the early period of the "industrial revolution."

6. In spite of all the endeavors of popular governments and labor unions, it is argued, the lot of the wage earners is desperate. Marx was quite right in predicting the inevitable progressive pauperization of the proletariat. The fact that accidental factors have temporarily secured a slight improvement in the standard of living of the American wage earner is of no avail; this improvement concerns merely a country whose

population is not more than 7 percent of the world's population and moreover, so the argument runs, it is only a passing phenomenon. The rich are still getting richer; the poor are still getting poorer; the middle classes are still disappearing. The greater part of wealth is concentrated in the hands of a few families. Lackeys of these families hold the most important public offices and manage them for the sole benefit of "Wall Street." What the bourgeois call democracy means in reality "pluto-democracy," a cunning disguise for the class rule of the exploiters.

7. In the absence of government price control, commodity prices are manipulated *ad libitum* by the businessmen. In the absence of minimum wage rates and collective bargaining, the employers would manipulate wages in the same way too. The result is that profits are absorbing more and more of the national income. There would prevail a tendency for real wage rates to drop if efficient unions were not intent upon checking the machinations of the employers.

8. The description of capitalism as a system of competitive business may have been correct for its early stages. Today it is manifestly inadequate. Mammoth-size cartels and monopolistic combines dominate the national markets. Their endeavors to attain exclusive monopoly of the world market result in imperialistic wars in which the poor bleed in order to make the rich richer.

9. As production under capitalism is for profit and not for use, those things manufactured are not those which could most effectively supply the real wants of the consumers, but those the sale of which is most profitable. The "merchants of death" produce destructive weapons. Other business groups poison the body and soul of the masses by habit-creating drugs, intoxicating beverages, tobacco, lascivious books and magazines, silly moving pictures, and idiotic comic strips.

10. The share of the national income that goes to the propertied classes is so enormous that, for all practical purposes, it can be considered inexhaustible. For a popular government, not afraid to tax the rich according to their ability to pay, there is no reason to abstain from any expenditure beneficial to the voters. On the other hand, profits can be freely tapped to raise wage rates and lower prices of consumers' goods.

❧

These are the main dogmas of the "un-orthodoxy" of our age, the fallacies of which economic education must unmask. Success or failure of endeavors to substitute sound ideas for unsound will depend ultimately on the abilities and the personalities of the men who seek to achieve this task. If the right men are lacking in the hour of decision, the fate of our civilization is sealed. Even if such pioneers are available, however, their efforts will be futile if they meet with indifference and apathy on the part of their fellow citizens. The survival of civilization can be jeopardized by the misdeeds of individual dictators, Führers or Duces. Its preservation, reconstruction, and continuation, however, require the joint efforts of all men of good will.

43

On Current Monetary Problems

PROFESSOR GREAVES: *What is the most important political problem for the world today?*

PROFESSOR MISES: The prevention of a third world war which might doom our entire civilization.

GREAVES: *What is the most important problem from the viewpoint of domestic economic policies?*

MISES: The reestablishment of financial integrity and making an end to inflation.

GREAVES: *What do you mean by the term "inflation"?*

MISES: Inflation is a policy of increasing the quantity of money in order to make it possible for the government to spend more than it collects in taxes or borrows from the public. It is first of all a way to avoid the necessity of explaining to the people why higher taxes are necessary. The government wants to spend more than the duly elected representatives of the nation are ready to permit it to collect in taxes. Out of nothing, the government creates money by fiat, and then spends it. The government's action does not add anything to the available supply of useful goods and services. It merely provides more money and thus brings about a tendency to make prices soar. Those groups of the population to whom the government gives some of this increased quantity of money are now in a position to buy more than they used to buy before. Their appearance on the market leaves a smaller share of the previously available commodities for those persons to whom the government did not give any of the increased money. Faced with higher prices, these people with no

An interview by Professor Percy L. Greaves, Jr., reprinted from the minibook published in 1969 by Constitutional Alliance, Inc.

additional money are forced to restrict their purchases. Thus every inflationary action on the part of the government — and no other group or institution is able to resort to inflationary measures — results in a boon for some people and necessarily a disaster for the rest of the nation.

There cannot be justice in the distribution of the additional quantity of money that the government creates. It is impossible to deal out this additional quantity of new money in a way which will be acknowledged by all people as a "just" distribution. This is what economists have in mind when they refer to what they call the "non-neutrality of money." The pseudo-economists are completely ignorant of this fundamental fact about government interference with the quantity of money. Thus many of them suggest that the government ought to increase the quantity of legal tender money year by year by a definite quantity — 2 percent or 5 percent or 7 percent — they change it from year to year. They make these suggestions without realizing that such increases necessarily mean that one group of the population is helped while the rest of the population is hurt.

These advocates of annual increases in the quantity of money never mention the fact that for all those who do not get a share of the newly created additional quantity of money, the government's action means a drop in their purchasing power which forces them to restrict their consumption. It is ignorance of this fundamental fact that induces various authors of economic books and articles to suggest a yearly increase of money without realizing that such a measure necessarily brings about an undesirable impoverishment of a great part, even the majority, of the population.

GREAVES: *Whom does the inflation help? And whom does it hurt?*

MISES: The various groups of the population are not affected in the same way by the inflation. There are some people whose economic standard the inflation improves.

GREAVES: *Who are they?*

MISES: These are, this I mentioned already, the people to whom the government gives the newly created quantities of money. Then there are the people who are profiting from the fact that those first receivers of the additional money are buying goods and services which they are selling. But those who are selling goods and services for which the demand doesn't increase, or even drops, on account of the inflation, are losers.

Still worse is the situation of those who are living on pensions and the income from savings.

GREAVES: *What is the effect of inflation on the savings of the masses?*
MISES: This is a very important part of the problem. The servants of government say, "Who is against this increase in the quantity of money? The rich people. We are doing something very useful and necessary and beneficial for the masses. Why? Because if the quantity of money increases, the purchasing power of the dollar decreases. This means that the burden of debts becomes easier and thus the poor debtors are favored at the expense of the rich creditors."

This was perfectly correct twenty-five hundred years ago in Athens, when the great statesman Solon exacted economic reforms cancelling public and private debts. Solon had to deal with what we today call "social problems." At that time the debtor was typically the poor man and the creditor was the rich man. The rich people could save and increase their possessions by investing in real property, houses, businesses, forests, and other landed property. For the masses of the people things were different. Most of them couldn't save at all, and those who could save a few pieces of money could only hide them in a dark corner of their premises, but this was all. They were not in a position to make savings grow by lending them against interest.

But we no longer live in Athens in the days of Solon. Nor do we live under the conditions of the Middle Ages or of the sixteenth, seventeenth, and eighteenth centuries, when the poor people couldn't save. Under capitalistic conditions the situation is very different. Capitalism has enriched the masses, not all of them, of course, because capitalism still has to fight the hostility of the governments. But under capitalistic conditions it is no longer true that the creditors are the rich and the debtors the poor.

Capitalism has made it possible for the masses of the poorest strata of the population, the people who have less — I don't want to say they are poor in the sense in which one frequently uses the term, only that they are poorer than the rich people — to save and invest their savings indirectly in the operation of business. They invest in savings deposits, insurance policies, and bonds. The rich people who are familiar with business conditions invest their savings in the common stock of corporations and in the purchase of real estate. But corporations and owners of real estate owe money, either because they have issued bonds, or because they have some connection with a bank which lends them money for the conduct of their affairs. The banks obtain this money from the savings accounts of simple citizens and the large insurance companies buy bonds with premiums paid by these poorer people.

The masses, people with less wealth than the richer people, have invested their savings "for a rainy day" in bonds, savings deposits, pension funds, and insurance policies. The value of all these investments depends on the value of the monetary unit. When the purchasing power of the monetary unit drops, their value shrinks. The masses, therefore, on account of having invested their savings in these assets, are creditors; the millionaires, the owners of real estate, common stocks, and so on, are debtors. Then if the government embarks on a policy of inflation, the fact that the debts are getting smaller does not hurt the rich so much, but the middle classes and the masses of people who have saved all their lives in order to enjoy a better old age, or to take care of themselves during periods of sickness, or to make it possible for them to educate their children, and so on. These poorer people are the big losers from inflation. This is what people do not realize when they are talking about various plans for increasing the quantity of money. The main victims of an inflationary policy are the less fortunate members of the population, while those who experience a boom are the owners of business enterprises and real estate who owe money to banks, insurance companies, or bond holders.

GREAVES: *What is the effect of inflation on charitable, educational, and other endowed institutions?*

MISES: One of the effects of inflation is the financial destruction of all institutions and foundations based upon funds invested in bonds. One of the great evils that the fantastic inflations of world wars brought to the European countries was the almost complete disappearance of the funds of many humanistic, scientific, and charitable institutions. All European countries asked that the funds of such institutions be invested in bonds issued by the government or its subdivisions. The World War inflations wiped these funds out almost entirely.

For instance, an Austrian, who had been raised and educated in an Austrian orphan asylum, migrated to the United States. There, as a U.S. citizen, he acquired a considerable fortune. He died a short time before the outbreak of World War I, leaving about $2 million in U.S. funds for an orphan asylum in Austria. According to Austrian law, such funds had to be invested in domestic bonds while plans were made for new buildings. The construction had to wait, of course, until after the war. By that time, the inflation had entirely destroyed the purchasing power of this benefaction; nobody received any benefits from it at all.

GREAVES: *Could this happen again?*

MISES: We may say that can't happen here. But what we are now experiencing every day is that the savings of the majority of the American population invested in insurance policies, savings accounts, bonds, pension funds, and so on, are melting away.

GREAVES: *If the government stops inflating, must we have more unemployment?*

MISES: The unemployment problem consists of the fact that people are asking for too much. It would be better not to talk about unemployment but about wage rates that are too high. Unemployment is the necessary effect of the fact that workers are not ready to work at wage rates which consumers are prepared to refund to the employer in buying the product. In the case of wages, people do not wish to admit what they admit with respect to everything else. They do not realize that persons who overrate their own skills and ask for higher wages than the customers are prepared to repay their employer must remain unemployed.

An employer cannot pay more to an employee than the equivalent of the value the employee, according to the judgment of the buying public, adds to the value of the product. If the employer were to pay more, he would suffer losses and finally go bankrupt. In paying wages, the employer acts, as it were, as an agent of the consumers. It is on the consumers that the incidence of the wage rates falls.

If nominal wage rates — wage rates expressed in terms of money — are too high for the state of the market, a part of the potential labor force will be unemployed. If the government then increases the quantity of money, that is, inflates, the unemployed can get jobs again. However, this happens only because, under the changed monetary conditions, prices are rising, or, in other words, the purchasing power of the monetary unit is dropping. The same amount of *money* wages then means less in *real* wages — that is, in terms of the goods and services that can be bought with the money wages. Inflation can cure unemployment only by reducing the potential wage earner's *real* wage.

But then the unions ask for a new increase in wages in order to keep up with the rising cost of living and we are back where we were before, with large-scale unemployment. This is what has happened in this country in recent years, as well as in many other countries.

If you want higher wage rates, you have to accumulate more capital. The more capital — other things being equal — the higher wage rates climb in a free market, that is a market not manipulated by the government or the unions. At these market wage rates all who want to be employed can get jobs.

Now, as the majority of the consumers are precisely the same people who are working and earning wages, it is in fact the workers themselves who determine what wages are compatible with full employment. The idea that workers and consumers are different persons is erroneous. Ultimately the workers and the consumers are the same people. For instance, the railroad workers themselves are consumers who are consuming all those products which cannot be produced and brought to places of consumption without the cooperation of the railroads. If the railroad employees get an increase in wage rates, this means that the railroad employees, as consumers, will be among those who will also have to pay more for the services rendered by the railroads.

The faulty ideas which underlie all discussions concerning labor and wage rates is that the masses of wage earners are producing for an upper "class" of capitalists and do not themselves enjoy the fruits of their efforts. The truth is that by far the greater part of all that is produced by the wage earners is also consumed by them, the wage earners, who are members of the same "class." The main characteristic of capitalism is precisely the fact that it is mass production for supplying the masses. What is not understood by the philosophy underlying union policies is that by far the greater part of all the goods and services produced under capitalism is consumed by the same people who are working in the shops, yards, and factories.

Unemployment cannot be fought by inflation. Unemployment is always due to the fact that to employ a man at the wage rate he is asking for results in a loss for the employer. As long as the employment of an additional man is profitable, because there are buyers who are ready to refund to the employer what he has spent in hiring the worker, there is no unemployment.

There prevails on a free labor market a constant tendency toward full employment. In fact, the only reasonable and successful full employment policy is to let the free market determine the height of wage rates. If union pressure or government decrees raise wage rates above this free market height, unemployment of a part of the potential labor force necessarily develops.

GREAVES: *Then minimum wage laws do not raise workers' wages?*

MISES: People think that if they raise the minimum wage rates they will improve somebody's conditions. This is one of the most dreadful mistakes, for there are people whose work, in the opinion of the buying public — i.e., the consumers — is not worth the higher wage rates. Therefore these people remain unemployed. Legally decreed minimum wage rates are either useless or they create additional unemployment. If the consumers, in buying the product, are not prepared to refund to the employer all that he has spent in producing the product, he will be forced to stop production and therefore the employment of workers.

GREAVES: *Many influential people say the cause of our monetary trouble is the unfavorable balance of payments. They imply that the higher prices due to the fall in the purchasing power of the dollar are a result of the fact that Americans are spending abroad more than foreigners are spending in the United States. They think that the balance of payments determines the purchasing power of the dollar in foreign trade and consequently in domestic prices, so they want to stop the American inflation by passing laws to reduce imports and to stop American citizens from traveling or spending money abroad. What do you have to say about that?*

MISES: This interpretation of American monetary troubles is absolutely wrong. The balance of payments argument is made in order to deny the government's responsibility for inflation. It is an attempt to exonerate the government policy of increasing the quantity of money and to indict the American people for the tendency of prices to rise. From this point of view the government wants to restrict the importation of goods which they consider unnecessary and to prevent Americans from traveling abroad.

Now let us see what this means. When U.S. citizens buy some imported product, they must pay for it. When the government prevents them from buying this foreign product, let us say French champagne, they will not put these dollars into a package and send this package to the government so it will have more money to pay the deficits of its enterprises — the post office, for instance. The citizens will buy something else on the domestic market. The prices of the domestic products they purchase will then go up on account of the fact that there is now a greater demand for them. This will bring about higher prices for some things which were previously exported and these things will no longer be exported.

In addition, the fact that an American law makes it impossible or more expensive for Americans to buy certain foreign products that they used to buy will bring about a lowering of the demand for these foreign products. Consequently, in order to make it possible for the foreign producers to sell all their production, they will tend to drop the prices of these foreign products. As a result, the foreigners will no longer be in a position to buy as much, to maintain the same standard of living as they did before. They will have to restrict their consumption. They will, for instance, have to restrict the purchase of some imported commodities, let us say, American cars. Thus, it comes about that when a country restricts its imports, it necessarily also restricts its exports. When foreigners sell less on *our* markets, they then have less means to buy *our* products.

The truth is that exports and imports depend on one another and in this sense are balanced. If we restrict the quantity of U.S. funds in the hands of foreigners, by anti-import measures and anti–overseas travel measures, we are necessarily restricting the quantity of the means — the money — that these foreigners are able to spend on U.S. goods or visits to America.

If all the countries of the world, keeping consistently to this balance of payments theory, were to make imports impossible, they would thereby also make exports impossible. Then every country would remain economically isolated. Prices and living costs would go up, not only because the government increases the quantity of domestic money, but also because the consumers would no longer have access to products that could be produced abroad under more favorable conditions. The result of all these policies would be more and more restriction of international trade.

Foreign trade is not one-sided. It is always necessarily a mutual exchange of goods and services between various countries for the mutual advantage of their citizens. A restriction of foreign trade means a reduction in the standard of living of the citizens of the countries whose trade is restricted.

GREAVES: *Why does this "balance of payments" situation develop only between countries and not between different sections of one country? There are many states in the United States with populations larger than, or at least not much smaller than the populations of many independent European nations. Why don't we hear the same complaints about the citizens of Illinois spending their money in Florida that we hear about the people who go to Paris and buy French perfumes, supposedly enriching France while impoverishing the United States?*

MISES: Because the various American states have no independent monetary policies. There cannot be any inflation in Iowa that is not at the same time and to the same extent also an inflation in the forty-nine other states of the Union.

And you needn't think only of trade among the states. People say it is harmful that France produces and sells to the United States only goods which are very bad, frivolous, immoral—books, novels, champagne, concerts, theatrical performances, and opera productions in Paris. But you could say the same thing also about, let us say, Brooklyn and Manhattan. Manhattan sells concerts, conferences, theatrical performances, opera productions, and so on, to the people from Brooklyn. Brooklyn people are spending their money in Manhattan. A Brooklyn man could say: "Why does my neighbor spend his money to attend an opera performance in Manhattan? Why does he not spend his money in Brooklyn?" And if you carry this reasoning step-by-step farther in the same direction, you would arrive eventually at perfect autarky, i.e., self-sufficiency, economic isolation of every group and political unit.

GREAVES: *What needs to be done?*

MISES: What is needed in order to avoid all these unwelcome effects of inflation is to restore honesty in the conduct of monetary affairs. This means to restore integrity in the conduct of all governmental affairs also and especially in observing precisely the financial provisions of the Constitution.

GREAVES: *Which provisions do you mean?*

MISES: Those financial provisions which make it illegal for the government to spend more than the budget permits. Every penny the government spends ought to be collected by the tax authorities, proceeding in strict conformity with the laws of the country.

GREAVES: *Then you wouldn't permit the Federal Government to borrow?*

MISES: If Congress wants to spend more it should make legal the issuance of additional quantities of government bonds — to be sold to the public, not to the commercial banks.

GREAVES: *It has long been illegal for Americans to own gold.* * *Has this contributed to the problem?*

MISES: The law that forbids the holding of gold to U.S. citizens makes it impossible for them to prevent the government's attempts to inflate. If individual citizens had had the right to hoard gold, the lunacy of the attempts to substitute paper for gold would have become visible long ago.

GREAVES: *Then you don't believe in "paper gold"?*

MISES: There is gold and there is paper, but there is no such thing as "paper gold." If private citizens in this country had the right to buy and to hold gold, a considerable quantity of gold would be owned today by U.S. citizens and it wouldn't be difficult to restore the U.S. monetary standard, nor to restore the monetary standards of the whole Western civilization.

GREAVES: *Would increasing the "price of gold" help?*

MISES: What is called, in rather mendacious terminology, "raising the price of gold" means in fact acknowledging legally the effects of inflation. The raising of the "price of gold" is in fact the acknowledgment by the government of the depreciation of the country's legal currency system. An honest description of the case would not talk of raising the "price of gold" but of raising the price of all necessities, of all the things people need for daily consumption.

GREAVES: *Many people believe that money is necessarily a creation of the government. Is this so?*

MISES: Money is a phenomenon of the market, a medium of exchange. But governments think of money as a product of government activity. Money is not a creation of the government. This should be

---

* The right to own gold, denied to U.S. citizens in 1933, and still denied at the time of this interview (1969), was finally restored as of January 1, 1975.

repeated again and again. All these doctrines begin with the idea that there is something more in money than the agreement of the parties to exchange something against a definite kind and quantity of this money. It is government interference that has destroyed money in the past and it is government interference that is destroying money again.

Money, as such, is an institution of the market economy. It is one of the *fundamental* institutions of the market. A market without money is impossible. A market is precisely the freedom of the people to produce, to trade, and to consume. When money is destroyed, when monetary exchange becomes impossible, then the existence of the market economy also comes to an end. And a free system without a market is impossible.

A thing cannot serve as money if the government has the right to increase its quantity *ad libitum.*

GREAVES: *Would it be more satisfactory if the government didn't mint or print the money, but left that function to private institutions?*

MISES: That assumes the manufacture of money by private institutions would be free from government interference. The trouble is not due to the fact that the government has the mint and the printing presses. Even if the governments had never tried to manufacture money, their influence would not have been different from what it is today.

The problem comes from the fact that it is the function of governments to adjudicate all disputes which might otherwise give rise to violence involving any of its citizens. The opportunity for governments to deal with monetary problems comes about in the same way in which they are concerned with all contracts providing for the exchange of goods and services. For example, governments are called upon every day to decide whether or not one of the parties to an exchange contract has failed to comply with his contractual obligations. A court's finding of such a failure then justifies compulsion on the part of the governmental apparatus of violent oppression.

If both parties fulfill their contractual obligations instantly and simultaneously, no disputes are likely to arise which would induce either of the parties to appeal to the courts. However, if the obligations of one or both parties are deferred for a period of time, it may happen that the courts will be asked how the terms of the contract are to be enforced. If the payment of a sum of money is involved, this involves the task of determining what meaning is to be given to the monetary terms in the contract. Actually, the court is asked to define what must be legally accepted as money. The power to give certain pieces of paper *legal tender* quality is one that requires constant watching.

The transition from coins to paper made it easy to inflate. All the monetary troubles come from the fact that many governments, for financial purposes, abuse the power to determine that pieces of paper are the legal equivalent of the coins of the realm. The power that this abuse of the judicial supremacy of the laws and the courts confers on the governments is the sole source of all the monetary troubles. The private minting and printing of money would not eliminate this power.

GREAVES: *In your many writings on monetary problems you have always spoken highly of the gold standard. Why?*

MISES: The practical problem of money today in the whole world is precisely this: Taxes are unpopular. And the most unpopular thing is to substitute a higher tax for a lower tax. The government wants to spend more without increasing taxes. Now what does the government do in such a situation? The government increases the quantity of money — it resorts to inflation. Prices necessarily go up as a greater quantity of money appears on the market and "chasing" after a not-increased quantity of goods.

The gold standard did not fail. The governments sabotaged it and still go on sabotaging it. The governments established a legal ratio between gold and the monetary unit. (For the United States the ratio established by law is that one ounce of gold is the legal equivalent of $35.)* But then, by inflating, the government makes it impossible to maintain this *legal tender* ratio. This is the monetary problem. Governments do not want to admit that an increased quantity of paper money brings about higher prices, in terms of the government-issued paper money, for all commodities and, of course, also for gold.

The quantity of money is the decisive problem. The quality that makes gold fit for service as money is precisely the fact that the quantity of gold cannot be manipulated by governments. The gold standard has one quality, one virtue. It is that the quantity of gold cannot be increased in the way that paper notes can be increased. The usefulness

---

* This artificially maintained ratio of $35.00 to one ounce of gold was raised in December 1971 to $38.00, and in February 1973 to $42.42. And then the ratio of the U.S. paper dollar to gold was allowed to float on the international market.

of the gold standard consists in the fact that it makes the supply of money depend on the profitability of mining gold, and thus checks large-scale inflationary ventures on the part of governments.

Gold cannot be produced in a cheaper way by any governmental bureau, committee, institution, office, international agency, or so on. This is the only justification for the gold standard. One has tried again and again to find some method to substitute these qualities of gold in some other way. But all these methods have failed, and will ever fail as long as governments are committed to the idea that it is all right for a government, which has not collected enough money to pay its expenses by taxing its citizens or by borrowing on the market, to increase the quantity of money simply by printing it.

The eminence of the gold standard is to be seen in the fact that the gold standard alone makes the determination of the monetary unit's purchasing power independent of the ambitions and activities of dictators, political parties, and pressure groups. No government is powerful enough to destroy the gold standard as long as the market economy is not entirely suppressed. The gold standard alone is what the nineteenth-century champions of representative government, civil liberties, and prosperity for all meant by "sound money."

44

On the International Monetary Problem

What is nowadays called governmental monetary management encompasses two kinds of policy. It is, on the one hand, deficit spending, i.e., undisguised inflation to enable the government to spend over and beyond the amount of funds collected by taxation or borrowed from the public. It is, on the other hand, a policy of easy money, i.e., of attempts to lower the market rate of interest by credit expansion.

The governments as well as their henchmen are fully convinced that this expansionist policy is highly beneficial to the immense majority of all decent people. They emphatically deny that increasing the quantity of money in circulation is what economists, politicians, and all sane people used to call and still call "inflation." As they see it, inflation has nothing to do with the quantity of money in circulation; rather it is a reprehensible procedure of greedy businessmen that ought to be prevented by government control of prices. In the eyes of the official doctrine, interest is essentially a factor hindering the development of "really productive" business. Such a doctrine views interest as a tribute that the industrious members of society are compelled to pay to a race of lazy moneylenders.

Only a few outsiders have the courage to deviate from the government-decreed methods of dealing with the expansionist policy. Very seldom does one meet in public discussion of the problem of rising prices and wage rates any reference to the government-made inflation. It is not that the authors of books, articles, and speeches about the problems involved knowingly avoid dealing with the genuine cause of the phenomena investigated. They are honest in their argumentation. Their "new economics" has told them that nothing but evil can emerge from the "anarchy" of the market. Their panacea is the "plan,"

Reprinted, by permission of *The New American*, from *American Opinion*, March 1967.

i.e., the government's unlimited dictatorship in all economic and political affairs.

In monetary matters mankind has already for many years enjoyed
the benefits of a world-embracing planning office, but it seems that the
results do not satisfy anybody. There is irritating talk about an international or world problem of the nations' mutual monetary relations.
There are national and international committees and conferences for
the study of the matter. Many books and innumerable pamphlets and
articles deal with the subject. There is general agreement that the present state is unsatisfactory and that a change is unavoidable. With this in
mind, let us examine the international monetary problem.

Balance of Payments Doctrine

When the servants of a government search for the cause of some unsatisfactory condition, they always discover that the authorities have done
all that could be done for a perfectly satisfactory solution of the matter
in question. But the beneficial effects of their action failed to appear because the people frustrated the wise plan of their rulers. The best-known
doctrine of this type was once the balance of trade theory and later its
modern offshoot, the balance of payments theory.[1]

After all, it made some sense in the nineteenth century when some
people still referred to this long-since entirely refuted doctrine as
justification for some restrictions on the importation of foreign merchandise and on other payments to foreigners. It gave the government
an excuse — of course, a vicious one — for maintaining that by indulging
in foreign luxuries people were sabotaging their ruler's wise monetary
policy. When domestic money is shipped to foreign countries as payment for imported "superfluous luxuries," proclaimed the officials, it becomes superabundant abroad and therefore its price, in terms of foreign
money, falls, causing the price of the foreign money to rise in terms of
the domestic money. This unwelcome rise in the price of foreign exchange in terms of the domestic money is caused, it is said, by an "unfavorable balance of payments," due to sending money abroad to pay for
foreign imports. This doctrine explained the depreciation of the domestic money by the "unpatriotic" consumption habits of consumers. It

---

1. For a brilliant critique of the balance of payments theory of foreign exchange see Rothbard,
Man, Economy and State (Princeton, 1962), pp. 719–22.

is, therefore, the sacred duty of good government to prevent such bad citizens from damaging the interests of the nation.

But in recent decades the declarations of U.S. government authorities with reference to the "balance of payments" bogey could not even seemingly exonerate the government and make the people responsible. The government of the United States in this period not only spent scores of billions of dollars for the conduct of foreign wars and for garrisoning armed forces in far distant parts of the world. It distributed alms of many dozens of billions under the newfangled title of "foreign aid." It was ridiculous demagogy to mention the "balance of payments" issue in connection with the expenses of American tourists visiting the Acropolis, of American students attending the University of Paris, and to pass over in silence the subsidies that enabled various "Führers" of semi-barbarous countries to establish and to preserve their despotic regimes. Only ignorance on the part of the representatives of the "new economics" can explain their attempts to revive the long since entirely discredited "balance of payments" interpretation of mutual exchange ratios between various currencies.

The theory maintained by economists, the so-called *purchasing-power-parity theory*, says: the exchange ratio between different currencies tends toward a point at which it does not make any difference which currency is employed in selling or buying. The parity is characterized by the fact that no gains can be made by buying against units of A currency and selling against units of B currency or vice versa. Any deviation from this parity will be corrected — "automatically," as a frequently misinterpreted term says — by the actions of people who want to profit by such buying and selling. This insight was already implied in the reasoning of Gresham's law. When domestic inflation makes prices in the country of A currency rise while there is no inflation and therefore no general upward movement of prices in the country of B currency, the previous exchange ratio between the two currencies A and B must change.[2]

International Exchange Ratios

If all over the world there prevailed the strict and pure gold standard, no other monetary problems would exist other than technological ones,

2. For a detailed exposition see the writings of Gustav Cassel, Edwin Cannan, and Benjamin McAlester Anderson and my own contributions.

e.g., that of properly minting the coins. No government interference with the technical production of coins would be necessary. The same would be the case if there could be established a world monetary center, not a bank operated by angels removed from all earthly concerns and interests.

In our actual world every government claims national sovereignty in all monetary matters. Even this state of affairs could result, at least for a majority of civilized nations, in rather satisfactory conditions, i.e., a state of affairs characterized by the absence of any monetary problems and crises. In order to achieve and to preserve such a state of affairs every nation belonging to this group of civilized nations would have to abstain from any kind of "monetary welfarism." It would have to strictly avoid any policy that would interfere with the — once and for all time — established exchange ratio between its domestic currency and the currencies of all the other nations that proceeded in the same way and thereby belonged to this group of civilized nations.

The actual state of affairs is entirely different. Most of the civilized nations are officially committed to a policy of a stable exchange ratio either between their national currency and gold or, what ought to be the same, between their national currency and the currencies of countries that also aim officially at a stable exchange ratio between their own currency and those of other nations that are committed to the same principle. But the government economists maintain there are conditions that make it extremely difficult or even quite impossible for the monetary authorities of a nation to preserve this officially decreed exchange ratio. There are unpatriotic citizens whose business transactions impair the nation's balance of payments. And, still worse, there are speculators who aim directly at making the price of foreign exchange rise above the parity fixed by the authorities. To frustrate these "attacks" upon the stability of the foreign exchange rates is believed to be one of the foremost duties of good government.

In the terminology of economics, what the military jargon employed by monetary authorities qualifies as "attacks" is a rising demand for foreign exchange. Notwithstanding its policy of increasing the quantity of money and lowering interest rates, the government wants to maintain a definite exchange ratio between the domestic (national) currency on the one side and gold and foreign exchange of other countries committed to the same policy on the other side. As the demand for gold or foreign exchange rises, the government sees the amount of its "reserves" dwindle. This is the situation in which the governments and public opinion declare that "something must be done." There is no need to expatiate about this fact and its consequences. The question to be raised and answered is: What is it that increases the demand for foreign exchange and moves people to offer higher prices in domestic currency for it?

Inflation and Inflationism

Practically all governments consider the two foremost goals of monetary policy to be first, to inflate their nation's currency system in order to be able to spend more than the amounts collected by taxation or borrowed from the public; and secondly, to bring about credit expansion in order to lower the rates of interest below the height they would attain on a free money market. It is these policies that necessarily and inevitably produce all those phenomena which the monetary authorities ascribe to the alleged unfavorable state of the balance of payments and to the machinations of speculators.

Let us begin with inflation and inflationism. *Inflation* is an increase in the quantity of money in circulation that surpasses the increase in the demand for money for cash holding. *Inflationism* is a government policy of increasing the quantity of money in order to enable the government to spend more than the funds provided by taxation and borrowing. Such "deficit spending" is nowadays, as everybody knows, the characteristic signature of the U.S. government's financial policies. It is highly praised under the label of "the new economics."

Of course, these advocates of boundless inflation have adopted a terminology that attaches to the words a different meaning. They use the term "inflation" to refer to what is merely the unavoidable effect of inflation, namely the general tendency of prices and wages toward higher points, and they ascribe this tendency to the greed and avarice of businessmen. They pretend that the government is sincerely and honestly committed to a policy of price stability.

Let us see. The government plans an additional expenditure. Let us assume that the government wants to raise the salaries of a group of public servants. It collects the funds required by raising the taxes to be paid by certain people. Then the increase in purchases, in terms of the national money, on the part of those benefited by higher salaries corresponds to the drop in purchases on the part of those who were forced to pay higher taxes. By and large, no change in the purchasing power of the monetary unit results.

But if the government simply provides the funds required for the higher salaries by issuing an additional quantity of legal-tender money, things are different. Those benefited by the new additional money compete on the market with all those whose demand had already been instrumental in the determination of the previous prices. An increased quantity of money is offered to buy a not-increased quantity of goods. The outcome is higher prices for vendible merchandise, or, what is the same, a drop in the "purchasing power" of the country's monetary unit.

Let us assume the exchange ratio between the Ruritanian *rur* and the Maritanian *mar* was 1 to 2. Now the Ruritanian government inflates and consequently prices expressed in *rurs* are rising while no changes occur in Maritania. It is obvious that such a state of affairs must necessarily bring about a corresponding alteration in the price of *rurs* expressed in *mars* or, what is the same, in the price of *mars* expressed in *rurs*. For now one *rur* buys only a smaller quantity of merchandise than 2 *mars*. One can gain by buying against *mars*, selling against *rurs*, and then exchanging these *rurs* at the rate of 1:2 against *mars*. Such transactions are inevitably bound to transform the previous exchange rate and finally to establish again a purchasing-power-parity rate adequate to the altered purchasing power of the *rur*.

The regular course of events under present conditions is this: Ruritania inflates and consequently Ruritanian prices are rising. But the Ruritanian government is anxious to preserve the previous exchange rate against foreign currencies. It tries to maintain this rate in its own exchange operations. As it is profitable to buy *mars* at the official rate, the demand for them increases and the monetary authorities of Ruritania see their "reserves" of foreign exchange drop. This is the emergency that is called "illiquidity" and makes the official circles clamor for more "reserves."

Then there is a second kind of government policy that results likewise in an increased demand for foreign exchange. The governments want to lower the market rate of interest. They resort to various measures for the attainment of this end. As far as these measures bring about credit expansion, they produce the same effects which the simple inflation of deficit spending brings about. But they disarrange besides the equilibrium of the market for short-term loans. Funds are withdrawn from the country's market for short-term loans, usually called *money market*, precisely because the authorities have temporarily succeeded in lowering domestic interest rates. This movement too results in a rising demand for foreign exchange.

We see now that this intensified demand for foreign exchange, these "attacks" upon the "reserves" in the hands of the monetary authorities, the central bank or its equivalent, are neither acts of God nor the outcome of machinations on the part of antipatriotic selfish citizens or of foreign enemies. They are the inevitable reaction of the market upon the monetary interventionism of the government, its misguided and misplaced monetary welfarism.

Inflationism is not a variety of economic policies. It is an instrument of destruction; if not stopped very soon, it destroys the market entirely. There is no need to refer to historical experiences, such as that of the German Weimar Republic of the years of 1920–23. It is a shame that in the discussions concerning present-day monetary problems some of the nonsense is revived that was brought forward in earlier periods of inflation.

Inflation Cannot Last

Any variety of inflationism and any attempts of institutionally lowering the rate of interest are incompatible with plans for the establishment of something that could be called an international system or order of monetary affairs. As long as the governments of many or even of most of the commercially important nations are committed to such policies, it is idle to talk about an efficient international organization of monetary matters.

Nothing characterizes the state of present-day "official" economic doctrine better than the fact that in the great flood of books and articles published about the international monetary problems there is hardly any reference to the issues of inflation and anti-interest measures. In the light of this literature and the pronouncements of the "monetary authorities" there prevails some mysterious evil, mostly called lack of liquidity, that thwarts the allegedly well-designed endeavors of governments and central banks to render international monetary conditions perfectly satisfactory. There is not enough "liquidity"; the "reserves" of the central banks, or of the institutions to which the functions of a central bank have been entrusted, are not large enough. The remedy is obvious: one needs more reserves. How can this be achieved? Of course, by "creating" more legal tender of those nations for whose notes and deposits the demand is most urgent.

Ruritania has succeeded in lowering its domestic loan market's interest rates. The result is a withdrawal of short-term funds from Ruritania, and a rising demand for *mars*. The Ruritanian central bank sees its reserve in *mars* and in other foreign currencies dwindle. There is, say the experts, a solution for this problem: let the Maritanian central bank or other central banks lend to their Ruritanian sister the *mars* or other foreign money required. That means let the foreign banks inflate up to a point at which their own currencies are no longer better than that of Ruritania.

The insufficiency of this suggestion moved some authors to elaborate plans for a "reserve currency." This currency should serve merely as an increase in the "reserve" of central banks. But the withdrawals of funds from Ruritania are made not only by other nations' central banks; they are made first of all by people who want to invest or to spend the funds withdrawn. For these people a "reserve currency" is useless. They want to get "real" money, not a "reserve" money.

Whatever people may say about a policy of increasing the quantity of fiat money, there is one aspect of it that even the most obstinate of its advocates cannot deny: Inflationism cannot last; if not radically stopped in time, it must lead inexorably to a complete breakdown. It is an expedient of people who do not care a whit for the future of their nation and its civilization. It is the policy of Madame de Pompadour, the mistress of the French King Louis XV—*Après nous le déluge*.

Today we are still able to stop the progress of inflation and to return to sound principles of financing government expenditure. But will we have the same opportunity tomorrow?

Appendix

To prevent a misinterpretation of the preceding statements concerning the height of the rate of interest and the height of profits some additional remarks are appropriate.

In dealing with the problems of an inflationary upward movement of prices, when one refers to the gross rate or market rate of interest, one must realize that the expectation of such a change in the height of prices will affect the size of the gross interest rate. People who expect a rise in definite prices are prepared to borrow at higher gross rates of interest than they would be ready to pay if they were to expect a less momentous rise in prices, or no rise at all. On the other hand the lender under such conditions grants loans only if the gross rate agreed upon is higher than it would be in the absence of such expectations. Thus, the expectation of rising prices has the tendency to make the market rate, the gross rate of interest, rise. There appears in this gross market rate a component—called the "price premium" by economists—that owes its existence to the cognition and anticipation of the inflationary movement of prices.

There is need to stress this point to show the futility of the usual methods of distinguishing between what people call low and high rates of interest. When the market rate rises above the height they consider "normal," people believe that everything possible has been done to keep "speculation" under control. From this point of view they gauge the raising of the rate of discount by one or a few percentage points by the monetary authorities as a "check" upon "inflationary speculation."

Another fact to be noted concerns the height of profits. All customary methods of accounting are necessarily based upon the unit of the nation's currency system. They do not pay heed to changes in this unit's purchasing power. One result of this neglect is that with the progress of inflation the habitual depreciation quotas shrink substantially, and that profits calculated without taking this fact into consideration are illusory. A second source of overvaluation of an enterprise's profits is due to the drop in the money's purchasing power occurring in the period between the acquisition and sale of merchandise. And then come the tax authorities and the labor unions and claim their share of these "excessive" profits that in fact, i.e., when calculated in gold or a not-inflated foreign currency, may be not profits at all, but losses.

45

Small and Big Business

A characteristic feature of the contemporary policies of all the not out-right socialist nations is animosity against business. Public opinion contrasts the mean selfishness of those engaged in the conduct of business with the lofty altruism of the politicians and the public servants. The profits made by those enterprises that succeed in filling, in the best possible and cheapest way, the most urgent wants of the consumers, i.e., of everybody, are called "unearned" income in the tax laws and are subject to confiscatory and discriminatory imposts. To restrict as much as possible the sphere in which private enterprise is free to operate — the so-called private sector of a nation's economy — and to expand concomitantly the public sector is considered as one of the foremost goals of economic policies. While paying lip service to the principle of free enterprise, nations are step-by-step adopting the principles of socialism and totalitarianism.

In spite of all the obstacles put in its way, private enterprise demonstrates anew each day its incomparable efficiency. New and better products appear again and again on the market and are made accessible to the many, not only to a small minority of privileged nabobs. The "common man" enjoys in the capitalistic countries amenities of which the richest people of ages gone by did not even dream. Not so long ago the socialist critics of capitalism used to blame the market economy for the penury of a part of the population, that is, for the fact that capitalism had not yet totally wiped out the unfortunate effects of the pre-capitalistic methods of production. Today they criticize capitalism for the "affluence" of the private citizen and suggest methods for depriving them of a great part of this "affluence" in order to enable their rulers to spend more for objectives for which the individual citizens do not spend, obviously because they do not approve of them.

Paper presented at the 1961 (Turin, Italy) meeting of the Mont Pelerin Society.

The only goal of production is to provide for consumption in the best possible and cheapest way. To serve the consumers is the objective of all business activities. Profits can be earned only by supplying the consumers in the best possible and cheapest way with all those things they want to use. In the market economy the consumers — the people — are supreme.

In competing for the patronage of the consumers, the capitalistic factory outstripped the traditional handicrafts that had prevailed in precapitalistic ages. Romantic dreamers whose information about the old artisans stems from works such as Richard Wagner's *Meistersinger** may deplore this fact. But consumers are now getting more, better, and cheaper shoes than in the time of artisan cobblers. It would be a boon for the barefooted masses of India if the old-fashioned workshops of their shoemakers had to give way to modern shoe factories.

Small Businesses

In the present there is in capitalistic countries, by and large, no longer a keen rivalry between big business and small business. There are lines in which the small-size enterprise can hold its own. Again and again changes in technological conditions and in marketing methods give bigger enterprises the opportunity to enter fields which hitherto have been a domain of small outfits. But on the other hand new specialties develop in which the small shop prevails. There is still room left for small-scale enterprise not only in the repair business, in the service trades, and in some fields of retailing, but even in some highly specialized processing jobs and certainly also in many categories of agriculture.

It is, of course, misleading to seek from statistics information about the role small units play in the structure of modern business. The features on the basis of which statistics classify an outfit as independent refer to legal, administrative, and technological characteristics. They qualify as independent businesses many jobs that substantially depend on a big-size concern. In many branches the distribution of the products and the rendering of the various services which the buyer expects and regularly gets from the seller is customarily accomplished by firms or

---

* *Die Meistersinger von Nürnburg*, an opera by Richard Wagner (1813–83) laid in sixteenth-century Nuremburg. Hans Sachs, a kind and elderly Meistersinger (master singer), a cobbler whose shop is seen in a couple of scenes, enables a young knight to become a Meistersinger and win the hand of his ladylove.

individuals whose business has the legal character of an autonomous existence, although it is essentially merely an outlet of a big concern.

Neither can we obtain more reliable information about the actual number of flourishing small business outfits by observing the purchasing habits of people. Even in the shopping districts of the big urban agglomerations we see interspersed among the numerous outlets of chain stores a rather impressive variety of seemingly independent retailers and artisans. But here again it is impossible, without a searching scrutiny of every individual case, to sift those that are really independent from those that are not.

A substantial antagonism between big concerns and small independent businessmen still prevails in retailing. Chain stores, department stores, and supermarkets are annexing more and more of the field previously served by the small shopkeeper. In almost every country trade associations of small businesses try to delay or even to stop this evolution. They aim at a privileged position for themselves and at legal and administrative restriction of the operations of their financially more potent competitors. Public opinion sympathizes with their claims and political parties promise to support them. But the consumers do not back up these endeavors. More and more people stop patronizing the small shops and turn to their competitors.

Those trade associations and pressure groups of small businesses that plan to improve the competitive power of their members' outfits by legislative measures, restricting the operations of big-scale enterprises, are engaged in a hopeless venture. In the long run the consumers will not acquiesce in a policy the costs of which would burden them heavily.

Measures to "Help" Small Businesses

The main argument advanced in favor of measures aiding the small independent shop in its competition with bigger enterprises refers to the moral and civic values inherent in economic independence. People contrast the position of a businessman who is his own boss and is responsible only to himself with that of an employee who is integrated in a huge apparatus and subject to a hierarchy of superior officers. Whatever weight this argument may have, it is out of place in justifying government intervention for the benefit of definite groups of businessmen. The more effective the government's measures of such intervention become, the more do they deprive its beneficiaries of their autonomy and their independence. The outward appearance of economic independence may be retained, but in fact the beneficiary of government support turns more and more into a ward of the administration. He is no longer a self-reliant citizen, but depends on the disposition of government officers and politicians. His discretion is restricted and finally entirely nullified by a bureaucratic apparatus. The policy inaugurated for the preservation of independent middle-class individuals leads to subjecting them to a virtual guardianship.

The best example is provided by the American farm policy. Its objective was to preserve the "family farm" and the free independent farmer, the type of man that made the United States and laid the foundations of its greatness. But the champions of farm aid were not aware of the insoluble contradiction between the ideal aimed at and the methods resorted to for its realization. A farmer supported by the government at the expense of the rest of the population, the immense majority of the people, is no longer independent. The government tells him what to produce and in what quantity, and thus virtually converts him into a public servant. The free farmer depended on the market; his income came from the consumers. The supported farmer depends on the discretion of a huge apparatus of government agencies. He is the lowest subordinate of a hierarchy of superiors. It is true that at the top of this hierarchy stand the president and Congress in whose election he cooperates. Because they canvass his votes, the politicians promise him aid. But it is precisely this aid that necessarily obliterates his independence. One cannot subsidize a man to render him independent. The very fact of receiving aid deprives the recipient of his discretion to determine the conduct of his affairs. This is the dilemma that the men who, in the last years, directed the course of American farm policies had to face, and could not solve because it cannot be solved.

It is the same in all other spheres of business. If the government grants privileges to certain categories of small business, it must neatly circumscribe the conditions that entitle a man to claim these privileges and must enforce these regulations. But then the privileged entrepreneur forfeits his independence and turns into a subordinate of the administrative apparatus entrusted with the enforcement of the law.

There is need to stress the fact that the terms "small business" and "big business" are rather vague and that the classification of a unit of business as big or small is different in different countries and has changed considerably with the passing of time. Those politicians and reformers who in the last decades of the nineteenth century in some of the continental countries of Europe aimed at legislative measures to protect "small business" against the competition of bigger enterprises, were guided by a nostalgic desire to reestablish the conditions of the precapitalistic ages in which artisans — such as tailors, shoemakers, carpenters, and bakers — prevailed in many or most of the branches of processing. But the ideas that inspired in the eighties of the past century the German Baron Vogelsang and the Austrian Prince Liechtenstein find today hardly any support. Perhaps they are a factor in the popular appeal of the French Poujade movement.* But no nation can today seriously consider "abolishing" factories and chain stores and replacing them by independent artisans or by cooperative organizations of craftsmen. In the field of the processing industries the era of the handicrafts is gone.

In the industrially most advanced countries people in speaking nowadays of small business in production more often than not have in mind enterprises that, in regard to the amount of capital invested, the size of their turnover, and the number of employees, fifty or a hundred years ago would have been called big business. These companies and firms are called small only when compared with the mammoth concerns. Here again we must realize that statistics do not provide any reliable information about the number of such really independent enterprises. For many of the corporations belonging to this group are more or less controlled or even fully owned by big concerns.

In dealing with these medium-size business units one must stress the fact that what makes it rather inconvenient for such enterprises to preserve their independence and causes them to sell out to bigger concerns is very often conditions that are not the effect of the state of the market, but of government policies. While the governments and political parties pretend to condemn "concentration," they are committed to policies that are furthering it.

---

* Prince Alois von Liechtenstein (1846–1920), a leader of the Austrian Christian-Socialist Party and a social reformer. K. Frelherr [Baron] von Vogelsang, a convert to Catholicism, and a theoretician of the Christian Socialists. Pierre Poujade, a French politician, responded to the dissatisfaction of farmers and small merchants with tax and economic policy, founding a short-lived movement, the Union de Défense des Commerçants et Artisans (UCDA), which in January 1956 won fifty-two seats in the National Assembly, but won none in 1962.

A typical example: An enterprising man in his twenties starts a new business. He succeeds very well and after twenty or thirty years of strenuous work his firm is rather flourishing. But then it is time for the owner to think of what may happen after his death. His heirs will be liable to pay inheritance taxes of a height that will force them to sell the outfit. Such forced sales bring much less than the price that corresponds to the real worth and net yield of the going business. It could happen that the family will retain but little after having paid their tax liability. In view of these possibilities it appears to the owner more advantageous to sell, while he is still in full vigor, to a big concern for a price paid in stock of the buying corporation. These securities have a broad market and his heirs will be able to sell them without any discount. The inheritance tax will deprive them of a part of the heritage, but not of more than the law was designed to impose upon them.

Capitalism Is Mass Production

Capitalism is mass production for the provision of the masses. The many, the same people who are working in the offices, the shops, the factories, and the farms, consume the greatest part of all the products turned out. In their capacity as consumers they make small enterprises grow into big businesses and force inefficient enterprises to go out of business. It is the efficiency of business, especially also of the biggest — the mammoth — concerns, that provides the masses with the comparatively high standard of living that the common man, the "proletarian" of the Marxian terminology, enjoys in the capitalistic countries. Any further improvements in the average standard of living can be expected only from a still further development of bigness in business. Governmental measures designed to curb big business are slowing down or entirely checking further progress in the material well-being of the masses. They prejudice the interests of the consumers. The bigger an industrial or commercial concern is, the more it depends on the patronage of the masses and the more it is eager to satisfy them.

In the precapitalistic past there was a broad gulf between the voluptuous habits of the well-to-do and the strained circumstances of the many. There was a sharp distinction between the luxuries of the rich and the necessities of the poor. From its very beginnings business, by improving the methods of production, was intent upon making accessible to a greater number of people many of the amenities previously enjoyed only by a tiny minority of wealthy people. But it still took a long time, sometimes many centuries, until an innovation lost its character as a luxury of the few and turned into a commonly used necessity. Capitalism has more and more shortened this period of transition and finally succeeded in virtually eliminating it. In the case of the motor car it still took several decades before the new vehicle turned from a pastime of playboys into an implement of every family. But with the new products developed by contemporary big business this time lag is so short that it practically does not count any longer. There was no sensible period in which the canned and frozen foods, the new textile fibers, radio and television sets, moving pictures, and many other innovations were only within the reach of the wealthy. Products of big business as they are, they can only be designed for mass consumption.

In the precapitalistic ages the difference between rich and poor was the difference between travelling in a coach and four and travelling, sometimes without shoes, on foot. Today in the industrialized parts of the U.S. the difference between rich and poor is the difference between a late-model Cadillac and a second-hand Chevrolet. It is difficult to see how this result could have been achieved without bigness in business.

The instigators of the campaign against bigness in business know very well that there cannot be any question of splitting up the large concerns into medium-size enterprises and of preventing the further growth of firms into bigness. They expatiate about the alleged evils of big business in order to make popular their socialist program. They aim at "social control of business," i.e., at subjecting the conduct of business to the control of government agencies.

Nationalization

The original socialist, or communist, scheme as advanced by the pre-Marxian socialists, the Marxians, the Prussian "state socialists," and the Russian Bolshevists, aimed at wresting the conduct of business from private citizens and transferring it to the government. In order to distinguish his own brand of socialism from that of his foremost rival, the German socialist, Ferdinand Lassalle (1825–64), Karl Marx substituted the term "society" (*Gesellschaft*) for the terms "state" and "government." And he substituted the term "socialization" (*Vergesellschaftung*) of the means of production to distinguish his doctrine from "nationalization"

(*Verstaatlichung*) as practiced by the German Chancellor Prince Otto von Bismarck (1815–98). But the term "socialization" as employed by the German Social-Democrats and the Second International did not mean anything other than "nationalization." The distinction between "socialization" and "nationalization" was merely verbal, a makeshift invented to cope with the special conditions of the German political scene in the age of Bismarck and his successors in office. Both terms signified the same, viz., to take over plants hitherto operated by private citizens and to manage them by government employees. In this sense Lenin approved the opinion that the post office is "an example of the socialist system." He declared as the aim of socialism "to organize the *whole* national economy like the postal system" and promised that "this will free the laboring classes." [1]

What Marx, Lenin, and all their followers failed to see was the fact that all-round nationalization was impracticable in a modern industrial economy. The very idea of nationalization had been hatched by people who lacked the mental capacity to grasp the essential characteristics of the market economy. They looked upon the existing structure of business as upon something permanent. They planned to expropriate the various plants and shops and then to operate them in the way the expropriated "exploiters" had done. They failed to realize the fact that what matters is to adjust daily anew the conduct of affairs to changing conditions and that the eminence of the entrepreneurial system is in its unceasing craving after improvement and the satisfaction of previously latent needs. The entrepreneurs are not people who simply continue what has already been accomplished before. They are essentially innovators, creators of things never heard of previously. This is what those have in mind who speak of the "dynamism" inherent in the capitalistic system of production.

When a nation turns to all-round nationalization of industry, it deprives its people of the benefits they derived from this capitalistic "dynamism." The fanatically anti-capitalistic mentality of our age made the masses in Russia acquiesce in this outcome. It is probable that also the German people would have submitted to these effects willy-nilly if the Germans had adopted Bolshevist methods after their defeat in the first World War. However, the economic conditions of Germany made it impossible to proceed in this way.

1. Lenin, *State and Revolution* (New York: International Publishers, 1932), pp. 43 f.

Post–World War I Germany

Germany — like most of the other countries of Central and Western Europe — is a predominantly industrial country. This means it cannot feed and clothe its population and supply it with the most urgently needed manufactures out of domestic resources. It must import food-stuffs and many badly needed raw materials. It has to pay for these imports by exporting manufactures, most of them produced out of imported raw materials. It must compete on foreign markets with the industries of all other industrial nations. If its exports drop consider-ably, starvation must result. In 1918 all German political parties were ideologically biased against private enterprise and in favor of nation-alization. But the experience of several decades of nationalized and municipalized enterprises had shown them the inefficiency of public conduct of economic affairs. They were clear-sighted enough to real-ize that concerns operated by bureaucrats, according to the pattern of the postal service, would not be able to rebuild the German export trade shattered by the events of the four years of war. Not only the "bourgeois," but no less the majority of those who voted the Social-Democratic ticket were fully aware of the fact that only the much-abused "exploiters" and "jobbers" could succeed in competing on for-eign markets with the businessmen of all other nations. For Germany in 1918 there could not be any question of imitating the Soviet policies. The hard facts of Germany's economic situation caused Karl Kautsky [German socialist (1854–1938)] and his party comrades, who for many decades had impetuously advocated full socialization, to shrink from the realization of their program. Of course, they were not keen enough to see that their resignation implied the abandonment of the essen-tial policies recommended by the first [fl. 1864–74] and the second [fl. 1889–1914] Socialist International, and were bitterly offended when Lenin branded them as "social traitors."

The attitude that the German "majority socialists" adopted in 1918 and 1919 marks a turning point in the socialist movement in the coun-tries of Western industrial civilization. The nationalization issue re-ceded more and more into the background. Only some adamant vision-aries, entirely blinded by Marxian dogmatism and unfit to face reality, still cling in Germany, England, and the United States to the outworn nationalization slogan. With all other foes of the market economy the party cry is now "planning."

While the nationalization scheme was, at least in principle, developed by British and French authors, the all-round planning scheme is of German origin. In the first World War the German government, adopting the socialist ideas of Walter Rathenau (1867–1922), "centralized" one branch of business after the other, i.e., deprived the individual firms and corporations of the power to direct the conduct of their business affairs. Control of their enterprises was transferred to a committee whose members — the nominal entrepreneurs of the branch concerned — were merely an advisory board of a commissary appointed by the Reich's government and bound to obey its orders. Thus the government obtained virtual control of those branches of business that were most important for the provision of the armed forces. As the war went on, the authorities proclaimed in the "Hindenburg plan" the application of this system for all branches of German trade and production. But the Hindenburg program was not yet completely put into effect when the Kaiser's Reich collapsed and its administrative apparatus disintegrated.

As long as the war lasted, people grumbled about this system called "war socialism" or "*Zwangswirtschaft*" (compulsory economy). However, it became popular as soon as it had been abolished. In spring of 1919 a memorandum drawn up by Rudolf Wissell and Wichard G. O. von Moellendorff proclaimed planning, *Zwangswirtschaft*, as the royal road toward socialism and the only program proper for a sincerely socialist party. Henceforth the parties dubbed as the "right" openly advocated it, while the parties of the "left" undecidedly wavered between the support of planning (*Zwangswirtschaft*) and that of nationalization. When in 1930 Heinrich Brüning, an outstanding member of the Catholic Centrum Party, was appointed Chancellor, he began to prepare the return to all-round planning that a short time later was consummated by Hitler. The innovations added to the *Zwangswirtschaft* scheme by Hitler were merely verbal, such as the substitution of the term *Betriebsführer* (shop manager) for the term entrepreneur, the revival of the feudal term *Gefolgschaft* (retinue) to signify a plant's total labor force, and the suppression of the term "labor market."

Socialism in the United States and Great Britain

In the United States the National Industrial Recovery Act (NIRA) of 1933 was an attempt to impose at one stroke the *Zwangswirtschaft*. The attempt failed because the Supreme Court declared the Act unconstitutional. But as planning remained the great slogan of American "left-ism," entrepreneurial discretion in the conduct of business has been step-by-step restricted by vaguely defined powers delegated to an array of administrative agencies.

Great Britain in the second World War adopted by and large the war socialism of the German pattern. But the Labour Party in its stubborn dogmatism failed to realize the fact that this system of central planning was the only form of socialism that could be considered in a predominantly industrial country dependent on the export of manufactures. Just as the German Marxians had done during the first World War, they rejected war socialism as a "bourgeois" makeshift to which the appellation socialism ought to be denied. They proclaimed nationalization as the only method of converting a market economy into a socialist regime. They nationalized the Bank of England, the railroads, the coal mines, and the steel industry. However, this belated revival of the nationalization issue did not substantially affect the trend of British pro-socialist policies. As in the United States, Germany, and the other predominantly industrial countries, in Great Britain too the pro-socialist tendencies manifest themselves today [1961]* chiefly in the advocacy of planning, i.e., of measures restricting the individual enterprises' discretion by subjecting them more and more to "social control," i.e., to the control of government agencies.

"Social Control" or "Planning"

The characteristic feature of this system of social control or planning is to be seen in the fact that it preserves to some extent a sphere in which the initiative of the entrepreneurial spirit can benefit the consumers. The heads of the industrial and commercial concerns are still free to devise improvements and measures to adjust the operation of their plants to the changing conditions of the market. Of course, their discretion is limited by the powers assigned to the bureaucrats. But the inefficiency, indolence, and laxity of some of these controllers prevents them from crippling altogether the initiative of business. A modicum of initiative is still left to the enterprising promoter, especially in matters of foreign trade.

---

* This trend toward "planning" in Great Britain has slowed in recent years as a result of the privatization of some government enterprises.

The greatest of all the achievements of capitalism is to be seen in the fact that in spite of all the obstacles put in its way by governments and by labor unions it still continues to supply the masses with more, better, and cheaper goods. While governments, political parties, bureaucrats, and union bosses are indefatigably intent upon sabotaging the operations of business, private enterprise still succeeds in improving the services it renders to consumers. We can only guess what these much-maligned speculators, promoters, and jobbers could do for the benefit of the people if their initiative were not enchained by the policies of the welfare state.

The reasons why the powers that are prefer, although reluctantly, the "social control" or "planning" system to the system of nationalization are, of course, not to be seen in the inestimable bounties that accrue to the consumers. Politicians care little about such things. What counts for them is, apart from the considerations of export trade, the effect of the two systems upon government finance.

Take the case of the American railroads. The railroad companies are subject to the most rigid control on the part of various government agencies. The government determines the height of the rates the companies are permitted to charge for the services they render to travellers and to shippers. The government agencies cooperate with the unions in fixing the height of the wage rates the employees receive. They connive at the system of featherbedding which forces the companies to support a host of idle loafers. They force the companies to run trains for which the demand of the public is so small that their operation involves substantial losses. They prohibit many reforms that would reduce waste and unnecessary expenditure; they are especially opposed to mergers. Besides, the companies are hurt by heavy discriminatory taxation on the part of the local authorities. Yet most of the companies have avoided bankruptcy and earn surpluses out of which they have to pay to the federal government millions in taxes.*

Now compare this with the conditions of nationalized railroad systems operating in other countries. The management of most of these nationalized railroads involves year after year considerable losses, and these deficits must be made good by contributions out of the

---

* Since 1961, when this paper was written, government regulations and controls led to the bankruptcy of the country's major railroads and their reorganization in the 1970s into the quasi-governmental agencies, heavily subsidized Conrail and Amtrak, with local communities taking over the commuter lines.

government's revenue from taxes. For the United States Treasury the railroads — and equally the telegraph and the telephone systems — are a source of revenue. For many countries the nationalized railroads and telegraph and telephone systems are an item of expenditure.

If the American postal system were operated by private enterprise, it would, even when subject to the control of some government agencies, probably not only render better and cheaper service to the public but also produce a surplus of revenue over costs. It would figure in the Federal budget, not as an item of great expenditure, but as a source of revenue.

Whatever one may think about the inherent faults of the system of "social control" of business or "planning," the fact remains that it is, at least in its present shape, in every regard superior to nationalization, the alternative system of socialist management.

Government Regulation

The antagonism between the two methods available for the transformation of the capitalistic market economy into a socialist system dominates present-day economic discussion. There is practically no longer any political party that would stand for the unhampered market economy. What the politicians nowadays call economic freedom is a system in which the government "regulates" the conduct of business by innumerable decrees and administrative orders and prohibitions. The Western nations do not endorse the Soviet methods of all-round nationalization of all enterprises and farms. But they no less reject the market economy which they smear as Manchesterism [the theory of nineteenth-century advocates of free markets], laissez-faire system, or economic royalism. They give to their own system various names such as New Deal, Fair Deal, or New Frontier in the United States, and "*soziale Marktwirtschaft*" in Germany. The authorities credit their own activities that in manifold ways paralyze the entrepreneurial initiative to introduce improvements in the methods of production and to improve the people's standard of living, and they blame business for all the mischiefs resulting from their own interference with it.

Not only the politicians and bureaucrats committed to these policies of progressively restricting the sphere of private business, but also the authors of books and essays dealing with these problems fail to realize that their program leads no less to integral socialism than to the nationalization program. If it is within the jurisdiction of the authorities to determine which prices, wage rates, interest rates, and profits are to be considered as fair and legal and which not, and if the police and the penal courts are called upon to enforce these decisions, the essential functions of business are transferred to the government. There is no longer any market and no longer a market economy. It is obvious that the countries this side of the Iron Curtain are more and more approaching this state of affairs. The businessmen, threatened by the menace of such controls, are well aware of the fact that they can escape the enactment of "controls," i.e., full government control of all prices, only if they avoid asking prices of which public opinion does not approve. They have long since virtually lost any influence upon the determination of wage rates. Moreover there cannot prevail any doubt about the fact that the bulk of the funds required for financing the ambitious plans for additional government projects will be collected by taxing away what is still left of the "unearned income" of the shareholders. Even with the present height of the rates of income and inheritance taxation, the greater part of the capital invested in business will in a few decades be expropriated and government-owned.

What the advocates of planning and of social control of business consider as a fair arrangement of economic conditions is a state of affairs in which the various enterprises do precisely what the authorities want them to do and every individual's income after taxes is determined by the government. Although all political parties again and again protest their abhorrence of the Hitler regime, they are eager to duplicate Hitler's economic methods. This is what they have in mind when talking about "discipline." They do not realize that discipline and control are incompatible with freedom. Obsessed with the idea that the entrepreneurs and capitalists are irresponsible autocrats and profits are an unfair lucre, they want to deprive the consumers of the power to determine, by their buying and abstention from buying, the course of all production activities, and to entrust this power to the government.

The political corollary of the supremacy of the consumers in the market economy is the supremacy of the voters under the system of representative government. Where the individuals *qua* consumers become wards of the government, representative government gives way to the despotism of a dictator.

Bureaucratic Management

Among the many spurious arguments advanced against big business, the reproach of bureaucratization plays an important, but somewhat peculiar role. Those censuring big business for bureaucratization implicitly admit that the business method of profit management is by far superior to bureaucratic management. But, they maintain, with the growth into bigness an enterprise necessarily becomes more and more bureaucratic. The subjection of an economic system in which big concerns prevail, to the supremacy of a governmental bureaucracy, therefore does not amount, they say, to a substitution of the less efficient bureaucratic methods of management for the more efficient profit management. It merely means the replacement of one bureaucracy by another bureaucracy. It will therefore not result in a diminution of the quantity and an impairment of the quality of the goods available for consumption.

It is certainly true that bureaucratic methods are adopted to some extent by big concerns. But the critics of this phenomenon not only grotesquely exaggerate its scope, they blame the enterprise — as is the case with most of the faults they find in big business — for something that is the outcome of their own cherished policies of restricting and sabotaging the operation of business by government interference.

Business management, also called profit management, is the method of conducting affairs for the best possible and cheapest provision of the consumers with all the commodities and services they are most urgently asking for. For the businessmen nothing counts but the approval of their actions by the buying public. Those who best succeed in satisfying the consumers earn profits. Those who fail in these endeavors suffer losses; if they do not learn the lesson and do not improve their conduct, they are forced to go out of business. Profit management means the full supremacy of the consumers. In this sense some economists called the market a democracy in which every penny gives a right to vote.

Bureaucratic management is the management of affairs rendering services that on account of their peculiar character cannot be sold on the market to those benefitted by them. The services a police department renders in curbing gangsterism are of the highest value for every citizen. But they cannot be sold piecemeal to the individuals in the way a railroad sells its services. As the "product" of the police activities has no market price, it is impossible to compare the effect of these activities with the costs expended in the way a business compares the costs expended in producing merchandise with the price at which it is sold on the market.

The services the shoe industry renders to the public could be considerably improved by increasing the amount of capital invested in this line of business. There would be more and cheaper shoes available for the consumers. But such an expansion of one industry could be brought about only by withholding or withdrawing capital and labor from other lines, e.g., from the production of shirts. The question is therefore whether or not the consumers approve of such an expansion of one industry and the restriction of some other industry necessarily induced by it. It is the consumers who by their comportment in buying shoes and shirts determine how much capital and labor should be dedicated to each of these industries. It is the profit motive that forces the entrepreneurs to employ to the best of their ability the material as well as the human factors of production according to the wishes of the consumers. The size of each industry and the quantity and quality of products it turns out are thus ultimately determined by the consumers. An entrepreneur who, defying the wishes of the consumers, would use — waste — capital and labor for the production of something for which the demand of the consumers is less urgent would be penalized by losses.

The service that the police department of a city renders to the public could certainly be improved by multiplying the funds devoted to it. But the question of whether or not the citizens consider the advantages to be expected from such an enlargement of the police department as a sufficient compensation for the additional expenditure with which it burdens them cannot be decided in the way it is done in the case of commodities and services negotiated on the market. The accounts of the police department can only provide information about the expenses incurred. The results obtained by the money expended cannot be expressed in money equivalents. The citizens must directly determine the amount of services they want to get and the price they are prepared to pay for them. They discharge this task by electing councilmen whose duty it is to allocate the available funds to the various municipal services.

This is the fundamental difference between profit management and bureaucratic management. The activities of profit-seeking private business enterprise are subject to the most rigid control on the part of the buying public. Every firm, each of its subdivisions and branches, every employee is in all activities forced to comply with the wishes of the consumers. The ultimate standard in the conduct of business is provided by the accounts that confront expenditure with proceeds. An employee or a branch that absorbs more money than it contributes to the concern's gross yields is looked upon as a failure. All parts of a business concern whether large or small are committed to one principle only: make profits and avoid losses. That means serve the consumers.

But it is different with the administration of affairs the product of which has no price on the market. Here the confrontation of costs expended and prices paid by the public for the resulting services cannot serve as guidance. The constitutional institution that allocates a definite sum out of public revenue for their conduct must prescribe what quantity and what kind of services it wants to get from the department concerned. The budget and the instructions issued for the spending of the allocation provide the ultimate standard. In business there prevails the rule, provide what the consumers want to buy at prices exceeding the costs expended. In bureaucratic affairs the rule is to comply strictly with the instructions issued. There is no excuse for a man in business who does not satisfy the consumers. There is no excuse for a bureaucrat who defies the instructions issued by his superiors. The first thing a bureaucrat must try to find out when faced with a new problem is: what do the regulations say?

Bureaucratic management as such is not an evil. It is the only method available for the administration of the proper affairs of government. The public servants would become irresponsible despots if they were not obliged to behave in the conduct of the affairs entrusted them precisely in the way the authorities, the officeholders elected by the people, order them to behave. But bureaucratism turns into a nuisance if it invades the conduct of profit-seeking business and induces it to substitute for the business principle "serve the customer" the bureaucratic principle "comply with the regulations and instructions."

What makes big business adopt in some regards bureaucratic methods is not its size but the policies practiced today of government interference with business. As conditions are today it is more profitable for a concern to be on good personal terms with men in the various government agencies that are harassing business than to improve the services it renders to the consumers. The main problem for many enterprises is how to avoid as much as possible the animosity of officeholders. Men who for some reasons are not popular with the ruling party are considered unfit to manage the affairs of a company. Former employees of government agencies are hired by business, not on account of their abilities but on account of their connections. The boards of directors find it necessary to spend large sums out of the shareholders' property for purposes that have no relation to the company's business and do not yield anything for it but popularity with the administration and the party in power. In considering changes in production and marketing, the first question is often: "How will this move affect our 'public relations'?" Big business is fully aware of the fact that the authorities have the power to harm it by proceeding further in the discriminatory methods of taxation and in many other regards. Big business is the main target in the undisguised war that government is waging against private enterprise.

In the last years a number of books — fiction and non-fiction — were published in which the bureaucracy of big companies has been taken to task. It escaped the notice of the public that the experience with which the authors of these books deal refers to those bureaus of the corporations that handle public relations and government affairs and not to the production and marketing of the goods they turn out. Apart from the effects of the union-enforced seniority rules, there is fortunately not yet too serious mischief done by bureaucratization in the conduct of the genuine operations of the plants.

People as Consumers versus People as Voters

In their beginnings the attacks upon big business were prompted by the aspiration of some groups of artisans, shopkeepers, and small farmers for special privileges that would enable them to meet the competition of bigger outfits. In some countries this motive still plays a role. But with the further evolution of economic affairs all people had to realize that there cannot be any question of a return to the conditions of the precapitalistic ages in which small units prevailed in almost all branches of production and distribution. Thus the meaning of the condemnation of bigness in business radically changed. It no longer suggests a return to medieval handicrafts. It is a plea for the establishment of all-round "planning" and "social control," i.e., government control of business. It is a plea for a step-by-step substitution of socialism of the *Zwangswirtschaft* (compulsory) type for the market economy. The long lists of the alleged crimes of big business compiled by the advocates of socialism cannot invalidate the fact that a nation is the more prosperous the more big business it has. The people of the United States enjoy the highest average standard of living because their country has up to now hindered less the growth of enterprises into bigness than other countries.

The question to be decided is: Who should determine the size of the enterprises, the consumers by their striving to buy what suits them best or the politicians who know only how to tax away and to spend?

It is true that the same people who in their capacity as consumers make the efficient suppliers' business grow into bigness, in their capacity as voters entrust the politicians with the power to give free rein to their antibusiness ventures. But in considering this blatant inconsistency and contradiction in the behavior of our contemporaries we must not forget the fact that the ability of the average citizen to deal with the issues of his own household and with those of economic policies is different. The housewife who buys one brand knows what is best for herself and her family. She has learned from experience and is fully competent to manage the affairs of her household. But she and likewise her husband are certainly less able to choose among various political and economic programs. Thus we see that the voters support policies that contradict their own wishes and vital interests as manifested by their behavior *qua* buyers and consumers. Here again the most instructive example is provided by the American farm policies. The immense majority of the nation are in favor of cheap prices for agricultural products. Nonetheless they have been, for many decades, electing senators and congressmen committed to a policy of spending billions of the taxpayers' money for measures to raise the prices of farm products far above the height that would prevail on an unhampered market. This policy of raising the prices of the vital necessities is so obviously nonsensical from whatever point of view you may judge it that even Cabinet Secretaries of Agriculture and members of the President's Council of Economic Advisers condemned it. But the voters are still voting for it.

Incidentally, we may add that most of the predominantly industrial countries of Europe are also committed to a policy of artificially raising the prices of essential foodstuffs high above the level they would attain on a free market.

Thus we must not be too much astonished to realize that also in the matter of big business the average voter, deceived by ruthless propaganda, supports what hurts his own interests. There is only one means available to change this mentality. One has to try to instruct the public.

46

Economics as a Bridge for
Interhuman Understanding

We intend to deal with the achievement of Utilitarian Philosophy and Classical Political Economy as far as they constitute a theory of peaceful human cooperation. One of the fundamental theses of Classical Economics is the theory of the harmony of the *rightly understood* — we prefer today to speak of the *long-run* — interests of all individuals and groups of individuals within a society of private ownership of the means of production and free enterprise.

Conflict of Interest Philosophies

Older social philosophies saw only conflicts of interests. They were prepared to assume that every individual is impelled by his own selfish interests to prejudice the interests of his fellow men. A nation cannot thrive but by damaging other nations. If every individual were to look only after his own well-being, no social cooperation would be possible. If every nation were intent only upon its own national prosperity, no peace could last. Peace, both within a country and in international relations, is therefore possible only if individuals and nations are prepared to renounce their selfishness for its sake. State and Church, it was held, are disciplinarian institutions whose aim it is to subdue the selfish and antisocial instincts of man. Civilization and social cooperation and the moral law are not of human origin. They are instruments by means of which God or Nature directs human action according to inscrutable design. The individual, in forsaking some selfish advantage for the benefit of society, and the king, in forsaking some conquest to avoid dis-

Paper presented at the Sixth Meeting of the Conference on Science, Philosophy and Religion in Their Relation to the Democratic Way of Life, August 1945.

turbing the peace, will be rewarded in the beyond, and they may find an earthly reward in the quiet of their conscience. The just should abide by the moral law. But this obedience is, from the point of view of his selfish interests, a burden. It is true that Heaven as a rule blesses the just citizen and the fair king in their earthly pilgrimages. But this is not always the case. In many instances the unjust, precisely on account of his wrongdoing, fares in this life better than the just.

What is needed to make social life satisfactory is, therefore, a powerful state which forces its citizens to behave in a fair way and does not covet what is rightly the domain of other states. For the inescapable laws of nature result in irreconcilable conflicts between the selfish interests of various men and groups of men. Nature has limited the means for human subsistence. Equally distributed, they are sufficient for all. However, they are not rich enough to quench entirely the appetite for more. Hence, covetousness, the propensity to appropriate other people's portions, originates. If men or groups of men take more than their fair share, they rob others of as much of their welfare as they increase their own portions above the mean.[1]

From the point of view of "natural law" the only just state of affairs is equality of income. The unfathomable decrees of Heaven have brought about inequality. It would be tantamount to a rebellion against divine and human law for the underprivileged to resort to violence in order to abolish this injustice. By such methods they could profit on earth, but they would imperil their spiritual salvation. On the other hand, the rich have only one means to atone for their questionable riches. They must make the proper use of their wealth, that is, they must be charitable and must subordinate their greed to justice and fairness.

The selfish earthly interests of individuals and of groups of individuals are antagonistic. If left alone, they would result in violent conflicts. Social cooperation and peace are possible only where men are motivated — either by voluntary obedience to the moral law or by compulsion on the part of the powers that be — to curb their egoism.

Social Cooperation and the Division of Labor

Utilitarianism and classical economics have entirely overthrown this philosophy.

---

1. Cf. Kant, *Fragmente aus dem Nachlass*, Collected Works, ed. Hartenstein, vol. 8 (Leipzig, 1868), p. 622.

Their reasoning runs this way: The means of subsistence are scarce, and their limited quantity puts a check upon the number of animals that may occupy the surface of the earth. But, while the beasts know no method of improving their own conditions other than to snatch food away from their rivals, man is in a much more propitious position. Reason taught him the advantages of social cooperation and its corollary, the division of labor. Labor performed under the system of the division of tasks is much more productive than the isolated efforts of self-sufficient individuals. Every step forward to a higher degree of the division of labor directly and immediately improves the material well-being of the individuals and groups concerned. The advantages of social cooperation are so manifest that nobody can ignore them. Their acknowledgment is the motive that pushes man toward social behavior.

It is, therefore, a mistake to assume that an individual in adjusting his conduct to the requirements of life within society and a nation in renouncing war to avoid endangering the international division of labor, sacrifice, for the sake of a heteronomous morality, their own selfish interests for reasons not open to rational explanation. What pushes a man toward social behavior and law abidance is his own *rightly understood* selfishness. What speaks in favor of international peace is precisely the consideration of a nation's own *rightly understood* selfish interests. If a man abstains from robbing a fellow man or if a nation abstains from aggression against other nations, each forgoes a smaller immediate gain in order to reap a bigger indirect profit. Society is for every individual the foremost means for the attainment of all ends sought.

It is furthermore erroneous to believe that individuals, in renouncing the alleged blessings of a fabulous state of nature and entering into society, have forgone some advantages and have a fair claim to be indemnified for what they have lost. The idea that anybody would have fared better under an asocial state of mankind and is wronged by the very existence of society is absurd. The natural condition of man is extreme poverty and insecurity. It is romantic nonsense to lament the passing of the happy days of primitive barbarity.

It is no less vain to deplore the inequality in the distribution of income and wealth. The notion of "distribution" is itself preposterous. There is in the framework of a market society no such thing as an apportionment of shares out of a fund accumulated before. Goods are not produced into a common chest from which they must be doled out to various people. The mode of production is such that they already come into existence as somebody's property.

It is a fallacy to assume that society is responsible for the fact that not everybody enjoys the advantages that riches give to a small number of people. The relative poverty of the poorer members of society is not the corollary of the relative abundance of the richer members. Poverty is precisely the condition of all in the state of nature. Society has not only created wealth for those who possess it; it has also immensely improved the material well-being of those who are considered poor when compared with the richer.[2] Those whose income is lower than the average would prejudice their own rightly understood interests if they were to overthrow a social system which makes them much more prosperous than any other realizable organization of society.

The eulogists of the social institutions of ages gone by can easily be dismissed. A return to the social conditions of the Middle Ages would require both a drastic decrease in population and a tremendous lowering of the standard of living for those surviving. Mankind is not free to go back with impunity from a higher degree of the division of labor to a lower degree.

It is different with the schemes drafted by the interventionists and the socialists. These schools do not suggest an abandonment of the division of labor. They pretend that the realization of their plans would increase the productivity of labor to an unprecedented extent and, at the same time, distribute income among the citizens in a way which they consider fairer than the distribution of incomes within a market society. To investigate the soundness of such suggested reforms is one of the main tasks of economics.

Now the economists are convinced that their careful scrutiny of the socialist and interventionist utopias has proved in an irrefutable way that all these schemes are impracticable and unfeasible and that every attempt to realize them must result in social disintegration and in misery for all. The champions of the doctrines exploded were at a loss to find any argument for the invalidation of the economists' devastating criticism of their plans.

Karl Marx and his disciples do not waste any words upon the hopeless tasks of proving the soundness of socialist ideas and of refuting the pertinent critique of these ideas by the economists. They declare taboo all discussions and investigations concerning the economic and social problems of a socialist society as "utopian" and utterly "unscientific."

---

2. Cf. Bentham, *Principles of the Civil Code*, Works, ed. Bowring, vol. 1 (Edinburgh, 1839), p. 309.

Finally, Marx renders these and other arbitrary and fallacious statements proof against any objections by establishing the principle of polylogism.* The logic of those who do not blindly accept the Marxian dogmas is disparaged as a spurious logic of the bourgeoisie. This bourgeois logic cannot produce truth, but only "ideologies" hatched merely for the defense of the unfair claims of an exploiting class. Thus Marxians appear to be relieved of the necessity of refuting by discursive reasoning the theorem of the harmony of the rightly understood interests of all members of a market society. They simply ridicule it as a piece of bourgeois ideology.

Critics of Liberalism

The foes of Liberalism (i.e., classical liberalism) view the nineteenth-century achievements of the natural sciences and especially Darwinism from two different aspects. Liberalism, says one group of these adversaries, is an outcome of the doctrine of natural law. All men are created equal and are by God or Nature endowed with certain inalienable and imprescriptible natural rights; one of these fundamental natural rights is the right to existence or even to affluence.

Now, observe these critics of Liberalism, it is an undeniable fact that men are not born or created equal. There exist very remarkable differences in the innate physiological and mental equipment of various individuals and groups of individuals. The basic assumption of Liberalism is thus exploded as contrary to fact. Furthermore, these critics reject the idea of natural rights. They go on to say, it is a fact that nature does not grant any rights to any living being, much less a right to existence or to a life in affluence. In limiting the means of subsistence nature condemns to death by starvation many of those who are born. In nature there is only a merciless struggle for survival. Nature does not accord to man more rights than to an amoeba. The whole doctrine of natural law and all conclusions drawn from it are illusory.

The second group of anti-Liberals maintains that no social philosophy can avoid acknowledging the fact that there exist among men irreconcilable conflicts of interests. Scholars differ, they say, only with regard to the determination of the roots of these conflicts. The racists

---

* The doctrine that members of different "classes" reason on the basis of their class's own unique logic.

see the conflicts among various races, the nationalists among various nations, the Marxians among various social classes. But all agree that conflict and not peace is the normal pattern of interhuman relations. Liberalism, they say, is inconsistent in its assertions. On the one hand, it establishes that ruthless competition is a fundamental principle of the social order and may therefore be called a forerunner of the Darwinian doctrine of the struggle for existence. But, on the other hand, it indulges in illusions concerning a fabulous harmony of the rightly understood interests of all men, classes, nations, and races.

All these anti-Liberals are mistaken because they are not familiar with the Liberal doctrine they want to refute. They do not realize that in the political movement of the eighteenth and early nineteenth centuries two quite different strains of thought were merged: the doctrine of inalienable natural rights, on the one hand, and the Utilitarian philosophy of the economists and of the champions of parliamentary government, on the other hand.

The doctrine of natural rights can be traced back to ancient and medieval philosophy. It was easy to coin this natural rights doctrine into popular catchwords which appealed to the masses. It supplied the revolutionaries with fanatical fervor. But its illusiveness again and again frustrated the initial success of the reforms inaugurated, and resulted in terrorism and tyranny.

Utilitarian Liberalism

The Utilitarian doctrine also can be traced back to an almost forgotten and generally loathed school of ancient philosophy, Epicureanism. But the teachings of classical political economy radically altered its application to the problems of social utility. The essence of the teachings of Utilitarian Liberalism is that the market system based on private property is the only workable pattern of social organization. Its operation results in a steady improvement of the material well-being of all individuals and groups of individuals. What is needed is a system of government that safeguards the undisturbed working of this beneficial mode of production. As violent conflicts disintegrate the division of labor, a system of government is required which prevents as far as possible both civil war and foreign war, namely, representative democracy. If all citizens, no matter how different they may be in their bodily and mental abilities, are equal under the law and are in a position to determine by majority vote who shall rule and according to what principles, there is no longer any cause left for revolution and civil war. Within a world of private property a democratic nation cannot derive any advantage from conquest, war no longer pays, and peace becomes durable. Thus reason and the consideration of each individual's and each nation's rightly understood selfish interests recommend Liberalism. The economic democracy of the consumers and its corollary, the political democracy of the voters, will bring about prosperity for all and durable peace.

In this cool reasoning there is no reference to the ideas of natural law and innate rights. The Utilitarians were vehemently hostile to them. The Utilitarian philosopher, Jeremy Bentham (1748–1832) opposed to the "terrorist language" of the champions of natural rights "the language of reason and plain sense." He shouted: "*Natural rights* is simple nonsense: natural and imprescriptible rights, rhetorical nonsense."[3] Both the nineteenth-century school of Historicism and the sect of Social Darwinism boast that they have demolished Liberalism by exploding the illusiveness of the ideas of natural law and of the origination of governments from a contract. However, Utilitarian Liberalism had nothing to do with these natural rights fictions. The Utilitarians themselves must be credited with the merit of having once and for all refuted them.

It is furthermore a grotesque mistake to consider competition among individuals in a market society as tantamount to the extermination of adversaries in wars and revolutions. Under capitalism, competition is the peaceful method to assign to every individual that place in society in which he renders the most valuable services to his fellow men. It is not a variety of struggle, but a mode of selecting the individual best fit for every assignment. One speaks of the "morality" of firms and of the "conquest" of markets. But the "death" of a firm is not a death; it is the elimination of an individual lacking entrepreneurial abilities from a position for which he is unfit and his transfer to a place which better fits his qualities. Neither is the "conquest" of a market a conquest; a newcomer offering better and cheaper commodities supplants a less efficient rival.

The short-run interests of the competitors are antagonistic. But the long-run — i.e., the rightly understood — interests are not. All people would be worse off under a social system that discriminates against more efficient competitors and thus grants privileges to the inefficient.

---

3. Cf. Bentham, *Anarchical Fallacies; Being an Examination of the Declaration of Rights issued during the French Revolution*, Works, ed. Bowring, vol. 2 (Edinburgh, 1843), p. 501.

The general aversion to any occupation with problems raised by the classical economists is best demonstrated by the oblivion into which Ricardo's law of association has fallen.

The economists deal with this law as the law of comparative costs only as far as it concerns problems of international trade. In fact the law is much more universal. It proves that cooperation under the division of labor always results in the mutual benefit of all individuals participating, even if one partner or group of partners is in every regard superior and more efficient than the other partner or group of partners. Ricardo's law is the fundamental law of human cooperation, the formation of society, and the inherent tendency of history toward a progressive intensification of the division of labor.

The law of association is extremely unpopular. It is assailed by all those anxious to be safeguarded against more efficient competitors. However, it provides, of course, the most powerful argument that can be advanced against discrimination and privilege.

The Montaigne Fallacy

The *Leitmotiv* of social philosophy up to the emergence of economics was: The profit of one man is the damage of another; no man profits but by the loss of others.[4] This is not a philosophy of social cooperation, but of dissociation and social disintegration. For the sake of expediency, we call this doctrine after its proponent, essayist Michel Eyquem de Montaigne (1533–92). In the light of this Montaigne fallacy, human intercourse cannot consist in anything but the spoliation of the weaker by the stronger.

There were, of course, philosophers who spoke of an exchange in which neither party profits or loses because the objects given away and received are of equal value. This Aristotelian idea was the core both of the Scholastic doctrine of the just price and of the tenets of Marxism. But what is the sense of exchanging things if both parties assign to the thing received the same value they assign to the thing given away? Why do they bother about exchanging if they do not improve thereby their own condition — i.e., if they do not derive any profit from the transaction?

4. Cf. Montaigne, *Essais*, book 1, chap. 22, ed. F. Strowski (Bordeaux, 1906), pp. 135–36. For the role played by this idea in social doctrines, cf. A. Oncken, *Geschichte der Nationaloekonomie* (Leipzig, 1902), pp. 152–53; E. F. Heckscher, *Mercantilism*, trans. M. Shapiro (London, 1935), vol. 2, pp. 26–27.

Contemporary foreign-trade policies provide a striking example of the logical consequences of the Montaigne fallacy. It is easy to explain why this fallacy when applied to the problems of merchant-consumer relations results in the belief that only selling is profitable while buying is tantamount to a loss. The businessman's profit becomes manifest in the entries of the books recording his transactions, while the consumer does not keep such books and records. In the field of international trade the Montaigne fallacy consequently leads to the statement that only exporting is profitable while importing is disastrous. Only a few people realize that restricting imports must concomitantly restrict exports and that protectionism, when carried out to its ultimate consequences, must bring about autarky [self-sufficiency]. People criticize only the protectionism of other nations and are slow in discovering the flaw in their own country's protectionist policy.

In the light of the Montaigne fallacy the mere fact that a nation imports merchandise is the proof that it is exploited by foreigners. It is hardly possible to exaggerate the role played by this idea in the domestic propaganda of the German Nazis, the Italian Fascists, and the nationalists in all other countries.

With regard to the employer-employee nexus it is not the employee-seller but the employer-buyer of labor whom the Montaigne fallacy brands as profiteer and exploiter. Here again the reason is that the profit of the employer appears in the books of the firm while the employees do not keep such books.

There are, of course, special conditions, as during an inflation or deflation, when the source of the buyer's or the seller's profit is the other party's loss. The main feature of an inflation or deflation is that the prices of various goods and services change neither at the same time nor to the same extent. But this is a special instance which unfortunately is not taken into consideration by those fanatically advocating an easy-money policy, credit expansion, and other similar inflationary measures as a patent medicine.

It is not correct to say that the doctor's profit is derived from the patient's disaster. The ailing man's misfortune is his illness. The doctor's profit stems from his relieving the patient's suffering. The source of the baker's profit is not the hunger of the buyers of bread, but his providing a merchandise which can remove hunger.

The source of the businessman's profits is always his successful foresight in providing for future needs. If the entrepreneur has correctly forecast the future needs, he earns a profit. If he has failed in this task, he suffers losses.

In a hypothetical world without economic improvement, the profits made by one group of entrepreneurs would be equal to the losses suffered by the other group. In such a world no part of the national income would go into profits. Our actual world is, however, a world in which there is improvement. Its most characteristic feature is its inherent tendency toward the production of more, better, and cheaper goods. As long as this tendency prevails, there is, in the whole of society, an excess of profits over losses.

The error of the Montaigne fallacy is that it looks at events as if they were isolated acts of God and does not judge them from the point of view of the working of the whole social system of production. It sees only the remedy which the pharmacist sells to a man who suffers from kidney trouble. It does not see that decades before the patient concerned was afflicted with his malady, a whole branch of business was eager to prepare an appropriate remedy and to furnish all pharmacists with it in order to supply without delay those who might one day need it. It does not see the entrepreneurs who established in some far remote corner of the earth plantations for the growing of one of the raw materials required for the production of this drug. Nor does it see the other entrepreneurs who built railroads and ships for the transportation of this raw material to the place in which the patient lives.

Social Cooperation

The economists do not fail to realize that in the short run there is a conflict of interests between buyer and seller. What they say is that these short-run conflicts are superseded by the harmony of the long-run interests, i.e., the rightly understood interests.

The only relevant question is whether any other system of the social organization of human cooperation could possibly succeed better in the satisfaction of human needs and wants.

The answer to this question can be provided only by economics. In the debates concerning society's social and economic organization, only people fully conversant with the most difficult and intricate problems of economics are in a position to form an independent opinion. To establish this fact does not mean to indulge in the habit of scientific specialists who overrate the importance of their own branch of knowledge and want to assign to themselves, as the representatives of this specialty, a controlling position in the conduct of all human affairs. Neither does it mean an acceptance of the Marxian materialist conception of history.

It is not the economists but the immense majority of our contemporaries who consider economic matters the most important thing. All political parties regard material interests as the primary problem; their programs promise their followers higher incomes and a higher standard of living. All political conflicts refer to antagonisms concerning economic issues. Present-day parties are fighting for prices, interest rates, and wage rates. Present-day wars are fought for raw materials and markets. The churches of all denominations are today speaking more about these problems than about questions of creed and Christian doctrine.

But while everybody's main concern is economic problems, nobody thinks it necessary to pay any attention to serious economic studies. The Montaigne fallacy is the universal substitute for economic knowledge. The logical outcome of this state of affairs is the popular conviction that the best method to further one's own interests is to inflict as much damage as possible on other people. Hence, domestic conflicts and foreign wars.

Blinded by the Montaigne fallacy, people are completely at a loss to see in the problems of social organization anything but the struggle for greater portions of a cake whose magnitude does not depend on the mode of social organization. Nobody seems to doubt that to prevent some people from acquiring riches is a policy extremely beneficial for the rest of society. Everybody is sincerely convinced that technological progress is an act of God not conditioned by the methods of social organization. Enjoying all the new products which free enterprise provides, they are tormented by one thought only: that some people have become rich in creating these new things.

A Consumers' Democracy

It is a faulty way of dealing with the subject to look at it as if it were a matter of ethics. People ask: "Why should the entrepreneur not be satisfied to sell his product at a price that does not allow for any profit at all or, at best, yields him not more than the average income of an employee?"

The social function of business profits and losses is to place the material factors of production in the hands of those men who are best fitted to use them in the most efficient way for the satisfaction of the wants of the consumers. The market of a capitalist society is a *consumers'* democracy. The consumers decide by their buying and their abstention from buying who should own the material factors of production. In a perfect market society, i.e., in a social system where there is no government tampering with commodity prices, wage rates, interest rates, and profits, the only method of acquiring and keeping wealth is to satisfy the needs of the consumers in the best and cheapest way. Business profits shift the means of production to those who have succeeded in these endeavors, and business losses take them away from those who have not. Profits and losses are instrumental in making the consumers sovereign and in forcing the entrepreneurs to adjust production to their wishes. In the absence of profits and consequently of losses, the entrepreneurs would lack any orientation concerning the desires of the consumers. There would be stagnation, not because the entrepreneurs are selfish, but because they would not know whether projected changes would suit the public.

The incessant tendency toward technological progress, which is inherent in the capitalist system, is the outcome of the fact that profits enlarge the sphere of action of the efficient entrepreneur and that losses restrict the influence of the inefficient. The confiscation of business profits does not benefit the masses. It prevents the efficient entrepreneur from expanding his efforts to supply the consumers in a better and cheaper way, and it shelters the less efficient against the competition of more efficient newcomers. It substitutes rigidity and immutability for progress and continuous improvement.

The inequality of wealth and income has a definite social function within a free-market society; it is the dynamic element safeguarding a permanent progress toward a better supply for the consumers. But when government interference curtails profits, this function ceases. Then the inequalities of wealth and income become privileges of those who have inherited wealth from preceding generations and are no longer useful to the whole of society and to each of its members.

The question is not whether it is just or not that a man who has succeeded in supplying his fellow men in the cheapest and best way should become rich. The question is not whether this man merits his affluence from any metaphysical point of view. The question is only whether any system other than that making the successful servant of the consumer's wishes rich could be more conducive to the constant progressive improvement of the masses' standard of living.

It is true that some of those rich today are the heirs of men who did not acquire their wealth by serving the consumers but by robbing people. Many aristocratic families of Europe are the descendants of expropriators or of men whom the expropriators presented with gifts out of their booty. However, in a free-market society these people too can preserve their wealth only by serving the consumers. If they succeed in this endeavor, they legitimize their wealth through the vote of the consumers. What is needed is only to deny them privileges which could protect them against the competition of other citizens more efficient in serving the consumers.

One of the poorest tricks of the champions of government omnipotence and of totalitarian methods of economic management is to stigmatize all their opponents as defenders of the vested interests of those who happen to be rich today. In fact, the advocates of the free-enterprise system are the most radical foes of any kind of protection of vested interests. The defenders of the vested interests are precisely those asking for tariffs, "parity" prices, price stabilization, and similar measures.

Economic liberalism does not fight for the interests of those who are rich today. On the contrary, what economic liberalism wants is a free hand left to everybody who has the ingenuity to supplant today's rich by providing consumers with better and cheaper products. Its main concern is to remove all obstacles to a future improvement of mankind's material well-being, or, in other words, to attain freedom from want.

It is therefore irrelevant to argue against those who recommend the free-enterprise system as the most appropriate method of removing want and raising the general standard of living by saying that the capitalists and entrepreneurs are themselves not blameless. Of course, capitalists and entrepreneurs are sinners too. But the economists do not advocate a market economy for the sake of these people. They do not intend to reward an alleged virtue on the part of the businessmen by allocating to them larger portions of wealth and income. They simply establish the fact that the free-enterprise system is better fitted to promote the well-being of the masses than any other social order.

The Conclusions of Economic Analysis

The logical deficiencies in the popular treatment of economic matters are really amazing. The most characteristic feature of the economic policies in the years between the two world wars was restriction of output of basic raw materials and foodstuffs. There were international agreements concerning the restriction of the production of rubber, tin, sugar, cocoa, coffee, and many other necessities. Domestic policies aimed at the same end. We cannot help recording the astonishing fact that the governments, statesmen, and politicians responsible for these restrictions could publicly boast that they are intent upon substituting an economy of plenty and abundance for what they disparaged as an economy of scarcity.

What is needed most seems to be a return to common sense and logical consistency.

It is not the aim of the foregoing casual observations to suggest any comprehensive answers to the most fervently discussed questions of our age. Their only aim is to make the conscientious reader realize that at the bottom of all these issues there are very intricate problems, which require a thorough and searching scrutiny.

In the field of economic studies no specialization is feasible. In the same way in which it is impossible for a mathematician to specialize in triangles and to neglect the study of circles, it is impossible to be an expert on wage rates without at the same time mastering the problems of profits and interest, commodity prices, and currency and banking. All the elements of the economic system are closely interconnected and influence one another. There are only economists and laymen. There are no such things as labor economists or farm economists.

Nobody is in a position to acquire an intuitive knowledge of economics from the mere opportunity provided by his vocation. Neither businessmen nor statesmen may pose as economic experts if they have not acquired special information by troublesome effort.

Economics is called inhuman because it shows what the inextricable consequences are of protecting less-efficient producers against the more efficient and of preserving by various means outstripped modes of production. However, the economists do not say: Thou shalt wear rayon and nylon stockings and thus hurt the cotton growers. It is the consumers who prefer rayon and nylon goods and thus restrict their demand for cotton.* Neither do the economists say: Thou shalt not subsidize submarginal cotton growers, i.e., those for whom producing does

---

* Since 1945 when nylon and rayon reigned supreme, chemists have developed blends of natural fibers — cotton, wool, and silk — with synthetics — nylon, rayon, polyester, lycra, spandex, etc. — creating new "miracle" textiles that are stretchable, washable, and wrinkle-proof. As a result, the market for cotton has been revived.

not pay at the lower market price of cotton. The economists merely point out on whom the burden of such subsidies falls and what the social consequences of generally espousing the policy of such subsidies must be. They dispel the fallacious belief that these subsidies could be granted by the *State* without any burden to the citizens and without lowering the productivity of labor and the general standard of living. If to say this is inhuman, then so is every expression of truth. If to say this is inhuman, then the physicians who exploded the myth of the healing power of mandrake were inhuman, too, because they hurt the people employed in gathering mandrake.

The main achievement of economics is that it has provided a theory of peaceful human cooperation. This is why the harbingers of violent conflict have branded it as a "dismal science" and why this age of wars, civil wars, and destruction has no use for it.

47

Economic Freedom in the Present-Day World

The program of liberalism (in the original sense of the term as it was understood in nineteenth-century Europe and not in present-day America where it is sometimes a synonym for radical interventionism, or more often for socialism and communism) was based upon cognizance that within the market economy, i.e., within the social system of private ownership of the means of production and the division of labor, harmony prevails among the rightly understood or long-term interests of all individuals and groups of individuals.

The Only Fact that Matters

Earlier ages had labored under the misapprehension that no man or group of men can profit but by the loss of others. In entirely demolishing this fallacy, eighteenth-century social philosophy and economics paved the way for the unprecedented achievements of modern Western civilization.

The decline of liberalism in its original sense consists precisely in the fact that the policy of all nations is again guided by the idea that there prevails an irreconcilable conflict between the interests of various classes in the Marxian sense, and of the various nations and races. The decline of liberalism is not one of a series of equally important events that can be lifted out of the context of the history of recent generations

Response to a 1957 questionnaire from French economist Jacques Rueff. Rueff was seeking to revive the Centre Paul Hymans, which, on account of World War II, had not met since its international conference in Paris in 1938. This article appeared in the January 17, 1958, issue of U.S.A. magazine.

and treated separately. It is the essence of this history, the only fact that matters. All that has happened during these decades was the consistent application of the philosophy of irreconcilable conflict.

Big Business, Great Service

In the market economy the consumers, by their buying or abstention from buying, ultimately determine what is to be produced, of what quality, and in what quantity. They are continuously shifting control of the material factors of production into the hands of those entrepreneurs, capitalists, and landowners who have succeeded in supplying them in the best possible and cheapest way with all they are asking for.

The characteristic principle of capitalism is mass production for the satisfaction of the wants of the masses. Industry serves, first of all the consumers, the much-talked-about common man. All the major branches of industry, all enterprises, which ignorance and envy belabor as "big business," produce for the many. Plants turning out what are considered luxury goods for the few never exceed small or medium size. Capitalism multiplies population figures and provides a standard of living for the average man which even the well-to-do of earlier ages would have deemed fabulous.

Economics shows that no other thinkable system of society's economic organization could attain the degree of productivity which capitalism attains. It has entirely refuted all the arguments advanced in favor of socialism and interventionism.

There are, of course, people who do not want to acquiesce in the verdict of economic theory. They reject economic thinking as an allegedly spurious waste of time and declare that they trust only the teachings of experience. If, for the sake of argument, we admit their claims, we may ask: "Where is the experience that bears witness to the merits of socialism and the evils of capitalism?"

If historical experience could teach anything, it would be that no nation has ever reached or preserved prosperity and civilization without the institution of private property. Recent experience of the United States, Great Britain, Germany, and other countries has again shown that the repeal of any of the interventionist measures — the abandonment of inflationary policies, and even the limited reestablishment of the supremacy of the market — has immediately improved the general economic situation.

Blessings of Capitalism

Again there are people who contend that to look upon the problems of social organization merely with a concern for an ample supply of various goods and services is the disclosure of a vicious mentality. They reject this "mean materialism" on moral grounds and want to deal with the issues involved from what they call a higher and loftier point of view. Such ideas certainly agree with the worldview of a Buddhist monk. In his eyes a life in dirt and penury has a positive value, and earthly possessions are dangerous because they could divert a man from the right path.

It is different with the theological and philosophical moralists of the West. These men find fault with capitalism because there are still people whom the blessings of capitalism have not yet benefited and who are, therefore, in an unsatisfactory condition. They wish that the quantity of goods made available to these poor could be increased. They know that this *could* be effected only by intensifying production, that is, by intensifying capitalism. But, lightheartedly and unthinkingly endorsing all the socialist fallacies, they recommend methods that would decrease the total amount of goods available for sustenance and thereby impair the standard of living.

The anti-capitalistic attitudes of a great many contemporary religious leaders and teachers of a secular morality are dictated by resentment and ignorance. The achievements of capitalism — e.g., the drop in infant mortality, the successful fight against plagues and famines, the general improvement of the standard of living — are to be highly valued also from the point of view of the teachings of any religious creed and of any system of ethical doctrines. No religious or ethical tenet can justify a policy that aims at the substitution of a social system under which output per unit of input is lower for a system in which it is higher.

Mistaken "Moderates"

The dismal conditions that the Bolshevik "experiment" has brought about and the lamentable failure of all ventures of partial socialization and nationalization have to some extent damped the fanatical bigotry with which several generations of zealots were fighting for Georges Sorel's ideal, the destruction of all that exists.

The design of a "social revolution" which at one blow would transform the earth into the land of Cockaigne has lost a good deal of its attraction. It was a tremendous shock for the parlor Communists, the socialist professors and bureaucrats, and the union bosses when they discovered that the revolutionary Moloch devours not only the capitalists, "sycophants of the bourgeoisie," and kulaks, but also people of their own kind. They stopped talking about the necessity of "finishing the unfinished revolution" and turned to a program for bringing about socialism step-by-step in a series of interventionist measures. They returned to the plan that Marx and Engels had outlined in the *Communist Manifesto*, but virtually had dropped in the later development of their doctrine because it was incompatible with the essential dogmas of dialectic materialism and the Marxian scheme of a philosophy of history.

The few lines in which the *Communist Manifesto* explains and justifies its ten-point program for the gradual realization of socialism are the best Marx and Engels ever wrote about economic issues; they are in fact the only acceptable observations contributed by Marx and Engels to economics. They call the measures they suggest "despotic inroads on the rights of property and on the conditions of bourgeois production" and declare that these measures "appear economically insufficient and untenable," and that "in the course of the movement they outstrip themselves and are unavoidable as a means of entirely revolutionizing the mode of production."

Later, forty years after the first publication of the German text of the *Manifesto*, five years after the death of Marx, when an "authorized English translation" of the *Manifesto*, "edited and annotated by Frederick Engels," was published, Engels provided an addition to the text in order to explain what the rather puzzling words "outstrip themselves" (*über sich selbst hinaustreiben*) meant. He inserted between the words "outstrip themselves" and "and are unavoidable" the words "necessitate further inroads upon the old social order." In these eight words Engels condensed the teachings of classical economics concerning the effects of interference with the market and to some extent even anticipated the modern economists' theory of interventionism.

This theory of interventionism deals with the effects of coercion and compulsion on the part of the government or agencies, like the labor unions to whom the government has virtually granted the privilege of resorting to violence. Such coercion and compulsion force entrepreneurs and capitalists to employ some of the factors of production differently from what they would have if they were obeying only the dictates of the consumers as conveyed to them by the state of the market.

This theory points out that the effects of such an interference are — from the very point of view of the government and the advocates and supporters of the measure concerned — more undesirable than the previous state of affairs that it was designed to alter. If the government is prepared neither to repeal its intervention nor to acquiesce in the unsatisfactory state of affairs that it has generated, then it is forced to add to its first intervention a second one, and as the result is, again from the government's point of view, more unsatisfactory than the previous state, a third one, and so forth until its authoritarian decrees regiment every aspect of human activities and thereby establish the social system that is known under the terms socialism, communism, planning, totalitarianism.

When people who aim at the substitution of socialism for the market economy advocate interventionist measures, they are consistent from the point of view of their aims. But those people are badly mistaken who consider interventionism as a third solution of the problem of society's economic organization, a system which, as they say, is as far from socialism as from capitalism, while combining what is "good" in each of these two systems and avoiding what is "bad" in them.

Interventionism cannot be considered a lasting system of society's economic organization. It is a method of realizing socialism by installment. Production can be directed either by the wishes of the consumers — as shown in their buying or desisting from buying — or by the state, the social apparatus of coercion and compulsion. A concrete factor of production — for instance a specific piece of steel — can either be used according to the orders of the consumers or according to the orders of the police. There is nothing in between.

What optimists view as a revival of true liberalism is merely the slowing down of the march toward socialism that the spectacular failure of all socialist adventures has begotten. If the New Deal had not failed to do away with mass unemployment in the 1930s, and if the Tennessee Valley Authority had not been an extremely costly fiasco, if the nationalization of British coal mining and steel making had made any sense, if German Nazism and Italian Fascism had not ruined everything that could be ruined, if the state-operated post offices, telegraphs and telephones, railroads, and other services had not, through their deficits, jeopardized many nations' budgetary equilibrium, the self-styled "progressives" would still pursue their policies with the same vigor with which their forerunners proceeded some years ago.

It is a mistake to look upon these "moderates" as if they were liberals in the classical sense of the term. The American Eisenhower Republicans and the British Conservatives are not advocates of the market economy and of economic freedom. What distinguishes them from the New Deal Democrats and from the Labour Party is not principles, but the degree of their reformist ardor and the pace of their march toward statism. They are always retreating, putting up today with measures which they vehemently opposed some time ago. In a few years they will very likely adopt measures which make them shudder today.

The German Ordo-Liberalism is different only in details from the *Sozialpolitik* of the Schmoller and Wagner school.* After the episodes of Weimar radicalism and Nazi socialism, it is a return in principle to the *Wohlfahrtstaat* of Bismarck and Posadovsky.†

All these movements are, of course, moderate when compared with the thoroughness of the dictators. But there is no substantial difference between *more* or *less* moderate interventionism. All interventionist measures, as Engels pertinently observed, "necessitate further inroads upon the old social order" and thereby finally lead to full socialism.

The Need for Sound Money

Interventionism believes that lowering the rate of interest below the height it would attain in an unhampered market is very beneficial, and considers credit expansion as the right means for the attainment of this end. But the boom artificially created by credit expansion cannot last. It must end in a general depression of trade, an economic crisis.

From this explanation of the trade cycle, the so-called monetary or circulation credit theory, one must infer that there is only one means to avoid the return of periods of economic depression, viz., to abstain from any attempts to produce by credit expansion a passing artificial boom. But the interventionists are not prepared to renounce their cherished policy of making people happy for a short time by an illusory prosperity. Fully aware of the fact that it is impossible to refute and to discredit the monetary theory of the trade cycle, they pass over it in silence, or distort it and sneeringly deride it.

---

* Gustav Schmoller (1838–1917) and Adolf Wagner (1835–1917) were economists. Both men were advocates of social reform, the welfare state, and state socialism.
† Arthur Posadovsky (1845–1932), a prominent official in the German government from 1897 through World War I, was responsible for much of the social and economic reform of that era.

In place of this banished doctrine, officialdom and the universities propagate a doctrine which, like that of Karl Marx, interprets the periodical return of industrial crises as a necessary outgrowth of capitalism. The crises, declares the *Communist Manifesto*, disclose the inability of the capitalistic mode of production, of private property and free enterprise, to manage productive forces. Economic crises are an inherent feature of the bourgeois system, and will return at ever shorter intervals, each time more threateningly, as long as socialist all-around planning has not been substituted for the capitalistic "anarchy of production."

Socialists and interventionists agree that the crises are necessary outcomes of the very operation of the market economy. They disagree with regard to the methods to be resorted to for the prevention of future periods of economic depression.

The orthodox Marxians declare that there is but one means available for this purpose, the unconditional and total adoption of the Soviet type of socialist management.

The interventionists, however, ascribe to the government the power to prevent or, at least, to mitigate considerably the harshness and duration of the slump by measures which they call "anti-cyclical." Under this high-sounding name they recommend, for the emergency in which government revenue is shrinking on account of the depression, tax abatement, on the one hand, and, on the other hand, a huge increase in government spending through gigantic public works and an increase in unemployment compensation. Though the crisis is the inevitable outcome of the creation of additional quantities of money and money substitutes, the interventionists want to cure it by still further inflation. They blithely neglect to take cognizance of the teachings of both theory and history concerning the final outcome of a protracted inflationary policy.

Inflation is also the only solution interventionism suggests for the problem of mass unemployment. Here again the fateful concatenation of all attempts at tampering with the market wreaks havoc. First, the government or the labor unions decree and enforce minimum wage rates that are higher than the potential market rates. Then, as this inevitably results in prolonging mass unemployment indefinitely, the government proceeds to inflation. The inflation results in higher commodity prices and a higher cost of living which cause the government and the unions to interfere in order to raise wage rates anew above the potential market rate. And so on.

A liberal (in its original sense) movement must never forget that sound money is one of the fundamental principles of liberalism, old or new.

Fables Can Cause War

The legal foundations of Western civilization and prosperity were provided by the institution of private property. What separates East and West is precisely the fact that the Orient did not develop the ideological, legal, and political framework within which property rights and their efficacious protection against arbitrariness on the part of rulers could thrive. Under these conditions no capital accumulation and no large-scale investment could be effected and result in the development of industrial plants and factories.

The natural conditions for production were in large parts of Asia more favorable than in Europe north of the Alps. On the eve of the "Industrial Revolution," India and China were considered as richer than even the most flourishing European countries. In technological skill and in the talents required for success in scientific research, Asian students of Western methods seem not to be inferior to the Europeans. What was lacking and is still lacking in the East is the spirit of freedom, which generated that great concept of the individual's rights that no one must infringe upon.

The vital principle of a liberal constitution is the independence of the judiciary that protects the individual and his property against any violator, whether king or common robber. To the institutions which the "progressives" try to ridicule with ironical sneers by dubbing them "the divine rights of capital," the "proletarians" of the West owe all that distinguishes their conditions from those of the indigent masses in Asia and Africa.

The inhabitants of the "underdeveloped" countries hanker for the material paraphernalia of Western capitalism and thereby implicitly acknowledge the superiority of Western methods of economic management. But their governments, in this regard fully supported by the "intellectuals," are sabotaging any attempts to intensify production and thereby to improve the average standard of living. What these countries need, first of all, is more investment of more capital. Yet their policies prevent both the accumulation of domestic capital and the importation of foreign capital.

Conditions in England and other European countries were no less grievous on the eve of the "Industrial Revolution" than they are today in many Asian and African lands. But while England had to lift itself by its own bootstraps, assembling the capital acquired and accumulating technological experience in a time-consuming process, these latter countries can freely use the technology of the West. And they got, and could still get if they did not prevent it, substantial aid by the investment of foreign capital.

Confused by the Communist fables that depict foreign investment as an outgrowth of predatory imperialism, Western "progressivism" labors under a sense of guilt in dealing with the conditions of the East. Western European and later also North American capitalists built most of the railroads, canals, other transportation and communication facilities, and public utilities in the "underdeveloped" countries, developed their natural resources, and constructed factories. A great part, perhaps the greater part of the capital invested in this way in these "underdeveloped" countries, has been expropriated under various pretexts. The amazing thing is that these confiscatory measures were enthusiastically approved by the "progressive" countrymen of the capitalist victims of such expropriation. Many governments not only did not protest against the expropriation of these investments, but virtually encouraged its perpetrators.

One of the main paradoxes of the modern world is this: The achievements of laissez-faire liberalism and the capitalistic market economy have finally instilled in all Eastern peoples the conviction that what the Western ideologies recommend and the Western policies practice is the right thing to be done. But by the time the East got this confidence in Western ways, the ideologies and policies of socialism and interventionism had supplanted liberalism in Europe and America.

In adopting the doctrines that condemned all things labelled "bourgeois" as the worst of all evils, the East meant to adopt the ideas that had made for the West's prosperity and civilization. From these allegedly modern and progressive American and Western doctrines, the Easterners got the inspiration for the war cries they are using today in their fight against the West. This applies also to Russian Communism which, from the Russian point of view, is seen as Western ideology imported by disciples of Hegel, Fourier, Marx, Sorel, and the Webbs, with the outspoken intention of "westernizing" their backward nation.

Led by the Soviet power, the peoples of Asia and Africa are engaged in what they believe is a struggle for their emancipation from the "yoke of capitalism." From the point of view of the Western nations, their fanatical anti-Westernism is certainly a highly deplorable fact. But it also hurts the vital interests of the Eastern peoples more seriously than those of the West. And it may kindle a new, an atomic, world war.

Dissenters' Role

The advocates of socialism (communism or planning) want to substitute for private control public (government) control of the means of production.

The advocates of interventionism declare that they do not want to abolish the market economy entirely. They want, they say, only to improve its functioning by various acts of government interference with business.

These two doctrines are today taught at schools, expounded in books, magazines, and newspapers, professed by political parties, and practiced by governments. There are socialist schools, books, periodicals, parties, and governments, and there are interventionist schools, books, periodicals, parties, and governments.

There are also a few dissenters who think that the market economy, the laissez-faire system or capitalism, is the only system that makes for prosperity and civilization, and that it alone can prevent the ruin of the West and the relapse into chaos and barbarism. Some of these dissenters have published books and articles. But almost no politician or bureaucrat takes notice of their ideas. Public opinion is not aware of the fact that such doctrines exist. The political idiom of the United States does not even have a word to signify them and their supporters. The word "liberal" means in America today socialist or interventionist. . . .

The state of affairs we have to face is this: The interventionist policies adopted by all governments and supported by all parties this side of the Iron Curtain will sooner or later bring about, to put it mildly, very unsatisfactory conditions. Since public opinion mistakenly considers these interventionist policies as procapitalistic policies, or as the Communists and many allegedly anti-Communist authors say "as a last desperate effort to salvage capitalism," people will argue, "Now capitalism has failed; nothing is left to us except to try the Russian methods."

These people will not see that what failed was not capitalism, not the system of the unhampered market economy, but interventionism. How could they realize this, when there are so many groups eager to represent a policy of interventionism as a policy for the preservation of economic freedom and the market economy? . . .

Therefore nothing is more important today than to enlighten public opinion about the basic differences between genuine liberalism, which advocates the free market economy, and the various interventionist parties which are advocating government interference with prices, wages, the rate of interest, profits and investment, confiscatory taxation, tariffs and other protectionist measures, huge government spending, and finally, inflation.

The typeface used in setting this book is Electra, designed in 1935 by the great American typographer William Addison Dwiggins. Dwiggins was a student and associate of Frederic Goudy and served for a time as acting director of Harvard University Press. In his illustrious career as typographer and book designer (he coined the term "graphic designer"), Dwiggins created a number of typefaces, including Metro and Caledonia, and designed as well many of the typographic ornaments or "dingbats" familiar to readers.

Electra is a crisp, elegant, and readable typeface, strongly suggestive of calligraphy. The contrast between its strokes is relatively muted, and it produces an even but still "active" impression in text. Interestingly, the design of the *italic* form — called "cursive" in this typeface — is less calligraphic than the italic form of many faces, and more closely resembles the roman.

This book is printed on paper that is acid-free and meets the requirements of the American National Standard for Permanence of Paper for Printed Library Materials, z39.48–1992. ⊗

Book design adapted by Erin Kirk New, Watkinsville, Georgia, after a design by Martin Lubin Graphic Design, Jackson Heights, New York

Typography by G&S Typesetters, Inc., Austin, Texas

Printed and bound by Worzalla Publishing Company, Stevens Point, Wisconsin